BLACK&DECKER®

The Complete Guide to Withdrawn

SHEDS

2nd Edition

- Utility
- Storage
- Playhouse
- Mini-Barn
- Garden
- Backyard Retreat
- More

Creative Publishing international

MINNEAPOLIS, MINNESOTA

www.creativepub.com

Creative Publishing international

Copyright © 2011
Creative Publishing international, Inc.
400 First Avenue North, Suite 300
Minneapolis, Minnesota 55401
1-800-328-0590
www.creativepub.com
All rights reserved

Printed in China

10 9 8 7 6 5 4 3 2 1

Library of Congress Cataloging-in-Publication Data on file

President/CEO: Ken Fund
Group Publisher: Bryan Trandem

Home Improvement Group

Associate Publisher: Mark Johanson
Managing Editor: Tracy Stanley
Developmental Editor: Jordan Wiklund

Creative Director: Michele Lanci
Art Direction/Design: Brad Springer, James Kegley, Kim Winscher,
Brenda Canales

Lead Photographer: Corean Kormarec
Set Builder: James Parmeter
Production Managers: Laura Hokkanen, Linda Halls

Page Layout Artist: Danielle Smith
Contributing Writer: Karen Ruth
Technical Editor: Chris Marshall
Additional Photography: Susan Teare
Shop Help: Charles Boldt

The Complete Guide to Sheds
Created by: The Editors of Creative Publishing international, Inc., in cooperation with Black & Decker.
Black & Decker® is a trademark of The Black & Decker Corporation and is used under license.

NOTICE TO READERS

For safety, use caution, care, and good judgment when following the procedures described in this book. The publisher and Black & Decker cannot assume responsibility for any damage to property or injury to persons as a result of misuse of the information provided.

The techniques shown in this book are general techniques for various applications. In some instances, additional techniques not shown in this book may be required. Always follow manufacturers' instructions included with products, since deviating from the directions may void warranties. The projects in this book vary widely as to skill levels required: some may not be appropriate for all do-it-yourselfers, and some may require professional help.

Consult your local building department for information on building permits, codes, and other laws as they apply to your project.

Contents

The Complete Guide to Sheds

Contents (Cont.)

Introduction

Few spaces are as useful and enjoyable as the contemporary backyard shed. Yes, you can store your tools and lawnmower in one, but imagine how a shed might enrich other aspects of your life—what if you had more space for your favorite hobby, or another place to relax? Often, those qualities are found in the same activity, and a shed can be customized to suit that activity and act as a natural extension of your personal style, expression, and habits. Some simply like a few hours' bustling in the garden and a handy place to store their materials; others see their sheds as sacred and beloved environments to create and express themselves, an open invitation to get out and play. How will you use your shed?

The custom buildings in this book are intended to get you thinking about how your shed might be conceived, built, and eventually outfitted with whatever fits your scope and style. The sheds featured here are meant to be versatile, practical, and adaptable, as well as serving as handsome additions to your house and home. In terms of property value, a shed can either be an asset or a liability. Nobody wants to see—much less buy—a rusty, ill-used and dilapidated shed, one with jilted doors hanging by a hinge, propped up on sunken concrete blocks. With a little planning beforehand, your shed will never suffer the same fate, standing tall and functioning well for years on end. A well-built shed can evoke the house it stands near or act as a private cabin or playhouse. A good shed appeals to its environment and complements your interests, hobbies and styles.

When it comes to actually constructing your shed, you can do it in one of two ways: build it from scratch in true DIY fashion, or buy a kit shed for easy assembly. This book covers both options. Each of the custom shed projects features a complete set of construction drawings and photographs, a detailed materials list, and step-by-step instructions and photos for building the shed of your dreams. For those who prefer a prefabricated shed, there's a full section of what to consider when choosing a kit shed, as well as instructions for the basic steps of two popular projects.

Not everyone comes into a shed project with a scuffed tool belt and an outfitted work bench. No matter—the Building Basics section of the book walks you through the entire construction process. It will also help you choose the right foundation for your shed and give you the knowledge to make custom substitutions to the projects as shown. Many shed kits also involve a fair amount of freehand work, so you're covered even if your kit comes without roofing or a floor.

One of the best aspects of building a shed is that it doesn't disrupt the daily life in your home; there's no need to rearrange the furniture on a daily basis, much less sweep out the sawdust. So take your time, enjoy the process, and think about the future of your shed and how you'll use it—it might just become your home away from home, not more than a few yards away.

Choosing
a Design

The purpose and variety of sheds is as different as the people who build them. Storage shed or man-cave? A place to play or a place to study? Ask a dozen different people about how they'd use a shed and you might hear a dozen a different answers. How you use your shed will directly impact its construction and overall style. A shed doesn't have to be just a building in your backyard; it can be an opportunity for personal expression. In other words, each shed was built by someone, in a certain place for a specific reason, something to match their personality and ways-of-being. Or doing. Or living. That's what sheds are all about. One unsung trait of sheds is privacy—the ability to get away from it all, even in your own backyard.

Like most buildings, your shed's form follows its function. Answering *why* is a key factor in determining the scope of your shed. From floor space to headroom, natural lighting vs. electric lighting, storage vs. living space, level of security, amount of privacy, and certainly price—all these factors are decisions to make before pounding the first nail.

Once the *why* has been determined, the next question to answer is *how:* a wide variety of styles, features, and materials are at your disposal. Will your foundation be wood or concrete? Will the exterior complement or contrast with the environment? Possibly the most important decision to make is the manner in which your shed will be built—some may enjoy the relative convenience of a kit or contractor to help with their shed. Others will seek the satisfaction of building the whole shed from the ground up in true DIY fashion.

Wherever you decide to place it and however you decide to build it, the following pages will help you plan for your best shed, whatever its purpose may be.

This graciously ornamented shed is easily built from a panelized kit. Special details like the dormer appear to be the work of a highly skilled carpenter but can actually be created by an ambitious do-it-yourselfer.

This inviting sunlight shed combines the utility of a storage shed with the floral beauty of a garden shed. Clear polycarbonate roof panels work from the spring thaw through the late fall, filtering light onto the plants below and infusing the shed with a warm, natural glow. The Dutch doors add further charm to an already delightful shed, and a small ramp makes wheelbarrow access a breeze.

Some sheds defy easy categories; part Japanese pagoda and part Mississippi riverboat, this hybrid shed features unique architectural details and a bold paint job. A water spout attached to the back gutter powers a glass jug-tipped waterwheel, while a little bonsai-style hedge trimming complements the Eastern aspects of this wondrous outbuilding.

Just because it's square doesn't mean it's boring. This English-style shed stands like a sentinel and attracts the eye with a beacon-like finial, reinforced slate roof, metal rain gutters, and triple-hinged door.

A simple garden often demands a simple shed. The flowerbox, exterior tiles, and simple paint job are more than enough to accentuate this garden shed. Nestled between the cedar garden and sweeping privacy fence, the shed is small enough to not be obtrusive, yet retains a humble dignity all its own.

This cabana-style pool-house shed invokes the seaside structures of Martha's Vineyard, and also serves as a handy place to store poolside accessories. The nautical design motif is carried onto the surrounding deck.

Full-lite French doors, cedar shakes, and a brick foundation make this woodland getaway a popular summer destination. Read a book or watch a thunderstorm from a spacious interior. The relatively small size of a shed can make normally pricey materials affordable for the budget-minded builder.

Sheds and other outbuildings are perfect opportunities for green roof experiments. These popular living roofs help keep the shed interior cool during sultry summer days, and the natural absorption capabilities of grass and flowers limits water runoff into local sewers.

The warm wood tones, elegant gable roof, and simple, unadorned exterior make this shed a sublime addition to its suburban environment. Wired for electricity and equipped with a hasp and padlock, this shed serves equally well as a barbecue hotspot, summer workshop, and winter storage space. The deck-and-siding stain only needs to be touched up every few years, complementing the cobblestone sidewalk and cedar privacy fence.

This teahouse-style shed finds its inspiration in the Far East, and features many aspects of traditional Eastern architecture. The sliding panel doors, cherry tree, stone walkway, and bamboo fencing are subtle but significant additions to this pagoda-like haven.

Some sheds work hard while others play hard. This luxuriant Victorian play shed is as unique a garden fixture as you'll find: note the steeple spire, lattice trim, arched picture windows, and full-size swinging door, inviting imagination and intrigue. Gingerbread trim and a mini picket fence complete this storybook shed.

From a small suburban plot to a sprawling rural backyard, this armoire-style lean-to will keep your toys and tools high and dry during any season. A bold color scheme and natural stone foundation coupled with an attractive arched roof turn this shed into an attractive addition to any home.

A key factor in siting your shed is how its size informs its function and style. Even a small suburban shed like this makes a wonderful home for your tools and toys, and it's a perfect example of a shed whose simple beauty underscores its sizable utility.

The double barn-style doors on this carriage shed reveal a permanent home for a special project. The interior of a shed doesn't have to be adorned with shelves stacked with junk; a large shed with few distractions is perfect for tinkering with your favorite hobby.

While kit sheds are based on efficient, modern building concepts, you can still find them in traditional styles that feature custom details, such as this metal roof.

An oldie but a goodie, the gambrel-style shed offers more storage space than most, and fits equally well on the farm or in the backyard. The wide face of the shed invites customization; this shed is wired for electricity and features a paver apron, a window box, and even a bird house under the gable to top it all off.

A kit shed offers all the storage capacity of the best stick-built sheds, and almost instantly. Installing shelves or pegboard on the slat walls maximizes storage space. When the garage gets a little packed, a kit shed is a popular alternative for storing that riding mower or four-wheeler.

Sunny colors and Spanish tile turns this ordinary gable shed into an adorable gardener's delight. Blossoming flowerbeds and an old-world street lamp add a further sense of nostalgia and peace to this scene, while a side umbrella and outdoor patio allow one to take it all in.

The most beloved sheds tend to fill up over time, reflecting the passions and philosophies of their owners.

Cedar shingles and open eaves create a seaside-cottage feeling in this shed, even in the middle of a wooded lot.

Some sheds invite silence and reflection, while others waste no time getting down to business. This is an example of the latter. As a scaled-down garage, an extra vehicle, tractor, or riding lawn mower can easily be stored here, while the service door and sectional overhead door keep the contents safe.

Situated between the deck and the pool, this simple yet elegant shed doubles as a changing room for water-bound friends, and a quick escape when the rain starts to fall. The custom walkway, landscaping, and exterior lights make this shed even more appealing.

Just because it's on the shore doesn't mean it has to be fancy. This rustic, cabin-style shed ties perfectly to the weathered picket fence with its open porch and dovetail joinery.

The interior of a shed is an open invitation for customization and creativity. Besides the warm and rustic interior, this shed also features a workbench made from leftover floor tiles. The post-and-beam structural elements are decorative and functional. Sometimes a simple nail is the best way to hang tools, proving that a well-organized shed doesn't need to be overly fancy.

Integrating a shed into a patio plan can help define the space, block unwanted views, and provide shade and handy storage for patio items.

Because sheds are relatively small, material upgrades, such as cedar shingles instead of asphalt roofing or plywood siding, can still be affordable.

This gable shed has plenty of charm and the fieldstone foundation wall helps it blend perfectly with its surroundings.

This standalone shed/outbuilding is a contemporary design element in a natural landscape. The deck foundation and privacy screen conjure images of swanky summer parties. Fully wired and furnished with a built-in couch and bar, this is a shed that stays up late.

Designed to suit the setting, this shed's rustic materials and antique windows add an air of timelessness and easy country living. Many of the building materials were salvaged, including the barnwood siding.

When not functioning as a three-season oasis for a quiet read or family get-together, this screenhouse-style shed provides ample storage space during the colder months of the year. With room for a workbench, card table, patio set, or even hammock stand, a well-designed shed's function usually changes with the seasons.

Building Basics

After dreaming up your shed, now it's time to build it. Almost any answer you need can be found within this book. Each element of the construction process is covered in detail—from selecting a site to building the foundation to framing the floor, walls, and roof. You'll also learn about buying lumber and hardware. After your shed is built, return to this section for ideas about adding a ramp, deck, or steps.

Because the various elements are presented à la carte, you can pick and choose the designs and materials you like best. A shed's location often determines its foundation. A wooden skid foundation (the easiest to build) will often do just fine on a level plane. For sloping sites, a concrete block foundation may be the way to go. You'll find detailed instructions of both in this book.

Be sure to have your project plans approved by the local building department before starting construction. This is especially important if you're making substitutions to the plans featured in the Shed Projects section; customization is key in any shed project, so remember to have fun and make it yours.

In this chapter:

- Choosing a Site for Your Shed
- Anatomy of a Shed
- Lumber & Hardware
- Building Foundations
- Ramps, Steps & Decks

Choosing a Site for Your Shed

The first step in choosing a site for your building doesn't take place in your backyard but at the local building and zoning departments. By visiting the departments, or making calls, you should determine a few things about your project before making any definite plans. Most importantly, find out whether your proposed building will be allowed by zoning regulations and what specific restrictions apply to your situation. Zoning laws govern such matters as the size and height of the building and the percentage of your property it occupies, the building's location, and its position relative to the house, neighboring properties, the street, etc.

From the building side of things, ask if you need a permit to build your structure. If so, you'll have to submit plan drawings (photocopied plans from this book should suffice), as well as specifications for the foundation and materials and estimated cost. Once your project is approved, you may need to buy a permit to display on the building site, and you may be required to show your work at scheduled inspections.

Because outbuildings are detached and freestanding, codes typically govern them loosely. Many impose restrictions or require permits only on structures larger than 100, or even 120, square feet. Others draw the line with the type of foundation used. In some areas, buildings with concrete slab or pier foundations are classified as "permanent" and thus are subject to a specific set of restrictions (and taxation, in some cases), while buildings that are set on skids and can—in theory at least—be moved are considered temporary or accessory and may be exempt from the general building codes.

Once you get the green light from the local authorities, you can tromp around your yard with a tape measure and stake your claim for the new building. Of course, you'll have plenty of personal and practical reasons for placing the building in a particular area, but here are a few general considerations to keep in mind:

Soil & drainage: To ensure that your foundation will last (whatever type it is), plant your building on solid soil, in an area that won't collect water.

Access: For trucks, wheelbarrows, kids, etc. Do you want access in all seasons?

Utility lines: Contact local ordinances to find out where the water, gas, septic, and electrical lines run through your property. Often, local ordinances and utility companies require that lines are marked before

digging. This is an essential step not only because of legalities, but also because you don't want your building sitting over lines that may need repair.

Setback requirements: Most zoning laws dictate that all buildings, fences, etc., in a yard must be set back a specific distance from the property line. This setback may range from 6" to 3 feet or more.

Neighbors: To prevent civil unrest, or even a few weeks of ignored greetings, talk to your neighbors about your project.

View from the house: Do you want to admire your handiwork from the dinner table, or would you prefer that your outbuilding blend in with the outdoors? A playhouse in plain view makes it easy to check on the kids.

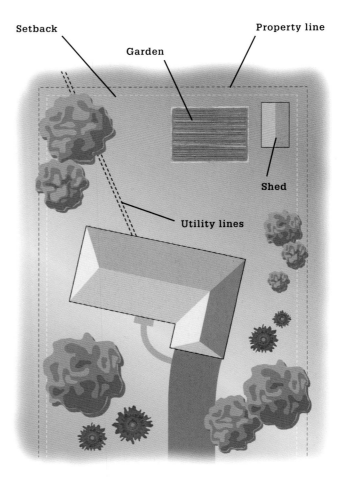

Visualize siting for your shed before it's built by simulating dimensions with stakes and a tarp. You can even move some of the items you plan to store into the staked-off area to see how they will fit.

Siting for Sunlight

Like houses, sheds can benefit enormously from natural light. Bringing sunlight into your backyard office, workshop, or garden house makes the interior space brighter and warmer, and it's the best thing for combating a boxy feel. To make the most of natural light, the general rule is to orient the building so its long side (or the side with the most windows) faces south. However, be sure to consider the sun's position at all times of the year, as well as the shadows your shed might cast on surrounding areas, such as a garden or outdoor sitting area.

SEASONAL CHANGES

Each day the sun crosses the sky at a slightly different angle, moving from its high point in summer to its low point in winter. Shadows change accordingly. In the summer, shadows follow the east-west axis and are very short at midday. Winter shadows point to the northeast and northwest and are relatively long at midday.

Generally, the south side of a building is exposed to sunlight throughout the year, while the north side may be shaded in fall, winter, and spring. Geographical location is also a factor: as you move north from the equator, the changes in the sun's path become more extreme.

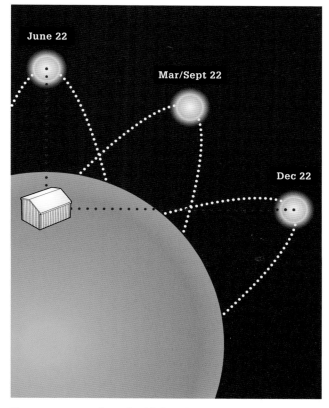

The sun moves from its high point in summer to its low point in winter. Shadows change accordingly.

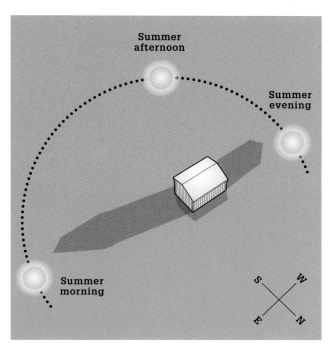

Shadows follow the east-west axis in the summer.

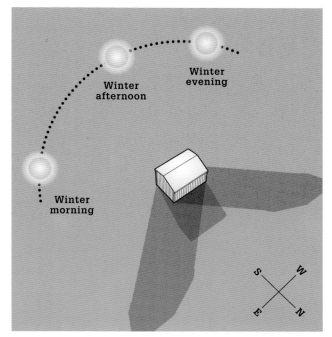

Winter shadows point to the northeast and northwest and are relatively long at midday.

Anatomy of a Shed

Shown as a cutaway, this shed illustrates many of the standard building components and how they fit together. It can also help you understand the major construction stages—each project in this book includes a specific construction sequence, but most follow the standard stages in some form:

1. Foundation—including preparing the site and adding a drainage bed;
2. Framing—the floor is first, followed by the walls, then the roof;
3. Roofing—adding sheathing, building paper, and roofing material;
4. Exterior finishes—including siding, trim, and doors and windows.

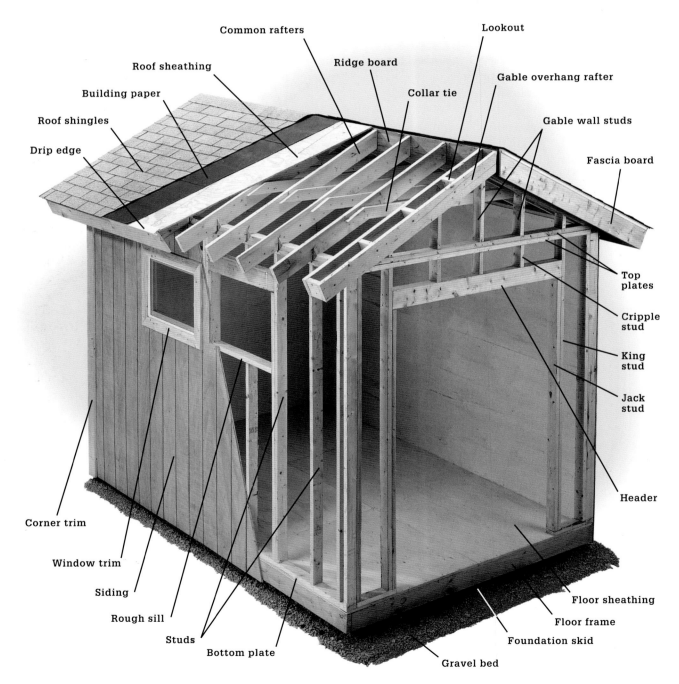

Common rafters

Ridge board

Lookout

Roof sheathing

Collar tie

Gable overhang rafter

Building paper

Gable wall studs

Roof shingles

Drip edge

Fascia board

Top plates

Cripple stud

King stud

Jack stud

Header

Corner trim

Window trim

Siding

Rough sill

Studs

Bottom plate

Floor sheathing

Floor frame

Foundation skid

Gravel bed

Lumber & Hardware

Lumber types most commonly used in outbuildings are pine—or related softwoods—or cedar, which is naturally rot-resistant and is less expensive than most other rot-resistant woods. For pine to be rot-resistant, it must be pressure-treated, typically with a chemical mixture called CCA (Chromated Copper Arsenate).

Pressure-treated lumber is cheaper than cedar, but it's not as attractive, so you may want to use it only in areas where appearance is unimportant. Plywood designated as exterior-grade is made with layers of cedar or treated wood and a special glue that makes it weather-resistant. For the long run, though, it's a good idea to cover any exposed plywood edges to prevent water intrusion.

Framing lumber—typically pine or pressure-treated pine—comes in a few different grades: Select Structural (SEL STR), Construction (CONST) or Standard (STAND), and Utility (UTIL). For most applications, Construction Grade No. 2 offers the best balance between quality and price. Utility grade is a lower-cost lumber suitable for blocking and similar uses but should not be used for structural members, such as studs and rafters. You can also buy "STUD" lumber: construction-grade 2 × 4s cut at the standard stud length of 92⅝". *Note: Treated lumber should be left exposed for approximately 6 months before applying finishes. Finishes will not adhere well to treated lumber that is still very green or wet. Lumber manufacturers likely have recommended times for their product.*

Board lumber, or finish lumber, is graded by quality and appearance, with the main criteria being the number and size of knots present. "Clear" pine, for example, has no knots.

All lumber has a nominal dimension (what it's called) and an actual dimension (what it actually measures). A chart on page 251 shows the differences for some common lumber sizes. Lumber that is greater than 4" thick (nominally) generally is referred to as timber. Depending on its surface texture and type, a timber may actually measure to its nominal dimensions, so check this out before buying. Cedar lumber also varies in size, depending on its surface texture. S4S (Surfaced-Four-Sides) lumber is milled smooth on all sides and follows the standard dimensioning, while boards with one or more rough surfaces can be over ⅛" thicker.

When selecting hardware for your project, remember one thing: All nails, screws, bolts, hinges, and anchors that will be exposed to weather or rest on concrete or that come in contact with treated lumber must be corrosion-resistant. The best all-around choice for nails and screws is hot-dipped galvanized steel, recognizable by its rough, dull-silver coating. Hot-dipped fasteners generally hold up better than the smoother, electroplated types, and they're the recommended choice for pressure-treated lumber. Aluminum and stainless steel are other materials suitable for outdoor exposure; however, aluminum fasteners corrode some types of treated lumber. While expensive, stainless steel is the best guarantee against staining from fasteners on cedar and redwood.

Another type of hardware you'll find throughout this book is the metal anchor, or framing connector, used to reinforce wood framing connections. All of the anchors called for in the plans are Simpson Strong-Tie® brand (see Resources), which are available at most lumberyards and home centers. If you can't find what you need on the shelves, look through one of the manufacturer's catalogs or visit the manufacturer's website. You can also order custom-made hangers. Keep in mind that metal anchors are effective only if they are installed correctly—always follow the manufacturer's installation instructions, and use exactly the type and number of fasteners recommended.

Finally, applying a finish to your project will help protect the wood from rot, fading and discoloration, and insects. Pine or similar untreated lumber must have a protective finish if it's exposed to the elements, but even cedar is susceptible to rot over time and will turn gray if left bare. If you paint the wood, apply a primer first—this helps the paint stick and makes it last longer. If you want to preserve the natural wood grain, use a stain or clear finish.

A combination of sheet stock, appearance-grade lumber, and structural lumber is used in most sheds.

Building Foundations

Your shed's foundation provides a level, stable structure to build upon and protects the building from moisture and erosion. In this section you'll learn to build four of the most common types of shed foundations. All but the concrete pier foundation are "on-grade" designs, meaning they are built on top of the ground and can be subject to rising and lowering a few inches during seasonal freezing and thawing of the underlying soil. This usually isn't a problem since a shed is a small, freestanding structure that's not attached to other buildings. However, it can adversely affect some interior finishes (wallboard, for example).

When choosing a foundation type for your shed, consider the specific site and the performance qualities of all systems in various climates; then check with the local building department to learn what's allowed in your area. Some foundations, such as concrete slabs, may classify sheds as permanent structures, which can affect property taxes, among other consequences. Residents in many areas may need to install special tie-downs or ground anchors according to local laws. If your building department requires a "frost-proof" foundation (so the building won't move with the freezing ground), you should be able to pass inspection by building your shed on concrete piers (see page 32). *Note: Information for forming, reinforcing, and bracing deeper foundation walls is not included here. A safe rule of thumb is that the depth required to get below the frost line in cold climates is 4 feet, though colder places like Canada and Alaska can have frost depths up to 8 feet.*

Wooden Skid Foundation

A skid foundation couldn't be simpler: two or more treated wood beams or landscape timbers (typically 4 × 4, 4 × 6, or 6 × 6) set on a bed of gravel. The gravel provides a flat, stable surface that drains well to help keep the timbers dry. Once the skids are set, the floor frame is built on top of them and is nailed to the skids to keep everything in place.

Building a skid foundation is merely a matter of preparing the gravel base, then cutting, setting, and leveling the timbers. The timbers you use must be rated for ground contact. It is customary, but purely optional, to make angled cuts on the ends of the skids—these add a minor decorative touch and make it easier to skid the shed to a new location, if necessary.

Because a skid foundation sits on the ground, it is subject to slight shifting due to frost in cold-weather climates. Often a shed that has risen out of level will correct itself with the spring thaw, but if it doesn't, you can lift the shed with jacks on the low side and add gravel beneath the skids to level it.

Tools & Materials ▸

Shovel	Circular saw
Rake	Square
4-ft. level	Treated wood timbers
Straight, 8-ft. 2 × 4	Compactible gravel
Hand tamper	Wood sealer-preservative

How to Build a Wooden Skid Foundation

STEP 1: PREPARE THE GRAVEL BASE

A. Remove 4" of soil in an area about 12" wider and longer than the dimensions of the building.
B. Fill the excavated area with a 4" layer of compactible gravel. Rake the gravel smooth, then check it for level using a 4-ft. level and a straight, 8-ft.-long 2 × 4. Rake the gravel until it is fairly level.
C. Tamp the gravel thoroughly using a hand tamper or a rented plate compactor. As you work, check the surface with the board and level, and add or remove gravel until the surface is level.

Excavate the building site and add a 4" layer of compactible gravel. Level, then tamp the gravel with a hand tamper or rented plate compactor (inset).

STEP 2: CUT & SET THE SKIDS

A. Cut the skids to length, using a circular saw or reciprocating saw. (Skids typically run parallel to the length of the building and are cut to the same dimension as the floor frame.)

B. To angle-cut the ends, measure down 1½" to 2" from the top edge of each skid. Use a square to mark a 45° cutting line down to the bottom edge, then make the cuts.

C. Coat the cut ends of the skids with a wood sealer-preservative and let them dry.

D. Set the skids on the gravel so they are parallel and their ends are even. Make sure the outer skids are spaced according to the width of the building.

STEP 3: LEVEL THE SKIDS

A. Level one of the outside skids, adding or removing gravel from underneath. Set the level parallel and level the skid along its length, then set the level perpendicular and level the skid along its width.

B. Place the straight 2 × 4 and level across the first and second skids, then adjust the second skid until it's level with the first. Make sure the second skid is level along its width.

C. Level the remaining skids in the same fashion, then set the board and level across all of the skids to make sure they are level with one another.

If desired, mark and clip the bottom corners of the skid ends. Use a square to mark a 45° angle cut.

Using a board and a level, make sure each skid is level along its width and length, and is level with the other skids.

2 × 4

Concrete Block Foundation

Concrete piers are columns of concrete that have their bases well below grade and the upper section sticking up out of the ground several inches or more. They provide a very stable shed base and, if you dig down past the frost line in your area, they eliminate heave and movement of the shed as the ground freezes and thaws. The most common method for building on concrete piers is to anchor the sole plate for a wall to the tops of the piers with a J-bolt or threaded rod that is attached to the pier. This method requires some precision when you lay out the positions of both the piers and—even more importantly—the J-bolts. A second option for building on concrete piers is to attach a thick, flat wood block to each pier with a j-bolt and countersunk nut and washer. This provides a flat, stable surface area that allows you to move your wall base plates around as needed and then anchor them to the block with lag screws.

Concrete block foundations are easy and inexpensive to build. In terms of simplicity, a block foundation is second only to the wooden skid. But the real beauty of this design is its ability to accommodate a sloping site: All you have to do is add blocks as needed to make the foundation level.

An easier option to pouring concrete piers is to purchase and install precast concrete piers. You simply position them on stable ground, level them, and set the joists for the deck directly into the grooved tops.

Mud Sill Buffer ▶

A 2 × 8 mud sill adds strength to a standard 2 × 6 floor frame. First, you fasten the side rim joists to the sill, then you set the assembly on top of the foundation blocks and install the remaining floor joists.

Tools & Materials ▶

Mason's lines & stakes
Excavation tools
Hand tamper
2-ft. level
4-ft. level
Long, straight 2 × 4
Caulking gun
Compactible gravel
Solid concrete blocks
Asphalt shingles or 1 × 8 pressure-treated lumber, as needed
Construction adhesive

A foundation created with solid concrete blocks on a prepared base is simple to build and makes an easy solution to dealing with low slopes.

How to Build a Concrete Block Foundation

STEP 1: PREPARE THE SITE

A. Using four mason's lines tied to stakes, plot the foundation layout. The foundation exterior should equal the outer dimensions of the floor frame. Use the 3-4-5 method to ensure perfectly square layout lines.

B. Mark the block locations onto the strings, and then onto the ground: Locate the corner blocks at the string intersections, and locate the intermediate blocks at equal intervals between the corner blocks. For an 8 × 10-ft. or 8 × 12-ft. shed, one row of four blocks (or block stacks) running down each side of the shed is sufficient.

C. Remove the mason's lines, but leave the stakes in place. At each block location dig a 16 × 20" hole that is 4" deep. Tamp the soil.

D. Add a layer of compactible gravel in each hole and tamp well, adding gravel if necessary to bring the top of the gravel up to grade. Tamp all added gravel.

STEP 2: SET THE BLOCKS

A. For the first block, retie the mason's lines. At the highest point on the gravel bed, square up a 4"-thick block to the layout lines.

B. Level the block in both directions, adding or removing gravel as needed.

C. Tape a 4-ft. level to the center of a long, straight 2 × 4.

D. Set up each of the remaining blocks or block stacks, using the level and 2 × 4 spanning from the first block to gauge the proper height. Start each stack with a 4"-thick block, and make sure the block itself is level before adding more blocks. Use 2" blocks as needed to add height, or shim stacks with trimmed pieces of asphalt shingles or 1 × 8 pressure-treated lumber.

E. Use the level and 2 × 4 to make sure all of the blocks and stacks are level with one another.

STEP 3: GLUE THE BLOCK STACKS

A. Glue stacked blocks together with construction adhesive. Also glue any shim material to the tops of the blocks.

B. After gluing, check to make sure all blocks and stacks are level with one another, and that they are on the layout lines, then remove the strings and stakes.

Create a bed of compacted gravel centered at each block location in your layout.

Set a block at the highest point on the site, check it with a level, and adjust as needed. (Inset) Use a level and board spanning across the blocks to establish the height of each stack so all the tops are level.

Bind stacked blocks together with exterior-rated construction adhesive to prevent shifting.

Concrete Pier Foundation

Foundation piers are poured concrete cylinders that you form using cardboard tubes. The tubes come in several diameters and are commonly available from building materials suppliers. For an 8 × 10-ft. shed, the minimal foundation consists of 8"-diameter piers at the corners.

You can anchor the shed's floor frame to the piers using a variety of methods. One method (shown here) is to bolt a wood block to the top of each pier, then fasten the floor frame to the blocks. Other anchoring options involve metal post bases and various framing connectors either set into the wet concrete or fastened to the piers after the concrete has cured. Be sure to consult your local building department for the recommended or required anchoring specifications.

Piers that extend below the frost line—the ground depth to which the earth freezes each winter—will keep your shed from shifting during annual freeze-thaw cycles. This is a standard requirement for major structures, like houses, but not typically for freestanding sheds (check with your building department). Another advantage of the pier foundation is that you can extend the piers well above the ground to accommodate a sloping site. *Note: All concrete should have compacted gravel underneath and against back walls as backfill. All reinforcing steel should have a minimum of 1½" concrete cover.*

How to Build a Concrete Pier Foundation

Tools & Materials ▸

Circular saw	Shovel	2½" screws	Concrete mix
Drill	Posthole digger	Stakes	J-bolts with washers
Mason's line	Reciprocating saw	Nails	and nuts
Sledgehammer	or handsaw	Masking tape	2 × 10 pressure-treated
Line level	Utility knife	Cardboard concrete forms	lumber (rated for
Framing square	Ratchet wrench	Paper	ground contact)
Plumb bob	2 × 4 lumber		

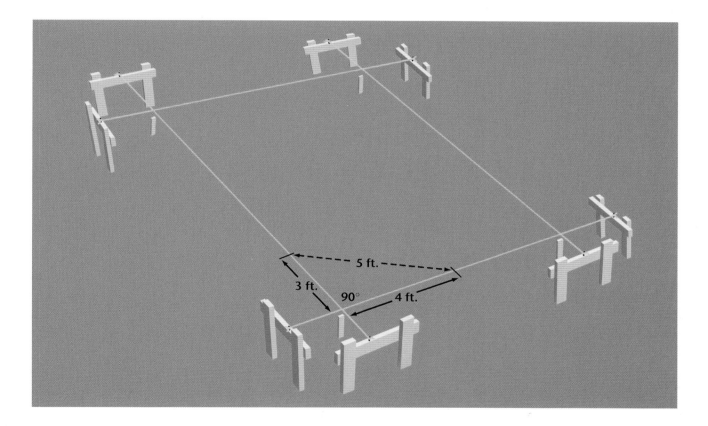

STEP 1: CONSTRUCT THE BATTER BOARDS

A. Cut two 24"-long 2 × 4 legs for each batter board (for most projects you'll need eight batter boards total). Cut one end square and cut the other end to a sharp point, using a circular saw. Cut one 2 × 4 crosspiece for each batter board at about 18".

B. Assemble each batter board using 2½" screws. Fasten the crosspiece about 2" from the square ends of the legs. Make sure the legs are parallel and the crosspiece is perpendicular to the legs.

STEP 2: SET THE BATTER BOARDS & ESTABLISH PERPENDICULAR MASON'S LINES

A. Measure and mark the locations of the four corner piers with stakes, following your project plan.

B. Set two batter boards to form a corner about 18" behind each stake. Drive the batter boards into the ground until they are secure, keeping the crosspieces roughly level with one another.

(continued)

Cut the batter board pieces from 2 × 4 lumber and assemble them with screws.

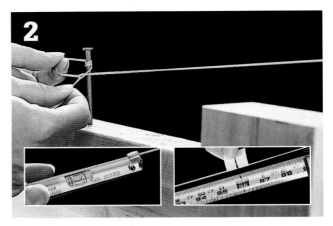

Tie the mason's lines securely to the nails, and level the lines with a line level (inset, left). Use tape to mark points on the lines (inset, right).

C. Stretch a mason's line between two batter boards at opposing corners (not diagonally) and tie the ends to nails driven into the top edge of the crosspieces; align the nails and line with the stakes. Attach a line level to the line, and pull the line very taut, making sure it's level before tying it.

D. Run a second level line perpendicular to the first: Tie off the end that's closest to the first string, then stretch the line to the opposing batter board while a helper holds a framing square at the intersection of the lines. When the lines are perpendicular, drive a nail and tie off the far end.

E. Confirm that the lines are exactly perpendicular, using the 3-4-5 method: Starting at the intersection, measure 3 ft. along one string and make a mark onto a piece of masking tape. Mark the other string 4 ft. from the intersection. Measure diagonally between the two marks; the distance should equal 5 ft. Reposition the second string, if necessary, until the diagonal measurement is 5 ft.

STEP 3: MARK THE FOOTING LOCATIONS

A. Following your plan, measure from the existing lines and use the 3-4-5 method to add two more perpendicular lines to form a layout with four 90° corners. Use the line level to make sure the mason's lines are level. The intersections of the lines should mark the centers of the corner piers, not necessarily the outside edge of floor framing.

B. Check the squareness of your line layout by measuring diagonally from corner to corner: when the measurements are equal, the frame is square. Make any necessary adjustments.

C. Plumb down with a plumb bob and place a stake directly under each line intersection. Mark the locations of intermediate piers onto the layout strings, then plumb down and drive stakes at those locations.

D. Untie each line at one end only, then coil the line and place it out of the way. Leaving one end tied will make it easier to restring the lines later.

STEP 4: SET THE FORMS

A. Dig holes for the forms, centering them around the stakes. The holes should be a few inches larger in diameter than the cardboard forms. The hole depth must meet the local building code requirements—add 4" to the depth to allow for a layer of gravel. For deep holes, use a posthole digger or a rented power auger. Add 4" of gravel to the bottom of each hole.

B. Cut each cardboard form so it will extend at least 3" above the ground. The tops of all piers/forms should be level with each other. Also, the top ends of the forms must be straight, so place the factory-cut end up, whenever possible. Otherwise, mark a straight cutting line using a large piece of paper with at least one straight edge: Wrap the paper completely around the form so that it overlaps itself a few inches. Position the straight edge of the paper on the cutting mark, and align the overlapping edges of the paper with each other. Mark around the tube along the edge of the paper. Cut the tube with a reciprocating saw or handsaw.

C. Set the tubes in the holes and fill in around them with dirt. Set a level across the top of each tube to make sure the top is level as you secure the tube with dirt. Pack the dirt firmly, using a shovel handle or a stick.

Use a plumb bob to mark the pier locations. Drive a stake into the ground directly below the plumb bob pointer.

Wrap paper around the form to mark a straight cutting line (inset). Set the forms in the holes on top of a 4" gravel layer.

Fill the forms with concrete, then set the J-bolts. Check with a plumb bob to make sure the bolts are centered.

Anchor a block to each pier with a washer and nut. If desired, countersink the hardware (inset).

STEP 5: POUR THE CONCRETE

A. Restring the mason's lines and confirm that the forms are positioned accurately.

B. Mix the concrete following the manufacturer's directions; prepare only as much as you can easily work with before the concrete sets. Fill each form with concrete, using a long stick to tamp it down and eliminate air pockets in the concrete. Overfill the form slightly.

C. Level the concrete by pulling a 2 × 4 on edge across the top of the form, using a side-to-side sawing motion. Fill low spots with concrete so that the top is perfectly flat.

D. Set a J-bolt into the wet concrete in the center of the form. Lower the bolt slowly, wiggling it slightly to eliminate air pockets. Use a plumb bob to make sure the bolt is aligned exactly with the mark on

the mason's line. *Note: You can set the bolt at 1½" above the concrete so it will be flush with the top of the block, or extend it about 2½" so the washer and nut will sit on top of the block; doing the latter means you won't have to countersink the washer and nut. Make sure the bolt is plumb, then smooth the concrete around the bolt and let the concrete cure.*

STEP 6: INSTALL THE WOOD BLOCKS

A. Cut 8 × 8" square blocks from 2 × 10 pressure-treated lumber that's rated for ground contact.

B. Drill a hole for the J-bolt through the exact center of each block; if you're countersinking the hardware, first drill a counterbore for the washer and nut.

C. Position each block on a pier, then add a galvanized washer and nut. Use the layout strings to align the blocks, then tighten the nuts to secure the blocks.

Concrete Slab Foundation

The slab foundation commonly used for sheds is called a slab-on-grade foundation. This combines a 3½"- to 4"-thick floor slab with an 8"- to 12"-thick perimeter footing that provides extra support for the walls of the building. The whole foundation can be poured at one time using a simple wood form.

Because they sit above ground, slab-on-grade foundations are susceptible to frost heave and in cold-weather climates are suitable only for detached buildings. Specific design requirements also vary by locality, so check with the local building department regarding the depth of the slab, the metal reinforcement required, the type and amount of gravel required for the subbase, and whether plastic or another type of moisture barrier is needed under the slab.

The slab shown in this project has a 3½"-thick interior with an 8"-wide × 8"-deep footing along the perimeter. The top of the slab sits 4" above ground level, or grade. There is a 4"-thick layer of compacted gravel underneath the slab and the concrete is reinforced internally with a layer of 6 × 6" $^{10}\!/_{10}$ welded wire mesh (WWM). (In some areas, you may be required to add rebar in the foundation perimeter—check the local code.) After the concrete is poured and finished, 8"-long galvanized J-bolts are set into the slab along the edges. These are used later to anchor the wall framing to the slab. *Note: All concrete should have compacted gravel underneath and against the back wall as backfill. All reinforcing steel should have a minimum of 1½" concrete cover.*

Tools & Materials ▸

Circular saw	Concrete edger
Drill	Compactible gravel
Mason's line	2 × 3 & 2 × 4 lumber
Sledgehammer	1¼" & 2½"
Line level	deck screws
Framing square	¾" A-C plywood
Shovel	8d nails
Wheelbarrow	5 × 10-ft. welded wire
Rented plate compactor	mesh (WWM)
Bolt cutters	1½" brick pavers
Bull float	J-bolts
Hand-held	2"-thick rigid
concrete float	foam insulation

Labels: 8"-thick perimeter · Plywood form · 4" compacted gravel · Trench sloped 45° · Welded wire mesh · 3½"-thick slab · #4 bars

How to Build a Concrete Slab Foundation

STEP 1: EXCAVATE THE SITE

A. Set up batter boards and run level mason's lines to represent the outer dimensions of the slab. Use the 3-4-5 method to make sure your lines are perpendicular, and check your final layout for squareness by measuring the diagonals.

B. Excavate the area 4" wider and longer than the string layout—this provides some room to work. For the footing portion along the perimeter, dig a trench that is 8" wide × 8" deep.

C. Remove 3½" of soil over the interior portion of the slab, then slope the inner sides of the trench at 45°. Set up temporary cross strings to check the depth as you work.

D. Add a 4" layer of compactible gravel over the entire excavation and rake it level. Compact the gravel thoroughly, using a rented plate compactor. *Note: All areas are to be level (flat).*

Measure down from the layout lines and temporary cross strings to check the depth of the excavation.

Assemble the form pieces with 2½" deck screws, then check the inner dimensions of the form. For long runs, join pieces with plywood mending plates.

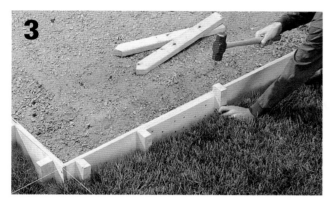

Drive stakes every 12" to support the form, using the mason's lines to make sure the form remains straight.

Lay out sheets of wire mesh, tie the rows together, then prop up the mesh with brick pavers or metal bolsters.

STEP 2: BUILD THE FORM

A. Cut sheets of ¾" A-C plywood into six strips of equal width—about 7⅞", allowing for the thickness of the saw blade. To make sure the cuts are straight, use a table saw or a circular saw and straightedge.

B. Cut the plywood strips to length to create the sides of the form. Cut two sides 1½" long so they can overlap the remaining two sides. For sides that are longer than 8 ft., join two strips with a mending plate made of scrap plywood; fasten the plate to the back sides of the strips with 1¼" screws.

C. Assemble the form by fastening the corners together with screws. The form's inner dimensions must equal the outer dimensions of the slab.

STEP 3: SET THE FORM

A. Cut 18"-long stakes from 2 × 3 lumber—you'll need one stake for every linear foot of form, plus one extra stake for each corner. Taper one end of each stake to a point.

B. Place the form in the trench and align it with the mason's lines. Drive a stake near the end of each side of the form, setting the stake edge against the form and driving down to 3" above grade.

C. Measuring down from the mason's lines, position the form 4" above grade. Tack the form to the stakes with partially driven 8d nails (driven through the form into the stakes). Measure the diagonals to make sure the form is square and check that the top of the form is level. Drive the nails completely.

D. Add a stake every 12" and drive them down below the top edge of the form. Secure the form with two 8d nails driven into each stake. As you work, check with a string line to make sure the form sides are straight and the tops are level, and measure the diagonals to check for square.

(continued)

Screed the concrete after filling the form, using two people to screed, while a third fills low spots with a shovel.

Float the slab with a bull float, then set the J-bolts at the marked locations (inset).

STEP 4: ADD THE METAL REINFORCEMENT

A. Lay out rows of 6 × 6" $^{10}/_{10}$ welded wire mesh so their ends are 1½" to 2" from the insides of the forms. Cut the mesh with bolt cutters or heavy pliers, and stand on the unrolled mesh as you cut, to prevent it from springing back. Overlap the sheets of mesh by 6" and tie them together with tie wire.

B. Prop up the mesh with pieces of 1½"-thick brick pavers or metal bolsters. The WWM should be just below the center of the slab (about 2" down in a 3½" slab).

C. Mark the layout of the J-bolts onto the top edges of the form, following your plan. (J-bolts typically are placed 4" to 6" from each corner and every 3 ft. in between, but may vary.)

STEP 5: POUR THE SLAB

A. Estimate and order concrete (see page 39). Starting at one end, fill in the form with concrete, using a shovel to distribute it. Use the shovel blade or a 2 × 4 to stab into the concrete to eliminate air pockets and settle it around the wire mesh and along the forms. Fill with concrete to the top of the form.

B. As the form fills, have two helpers screed the concrete, using a straight 2 × 4 or 2 × 6 that spans the form: Drag the screed board along the top of the form, working it back and forth in a sawing motion. Throw shovelfuls of concrete ahead of the screed board to fill low spots. The goal of screeding is to make the surface of the concrete perfectly flat and level, if not smooth.

C. Gently rap the outsides of the form with a hammer to settle the concrete along the inside faces of the form. This helps smooth the sides of the slab, but too much will cause aggregate to settle and concrete will "scale" or "spall."

STEP 6: FINISH THE CONCRETE & SET THE J-BOLTS

A. Immediately after screeding the concrete, make one pass with a bull float to smooth the surface. Add small amounts of concrete to fill low spots created by the floating, then smooth those areas with the float. Floating forces the aggregate down and draws the water and sand to the surface.

B. Set the galvanized J-bolts into the concrete 1¾" from the outside edges of the slab (bottom should turn in toward the slab). Work the bolts into the concrete by wiggling them slightly to eliminate air pockets. The bolts should be plumb and protrude 2½" from the slab surface. After setting each bolt, smooth the concrete around the bolt, using a magnesium or wood concrete float.

C. Watch the concrete carefully as it cures. The bull-floating will cause water (called bleed water) to rise, casting a sheen on the surface. Wait for the bleed water to disappear and the surface to become dull. Pressure-test the concrete for firmness by stepping on it with one foot: if your foot sinks ¼" or less, the concrete is ready to be finished. *Note: Air-entrained concrete may have very little bleed water, so it's best to rely on the pressure test.*

D. Float the concrete with a hand-held magnesium or wood float, working the float back and forth until the surface is smooth. If you can't reach the entire slab from the sides, lay pieces of 2"-thick rigid foam insulation over the concrete and kneel on the insulation. Work backwards to cover up any impressions.

E. Use a concrete edging tool to round over the slab edge, running the edger between the slab and the form. If you want a very smooth finish, work the concrete with a trowel.

F. Let the concrete cure for 24 hours, then strip the forms. Wait an additional 24 hours before building on the slab.

Estimating & Ordering Concrete ▶

A slab for a shed requires a lot of concrete: an 8 × 10-ft. slab designed like the one in this project calls for about 1.3 cubic yards of concrete; a 12 × 12-ft. slab, about 2.3 cubic yards. Considering the amount involved, you'll probably want to order ready-mix concrete delivered by truck to the site (most companies have a minimum order charge). Tell the mixing company that you're using the concrete for an exterior slab.

An alternative for smaller slabs is to rent a concrete trailer from a rental center or landscaping company; they fill the trailer with one yard of mixed concrete and you tow it home with your own vehicle.

If you're having your concrete delivered, be sure to have a few helpers on-hand when the truck arrives; neither the concrete nor the driver will wait for you to get organized. Also, concrete trucks must be unloaded completely, so designate a dumping spot for any excess. Once the form is filled, load a couple of wheelbarrows with concrete (in case you need it) then have the driver dump the rest. Be sure to spread out and hose down the excess concrete so you aren't left with an immovable boulder in your yard.

If you've never worked with concrete, finishing a large slab can be a challenging introduction; you might want some experienced help with the pour.

ESTIMATING CONCRETE

Calculate the amount of concrete needed for a slab of this design using this formula:

Width × Length × Depth, in ft. (of main slab)
Multiply by 1.5 (for footing edge and spillage)
Divide by 27 (to convert to cubic yards)

Example—for a 12 × 12-ft. slab:
12 × 12 × .29 (3½") = 41.76
41.76 × 1.5 = 62.64
62.64 ÷ 27 = 2.32 cubic yards

Timing is key to an attractive concrete finish. When concrete is poured, the heavy materials gradually sink, leaving a thin layer of water—known as bleed water—on the surface. To achieve an attractive finish, it's important to let bleed water dry before proceeding with other steps. Follow these rules to avoid problems:

- Settle and screed the concrete and add control joints immediately after pouring and before bleed water appears. Otherwise, crazing, spalling, and other flaws are likely.
- Let bleed water dry before floating or edging. Concrete should be hard enough that foot pressure leaves no more than a ¼"-deep impression.
- Do not overfloat the concrete; it may cause bleed water to reappear. Stop floating if a sheen appears, and resume when it is gone.

Note: Bleed water does not appear with air-entrained concrete, which is used in regions where temperatures often fall below freezing.

Tips for Pouring Concrete ▶

- Do not overload your wheelbarrow. Experiment with sand or dry mix to find a comfortable, controllable volume. This also helps you get a feel for how many wheelbarrow loads it will take to complete your project.
- Once concrete is poured and floated it must cure. It should not dry. If it is a hot day it is a good idea to spray mist from a hose after it has "set" to keep it moist. Make sure you have a flat, stable surface between the concrete source and the forms.
- Start pouring concrete at the farthest point from the concrete source, and work your way back.

Ramps, Steps & Decks

Most of the sheds in this book with framed wood floors have a finished floor height that sits at least 10" above the ground. This makes for a fairly tall step up to the shed. On a sloping site, the approach to the shed may be considerably lower than the floor. But not to worry—you can quickly build a custom ramp or set of steps for safe, easy access. As an alternative, you might add a large platform that serves as both a step and a sun porch.

Simple Ramp

A basic, sturdy ramp is a great convenience for moving heavy equipment in and out of your shed. Using the simple design shown here, you can make the slope of the ramp as gentle or as steep as you like (within reason). Of course, the gentler the slope, the easier it is roll things up the ramp. Construct your ramp from pressure-treated lumber rated for "ground contact." If desired, set the bottom end of the ramp on a bed of compacted gravel for added stability.

Add a single ramp to your shed to facilitate moving heavy equipment.

How to Build a Shed Ramp

STEP 1: DETERMINE THE SLOPE & INSTALL THE LEDGER

A. Set a board onto the shed floor in front of the door opening with its end on the ground. Experiment with different placements until you find the best slope for your needs.
B. Mark where the end of the board meets the ground. Measure in toward the shed about 6" and make another mark—this represents the end of the ramp.

STEP 2: INSTALL THE LEDGER

A. Draw a level line onto the shed's floor frame 4⅝" below the shed's floor surface.
B. Cut a 2 × 4 ledger board to length so it equals the total width of the ramp.
    Note: The ramp should be at least as wide as the door opening.
C. Position the ledger on the level line so it is centered from side to side underneath the door.

Tools & Materials ▸

Saw	2 × 6 pressure-
Drill	treated lumber
Framing square	3" corrosion-
2 × 4 pressure-	resistant screws
treated lumber	

STEP 3: CUT THE FIRST STRINGER

A. To mark the angles for the stringer cuts, plot the layout of the ramp onto a sheet of plywood (or the shed floor). First, use a framing square to make two perpendicular lines representing the front of the shed and the ground. Measure the height of the shed floor, then subtract 1⅝". Transfer this dimension to one of the layout lines. Measure from the shed to the end-of-ramp mark on the ground, then transfer this dimension to the other layout line.

Place a board between the ground and the shed floor to find the desired ramp slope.

B. Place a 2 × 6 stringer board onto the layout lines so its top edge meets the two marks. Use the perpendicular lines to mark the angled end cuts on the stringer. Make the cuts.

C. Cut the upper end of the stringer to accept the ledger by making a 1½"-deep notch starting about 2¾" down from the top edge. The notch should be parallel to the end of the stringer.

STEP 4: CUT & INSTALL THE REMAINING STRINGERS

A. Test-fit the first stringer on the ledger. Make sure the 2 × 6 decking will not extend above the shed floor when installed. Make adjustments to the stringer cuts as needed.

B. Use the first stringer as a template to mark the cuts on the remaining stringers. You'll need one stringer for each end and every 12" to 16" in between. Cut the remaining stringers.

C. Fasten the stringers to the ledger and the shed's floor frame using 3" screws. The end stringers should be flush with the ends of the ledger.

D. Fasten the ledger to the floor framing with 3" corrosion-resistant screws.

STEP 5: INSTALL THE DECKING

A. Cut 2 × 6 decking boards to equal the width of the ramp.

B. Make sure the stringers are perpendicular to the shed, and then fasten the decking boards to the stringers with 3" screws. Leave a ¼" gap between boards to promote drainage and add traction on the ramp surface. *Note: If the top or bottom board will be narrower than 2", plan the decking layout so the first and last boards are roughly the same width.*

C. If desired, bevel the front edge of the board at the bottom of the ramp to ease the transition.

Mark a level line 4⅝" below the floor to locate the top edge of the ledger.

Use perpendicular layout lines to mark the angled end cuts on the first stringer.

Make sure the first stringer fits well, then use it to mark the remaining stringers for cutting.

Fasten the decking to the stringers with 3" screws to complete the ramp.

Traditional Stairs

A small set of framed wooden stairs is usually called for when a shed floor stands at about 21" or more above the ground (for lower floors, you might prefer to build a couple of simple platforms for three easy steps into the shed; see page 45). But regardless of the floor height, notched-stringer stairs add a nice handmade, built-in look to an entrance. And it's fun to learn the geometry and carpentry skills behind traditional stair building.

When planning your project, bear in mind that stairs in general are strictly governed by building codes. Your local building department may impose specific design requirements for your project, or they may not get involved at all—just be sure to find out. In any case, here are some of the standard requirements for stairs:

- Minimum tread depth: 10"
- Maximum riser height: 7¾" (7¼" is a good standard height)
- Minimum stair width: 36" (make your staircase at least a few inches wider than the shed's door opening)
- A handrail is often required for stairs with more than one riser, but this may not apply for storage sheds and the like (check with the local building department)

Because stairs are easier and safer to use when starting from a flat landing area, it's a good idea to include a level pad of compacted gravel at the base of your stairs. This also provides stability for the staircase and eliminates the potential for a slippery, muddy patch forming at the landing area.

Calculating Step Size ▸

Properly built stairs have perfectly uniform treads (the part you step on) and risers (the vertical section of each step).

To determine the riser height, all you have to do is divide the total rise—the distance from the ground to the shed floor—and divide by the number of steps. If you end up with risers over 7¾", add another step.

Determining the tread depth is up to you. However, because shallow steps are hard to climb and easy to trip on, you should make your treads at least 10" deep, but preferably 11" or more. The tread depth multiplied by the number of steps gives you the total run—how far the steps extend in front of the shed. When cutting the stringers, you cut the first (bottom) riser shorter than the others to account for the thickness of the tread material.

Stringer stairs are an easy and often necessary addition to elevated shed doors.

How to Build Notched-Stringer Stairs

Tools & Materials ▸

Framing square
Circular saw
Handsaw
Drill and bits
Sledgehammer

Compactible gravel
2 × 12 pressure-
  treated lumber
Corrosion resistant
  framing connectors

10d × 1½" galvanized nails
3" galvanized screws
2½" galvanized screws
2 × 4 pressure-
  treated lumber

2 16" lengths of
  #4 (½"-dia.)
  rebar
⅝ × 6 pressure-
  treated lumber

STEP 1: LAY OUT THE FIRST STRINGER

A. Use a framing square to lay out the first stringer onto a straight piece of 2 × 12 lumber. Starting at one end of the board, position the square along the board's top edge. Align the 12" mark of the blade (long leg of the square) and the 6½" mark on the tongue (short leg of the square) with the edge of the board. Trace along the edges of the blade and tongue. The tongue mark represents the first riser.

B. Use the square to extend the blade marking across the full width of the board. Then, draw a parallel line 1" up from this line. The new line marks the bottom cut for the stringer (the 1" offset accounts for the thickness of the tread material).

C. Continue the step layout, starting at the point where the first riser meets the top of the board.

D. Mark the cutting line at the top end of the stringer by extending the third (top) tread marking across the full width of the board. From this line, make a perpendicular line 12" from the top riser: this is where you'll cut the edge of the stringer that fits against the shed.

STEP 2: CUT THE STRINGERS

A. Make the cuts on the first stringer using a circular saw set to full depth. Where treads and risers intersect, cut just up to the lines, then finish the cuts with a handsaw.

B. Test-fit the stringer on the shed. The top tread cut should be 1" below the shed floor. Make adjustments to the stringer cuts as needed.

C. Use the first stringer as a template to mark the remaining stringers. You'll need one stringer for each end and every 12" to 16" in between. Cut the remaining stringers.

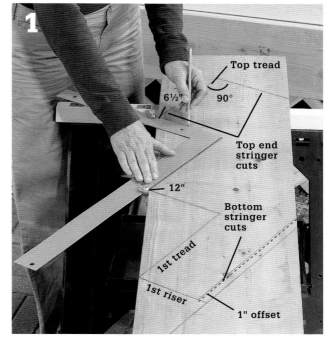

Use a framing square to mark the treads, risers, and end cuts on the stringer.

Cut out stringers with a circular saw, and finish the corners of the cuts with a handsaw.

(continued)

Mount the top ends of the stringers to the shed using framing connectors (shown). Anchor the bottom ends to blocking.

Trim the rear tread boards as needed to fit behind the front treads.

STEP 3: INSTALL THE STRINGERS

A. Mark a level line onto the shed's floor frame, 1" below the finished floor surface. Onto the level line, mark the center and outsides of the stairs. Transfer the side markings to the ground using a square and straightedge.

B. Cut 2× blocking to carry the bottom ends of the stringers. Fasten the blocking to the ground using 16" pieces of #4 rebar driven through ½" holes. For concrete or masonry, use masonry screws or a powder-actuated nailer.

C. Anchor the tops of the stringers to the floor frame with corrosion-resistant framing connectors, using 1½"-long 10d galvanized common nails. The tops of the stringers should be flush with the level line.

D. Anchor the bottom ends of the stringers with nails or screws.

STEP 4: ADD THE TREAD & RISER BOARDS

A. Cut the treads to length from 2 × 8" pressure-treated decking lumber or two 2 × 6" boards ripped to 4" each. You can cut the treads to fit flush with the outside stringers or overhang them by ½" or so for a different look.

B. On each step, position a full-width tread at the front with the desired overhang beyond the riser below. Fasten the tread to the stringers with 2½" galvanized screws. Rip the second tread to size and fasten it behind the first tread, leaving a ¼" gap between the boards. Install the remaining tread boards.

C. If desired, install 1 × 6 riser boards so the ends are flush with the outside stringers (no overhang). Or, you can omit the riser boards for open steps.

Option: Add riser boards to enclose each step.

Option: Leave off riser boards for an open staircase.

Platforms for Steps & Decking

This simple platform is a popular option for sheds because it's so easy to build and it provides a sturdy step for comfortable access. You can use the same basic design to make platforms of any size. A large platform can become an outdoor sitting area, while a stack of smaller platforms can create a set of steps that are accessible from three directions. For stability and longevity, set your platforms on top of solid concrete blocks—the same type used for block foundations. See page 30 for more information about building with concrete block.

Tools & Materials ▸

Shovel
Level
Saw
Drill
Compactible gravel
  (optional)

2× treated lumber
16d galvanized
  common nails
3" deck screws

How to Build a Basic Platform

STEP 1: BUILD THE PLATFORM FRAME

A. Cut two long side pieces from 2 × 6 lumber. These should equal the total length of the frame. Cut two end pieces to fit between the side pieces. For example, if your platform will measure 24 × 36", cut the sides at 36" and cut the ends at 23". Also cut an intermediate support for every 16" in between: make these the same length as the end pieces.
B. Fasten the end pieces between the sides with pairs of 16d galvanized common nails.
C. Fasten the intermediate support at the center of the frame or at 16" intervals.

STEP 2: INSTALL THE DECKING

A. Cut 2 × 6 decking boards to fit the long dimension of the platform frame (you can also use 5⁄4 × 6 decking boards). *Option: For a finished look, cut the decking about 1" too long so it overhangs the frame structure.*
B. Measure the frame diagonally from corner to corner to make sure it is square.
C. Starting at the front edge of the frame, attach the decking to the framing pieces with pairs of 3" deck screws. Leave a ¼" gap between the boards. Rip the last board to width so that it overhangs the front edge of the frame by 1".
D. Set the platform in position on top of the block foundation. If desired, fasten the platform to the shed with 3" screws.

Assemble the frame pieces with pairs of 16d common nails.

Install the decking with screws, leaving a ¼" gap between boards.

Shed Projects

It's time to get that tool belt dusty—it's time to build a shed. Each custom project in this section features a complete materials list to make shopping at your local home center and lumberyard a breeze. From the detailed drawings and how-to instructions you'll learn what length to cut each piece and where it goes in the finished product. The step-by-step instructions will walk you through the entire sequence, highlighting important and unique details along the way. Even if you don't find the exact shed you want in this chapter, you can easily alter the plans or even combine elements from different sheds to one that meets your needs perfectly. *Note: Making sheds larger than shown may require review of code/design criteria for lumber sizes, especially floor joists, roof joists, and headers.*

In this chapter:

- Lean-to Tool Bin
- Simple Storage Shed
- Modern Utility Shed
- Service Shed
- Timber-frame Shed
- Salt Box Storage Shed
- Mini Garden Shed
- Clerestory Studio
- Sunlight Garden Shed
- Gambrel Garage
- Convenience Shed
- Rustic Summerhouse
- Gothic Playhouse
- Metal & Wood Kit Sheds

Lean-to Tool Bin

The lean-to is a classic outbuilding intended as a supplementary structure for a larger building. Its simple shed-style roof helps it blend with the neighboring structure and directs water away and keeps leaves and debris from getting trapped between the two buildings. When built to a small shed scale, the lean-to (sometimes called a closet shed) is most useful as an easy-access storage locker that saves you extra trips into the garage for often-used lawn and garden tools and supplies.

This lean-to tool bin is not actually attached to the house, though it appears to be. It is designed as a freestanding building with a wooden skid foundation that makes it easy to move. With all four sides finished, the bin can be placed anywhere, but it works best when set next to a house or garage wall or a tall fence. If you locate the bin

out in the open—where it won't be protected against wind and extreme weather—be sure to anchor it securely to the ground to prevent it from blowing over.

As shown here, the bin is finished with asphalt shingle roofing, T1-11 plywood siding, and 1× cedar trim, but you can substitute any type of finish to match or complement a neighboring structure. Its 65"-tall double doors provide easy access to its 18 square feet of floor space. The 8-ft.-tall rear wall can accommodate a set of shelves while leaving enough room below for long-handled tools.

Because the tool bin sits on the ground, in cold climates it will be subject to shifting with seasonal freeze-thaw cycles. Therefore, do not attach the tool bin to your house or any other building set on a frost-proof foundation.

Keep your tools safe and dry in the lean-to tool bin located next to a house, garage, fence or wall.

Cutting List

DESCRIPTION	QTY./SIZE	MATERIAL
Foundation		
Drainage material	0.5 cu. yd.	Compactible gravel
Skids	2 @ 6'	4 × 4 treated timbers
Floor Framing		
Rim joists	2 @ 6'	2 × 6 pressure-treated
Joists	3 @ 8'	2 × 6 pressure-treated
Floor sheathing	1 sheet @ 4 × 8	¾" tongue-&-groove ext.-grade plywood
Joist clip angles	4	3 × 3 × 3" × 16-gauge galvanized
Wall Framing		
Bottom plates	1 @ 8', 2 @ 6'	2 × 4
Top plates	1 @ 8', 3 @ 6'	2 × 4
Studs	14 @ 8', 8 @ 6'	2 × 4
Header	2 @ 6'	2 × 6
Header spacer	1 piece @ 6'	½" plywood — 5" wide
Roof Framing		
Rafters	6 @ 6'	2 × 6
Ledger*	1 @ 6'	2 × 6
Roofing		
Roof sheathing	2 sheets @ 4 × 8'	½" ext.-grade plywood
Shingles	30 sq. ft.	250# per square min.
Roofing starter strip	7 linear ft.	
15# building paper	30 sq. ft.	
Metal drip edge	24 linear ft.	Galvanized metal
Roofing cement	1 tube	
Exterior Finishes		
Plywood siding	4 sheets @ 4 × 8'	⅝" Texture 1-11 plywood siding, grooves 8" O.C.

DESCRIPTION	QTY./SIZE	MATERIAL
Door trim	2 @ 8' 2 @ 6'	1 × 10 S4S cedar 1 × 8 S4S cedar
Corner trim	6 @ 8'	1 × 4 S4S cedar
Fascia	3 @ 6' 1 @ 6'	1 × 8 S4S cedar 1 × 4 S4S cedar
Bug screen	8" × 6'	Fiberglass
Doors		
Frame	3 @ 6'	¾" × 3½" (actual) cedar
Stops	3 @ 6'	1 × 2 S4S cedar
Panel material	12 @ 6'	1 × 6 T&G V-joint S4S cedar
Z-braces	2 @ 10'	1 × 6 S4S cedar
Construction adhesive	1 tube	
Interior trim (optional)	3 @ 6'	1 × 3 S4S cedar
Strap hinges	6, with screws	
Fasteners		
16d galvanized common nails	3½ lbs.	
16d common nails	3½ lbs.	
10d common nails	12 nails	
10d galvanized casing nails	20 nails	
8d galvanized box nails	½ lb.	
8d galvanized finish nails	2 lbs.	
8d common nails	24 nails	
8d box nails	½ lb.	
1½" joist hanger nails	16 nails	
⅞" galvanized roofing nails	¼ lb.	
2½" deck screws	6 screws	
1¼" wood screws	60 screws	

Note: 6-foot material is often unavailable at local lumber stores, so buy half as much of 12-foot material.

Floor Framing Plan

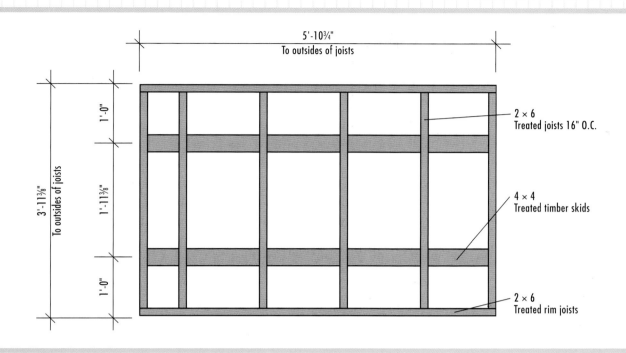

5'-10¾"
To outsides of joists

1'-0"

3'-11⅜"
To outsides of joists

1'-11⅜"

1'-0"

2 × 6
Treated joists 16" O.C.

4 × 4
Treated timber skids

2 × 6
Treated rim joists

Roof Framing Plan

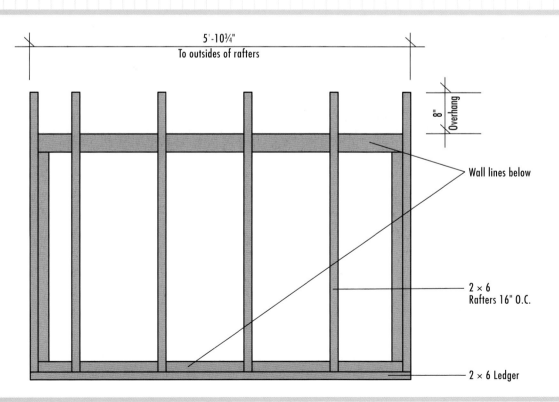

5'-10¾"
To outsides of rafters

8"
Overhang

Wall lines below

2 × 6
Rafters 16" O.C.

2 × 6 Ledger

Front Framing Elevation

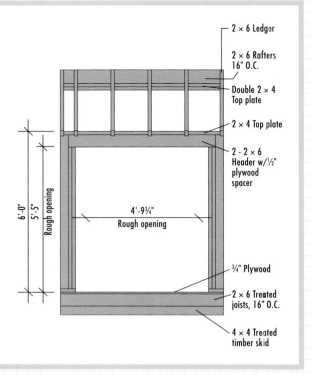

2 × 6 Ledger

2 × 6 Rafters 16" O.C.

Double 2 × 4 Top plate

2 × 4 Top plate

2 - 2 × 6 Header w/½" plywood spacer

6'-0"

5'-5" Rough opening

4'-9¾" Rough opening

¾" Plywood

2 × 6 Treated joists, 16" O.C.

4 × 4 Treated timber skid

Left Framing Elevation

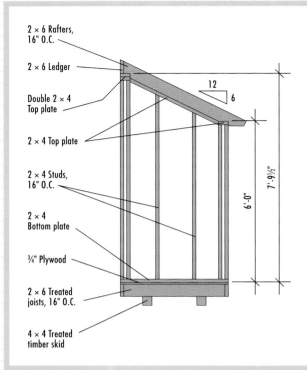

2 × 6 Rafters, 16" O.C.

2 × 6 Ledger

Double 2 × 4 Top plate

2 × 4 Top plate

12

6

2 × 4 Studs, 16" O.C.

2 × 4 Bottom plate

¾" Plywood

2 × 6 Treated joists, 16" O.C.

4 × 4 Treated timber skid

6'-0"

7'-9½"

Rear Side Framing Elevation

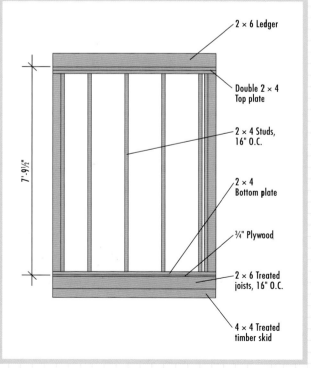

2 × 6 Ledger

Double 2 × 4 Top plate

2 × 4 Studs, 16" O.C.

2 × 4 Bottom plate

¾" Plywood

2 × 6 Treated joists, 16" O.C.

4 × 4 Treated timber skid

7'-9½"

Right Side Framing Elevation

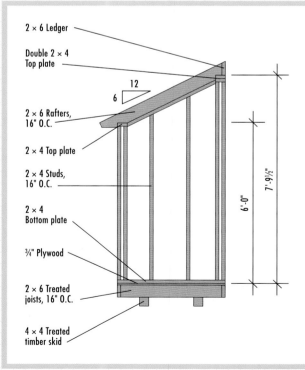

2 × 6 Ledger

Double 2 × 4 Top plate

12

6

2 × 6 Rafters, 16" O.C.

2 × 4 Top plate

2 × 4 Studs, 16" O.C.

2 × 4 Bottom plate

¾" Plywood

2 × 6 Treated joists, 16" O.C.

4 × 4 Treated timber skid

6'-0"

7'-9½"

Building Section

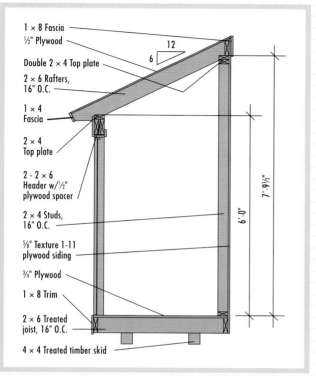

1 × 8 Fascia

½" Plywood

Double 2 × 4 Top plate

2 × 6 Rafters, 16" O.C.

1 × 4 Fascia

2 × 4 Top plate

2 - 2 × 6 Header w/½" plywood spacer

2 × 4 Studs, 16" O.C.

⅝" Texture 1-11 plywood siding

¾" Plywood

1 × 8 Trim

2 × 6 Treated joist, 16" O.C.

4 × 4 Treated timber skid

12
6

6'-0"

7'-9½"

Side Elevation

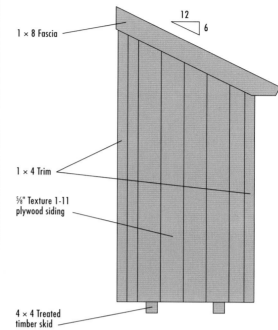

1 × 8 Fascia

12
6

1 × 4 Trim

⅝" Texture 1-11 plywood siding

4 × 4 Treated timber skid

Front Elevation

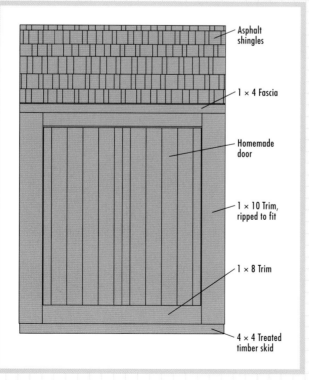

Asphalt shingles

1 × 4 Fascia

Homemade door

1 × 10 Trim, ripped to fit

1 × 8 Trim

4 × 4 Treated timber skid

Rear Elevation

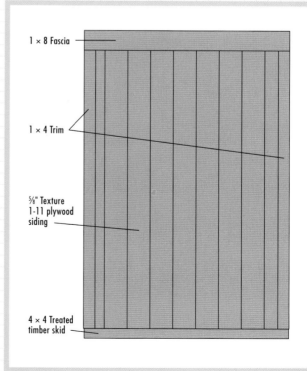

1 × 8 Fascia

1 × 4 Trim

⅝" Texture 1-11 plywood siding

4 × 4 Treated timber skid

Wall Plan

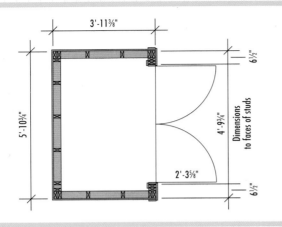

3'-11⅜"

5'-10¾"

4'-9¾"

Dimensions to faces of studs

2'-3⅝"

6½"

6½"

Rafter Template

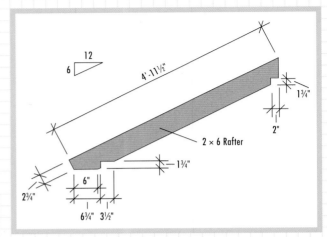

12

6

4'-11½"

1¾"

2"

2 × 6 Rafter

1¾"

6"

2¾"

6¾" 3½"

Side Roof Edge Detail

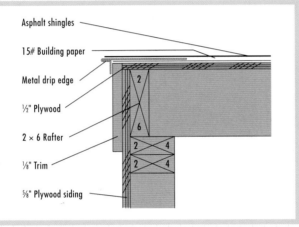

Asphalt shingles

15# Building paper

Metal drip edge

½" Plywood

2 × 6 Rafter

⅛" Trim

⅝" Plywood siding

2

6

2   4

2   4

Overhang Detail

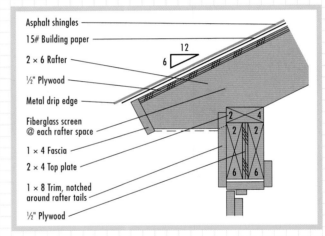

Asphalt shingles

15# Building paper

2 × 6 Rafter

½" Plywood

Metal drip edge

Fiberglass screen @ each rafter space

1 × 4 Fascia

2 × 4 Top plate

1 × 8 Trim, notched around rafter tails

½" Plywood

12

6

2   4

2   2

6   6

Door Jamb Detail

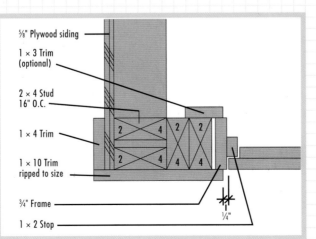

⅝" Plywood siding

1 × 3 Trim (optional)

2 × 4 Stud 16" O.C.

1 × 4 Trim

1 × 10 Trim ripped to size

¾" Frame

1 × 2 Stop

2   4   2   2

2   4   4   4

¼"

Door Elevation

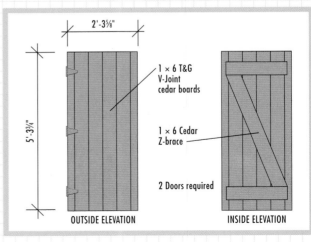

2'-3⅝"

5'-3¾"

1 × 6 T&G V-Joint cedar boards

1 × 6 Cedar Z-brace

2 Doors required

OUTSIDE ELEVATION

INSIDE ELEVATION

How to Build the Lean-to Tool Bin

Prepare the site with a 4" layer of compacted gravel. Cut the two 4 × 4 skids at 70¾". Set and level the skids following FLOOR FRAMING PLAN (page 51). Cut two 2 × 6 rim joists at 70¾" and six joists at 44⅜". Assemble the floor and set it on the skids as shown in the FLOOR FRAMING PLAN. Check for square, and then anchor the frame to the skids with four joist clip angles (inset photo). Sheath the floor frame with ¾" plywood.

Cut plates and studs for the walls: Side walls—two bottom plates at 47⅜", four studs at 89", and four studs at 69"; Front wall—one bottom plate at 63¾", one top plate at 70¾", and four jacks studs at 63½". Rear wall—one bottom plate at 63¾", two top plates at 70¾", and six studs at 89". Mark the stud layouts onto the plates.

Fasten the four end studs of each side wall to the bottom plate. Install these assemblies. Construct the built-up 2 × 6 door header at 63¾". Frame and install the front and rear walls, leaving the top plates off at this time. Nail together the corner studs, making sure they are plumb. Install the rear top plates flush to the outsides of the side wall studs. Install the front top plate in the same fashion.

Cut the six 2 × 6 rafters following the RAFTER TEMPLATE (page 54). Cut the 2 × 6 ledger at 70¾" and bevel the top edge at 26.5° so the overall width is 4⁵⁄₁₆". Mark the rafter layout onto the wall plates and ledger, as shown in the ROOF FRAMING PLAN (page 51), then install the ledger flush with the back side of the rear wall. Install the rafters.

(continued)

Complete the side wall framing: Cut a top plate for each side to fit between the front and rear walls, mitering the ends at 26.5°. Install the plates flush with the outsides of the end rafters. Mark the stud layouts onto the side wall bottom plates, then use a plumb bob to transfer the marks to the top plate. Cut the two studs in each wall to fit, mitering the top ends at 26.5°. Install the studs.

Sheath the side walls and rear walls with plywood siding, keeping the bottom edges ½" below the floor frame and the top edges flush with the tops of the rafters. Overlap the siding at the rear corners, and stop it flush with the face of the front wall.

Add the 1 × 4 fascia over the bottom rafter ends as shown in the OVERHANG DETAIL (page 54). Install 1 × 8 fascia over the top rafter ends. Overhang the front and rear fascia to cover the ends of the side fascia, or plan to miter all fascia joints. Cut the 1 × 8 side fascia to length, and then clip the bottom front corners to meet the front fascia. Install the side fascia.

Install the ½" roof sheathing, starting with a full-width sheet at the bottom edge of the roof. Fasten metal drip edge along the front edge of the roof. Cover the roof with building paper, then add the drip edge along the sides and top of the roof. Shingle the roof, and finish the top edge with cut shingles or a solid starter strip.

9

Cut and remove the bottom plate inside the door opening. Cut the 1 × 4 head jamb for the door frame at 57⅛" and cut the side jambs at 64". Fasten the head jamb over the sides with 2½" deck screws. Install 1 × 2 door stops ¾" from the front edges of jambs, as shown in the DOOR JAMB DETAIL (page 54). Install the frame in the door opening, using shims and 10d casing nails.

10

For each door, cut six 1 × 6 tongue-and-groove boards at 63¾". Fit them together, then mark and trim the two end boards so the total width is 27⅝". Cut the 1 × 6 Z-brace boards following the DOOR ELEVATION (page 54). The ends of the horizontal braces should be 1" from the door edges. Attach the braces with construction adhesive and 1¼" screws. Install each door with three hinges.

11

Staple fiberglass insect mesh along the underside of the roof from each side 2 × 6 rafter. Cut and install the 1 × 8 trim above the door, overlapping the side door jambs about ¼" on each side (see the OVERHANG DETAIL, page 54).

12

Rip vertical and horizontal trim boards to width, then notch them to fit around the rafters, as shown in the DOOR JAMB DETAIL (page 54). Notch the top ends of the 1 × 10s to fit between the rafters and install them. Add 1 × 8 trim horizontally between the 1 × 10s below the door. Install the 1 × 4 corner trim, overlapping the pieces at the rear corners.

Simple Storage Shed

The name of this practical outbuilding says it all. It's an easy-to-build, sturdy, 8 × 10-ft. shed with plenty of storage space. With no windows it also offers good security. The clean, symmetrical interior and centrally located double doors make for easy access to your stuff. The walls are ready to be lined with utility shelves, and you can quickly add a ramp to simplify parking the lawn mower, wheelbarrow, and other yard equipment.

This shed is indeed basic, but it's also a nicely proportioned building with architecturally appropriate features like overhanging eaves and just enough trim to give it a quality, hand-built appearance. Without getting too fancy—remember, simplicity is the central design idea—you might consider finishing the exterior walls and roof of the shed with the same materials used on your house. This easy modification visually integrates the shed with the rest of the property

and provides a custom look that you can't get with kit buildings.

Inside the shed, you can maximize storage space by building an attic: Install full-length 2 × 4 or 2 × 6 joists (which also serve as rafter ties) and cover them with ½" plywood. Include one or more framed-in access openings that you can easily reach with a stepladder. This type of storage space is ideal for seldom-used household items—like winter clothing and holiday decorations—that you can stow in covered plastic bins.

The simplicity and economy of this shed design also make it a great choice for cabins, vacation homes, and other remote locations. A heavy-duty hasp latch and padlock on the door, along with head and foot slide bolts inside, will provide the security you need when you're away for long periods.

Customize the simple storage shed with a ramp, shelves, or even a small loft for increased storage space.

Cutting List

DESCRIPTION	QTY./SIZE	MATERIAL
Foundation		
Drainage material	1.25 cu. yd.	Compactable gravel
Skids	2 @ 10'	4 × 6 pressure-treated landscape timbers
Floor		
Rim joists	2 @ 10'	2 × 8 pressure-treated, rated for ground contact
Joists	9 @ 8'	2 × 8 pressure-treated
Floor sheathing	3 sheets @ 4 × 8'	¾" tongue-&-groove ext.-grade plywood
Wall Framing		
Bottom plates	2 @ 10', 2 @ 8'	2 × 4
Top plates	4 @ 10', 4 @ 8'	2 × 4
Studs	36 @ 8'	2 × 4
Door header	1 @ 10'	2 × 6
Roof Framing		
Rafters	6 @ 12'	2 × 6
Rafter blocking	2 @ 10'	2 × 6
Ridge board	1 @ 10'	1 × 8
Collar ties	2 @ 12'	2 × 4
Exterior Finishes		
Siding	11 sheets @ 4 × 8'	½" Texture 1-11 plywood siding
Fascia	4 @ 12'	1 × 8
Corner trim	8 @ 8'	1 × 2
Gable wall trim	2 @ 8'	1 × 4
Siding flashing	16 linear ft.	Metal Z-flashing

DESCRIPTION	QTY./SIZE	MATERIAL
Roofing		
Sheathing (& door header spacer)	5 sheets @ 4 × 8'	½" exterior-grade plywood roof sheathing
15# building paper	1 roll	
Shingles	1¼ squares	Asphalt shingles — 250# per sq. min.
Drip edge	45 linear ft.	Metal drip edge
Door		
Frames	7 @ 8'	2 × 4 pressure-treated
Panels	1 sheet @ 4 × 8'	½" Texture 1-11 plywood siding
Stops & overlap trim	4 @ 8'	1 × 2 pressure-treated
Fasteners & Hardware		
16d galvanized common nails	4 lbs.	
16d common nails	10 lbs.	
10d common nails	2 lb.	
8d galvanized common nails	3 lbs.	
8d box nails	3 lbs.	
8d galvanized siding or finish nails	9 lbs.	
1" galvanized roofing nails	5 lbs.	
Door hinges with screws	6 @ 3½"	Galvanized metal hinges
Door handle	1	
Door lock (optional)	1	
Door head bolt	1	
Door foot bolt	1	
Construction adhesive		

Elevation

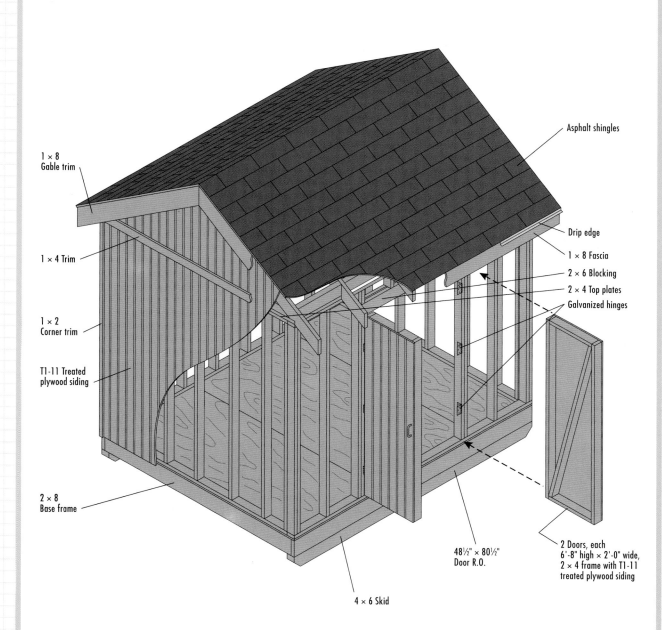

1 × 8
Gable trim

1 × 4 Trim

1 × 2
Corner trim

T1-11 Treated
plywood siding

2 × 8
Base frame

4 × 6 Skid

48½" × 80½"
Door R.O.

Asphalt shingles

Drip edge

1 × 8 Fascia

2 × 6 Blocking

2 × 4 Top plates

Galvanized hinges

2 Doors, each
6'-8" high × 2'-0" wide,
2 × 4 frame with T1-11
treated plywood siding

Framing Elevation

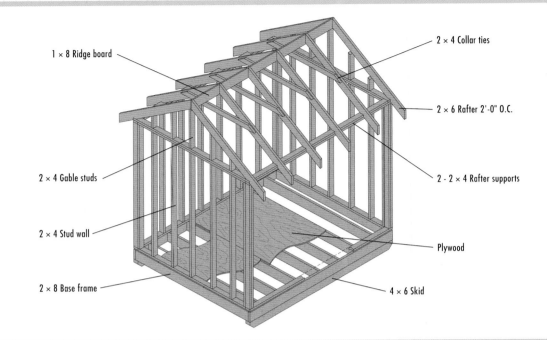

1 × 8 Ridge board

2 × 4 Collar ties

2 × 4 Gable studs

2 × 6 Rafter 2'-0" O.C.

2 - 2 × 4 Rafter supports

2 × 4 Stud wall

Plywood

2 × 8 Base frame

4 × 6 Skid

Side Framing

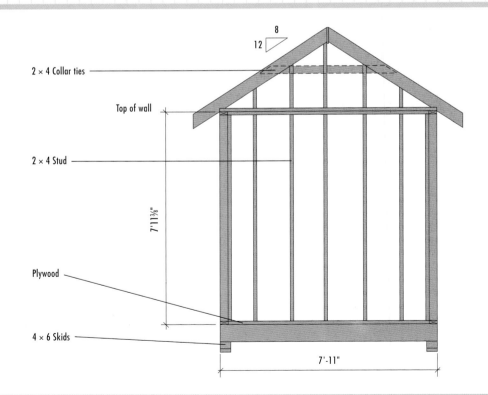

8
12

2 × 4 Collar ties

Top of wall

2 × 4 Stud

7'11⅜"

Plywood

4 × 6 Skids

7'-11"

Floor Framing

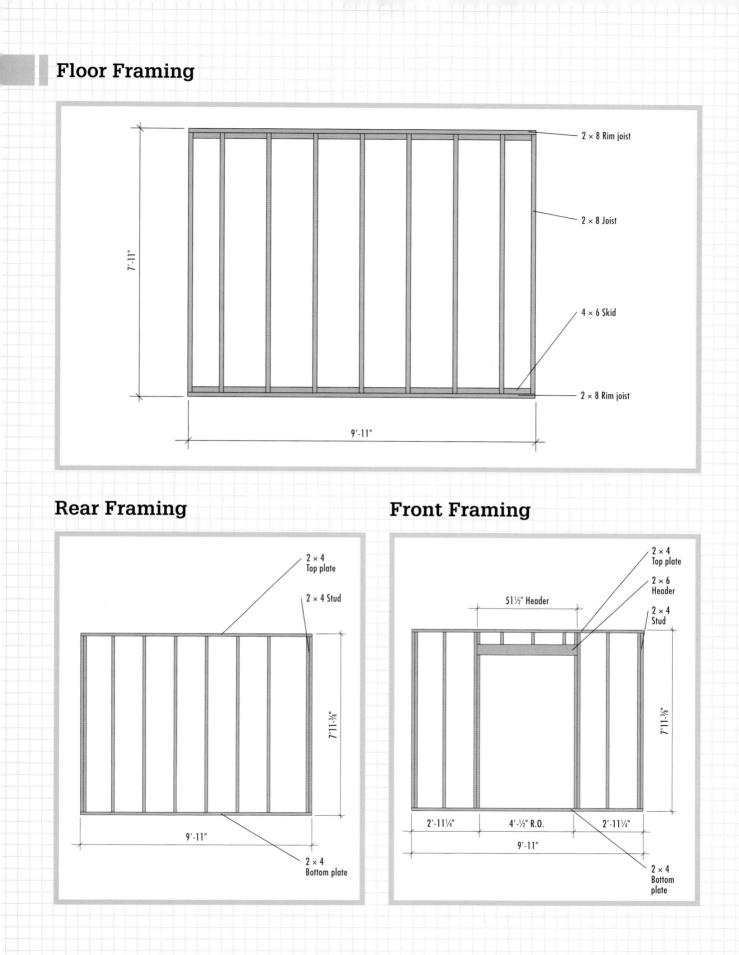

2 × 8 Rim joist

2 × 8 Joist

4 × 6 Skid

2 × 8 Rim joist

7'-11"

9'-11"

Rear Framing

2 × 4 Top plate

2 × 4 Stud

7'11-³/₈"

9'-11"

2 × 4 Bottom plate

Front Framing

2 × 4 Top plate

2 × 6 Header

2 × 4 Stud

51½" Header

7'11-³/₈"

2'-11¼"

4'-½" R.O.

2'-11¼"

9'-11"

2 × 4 Bottom plate

Roof Plan

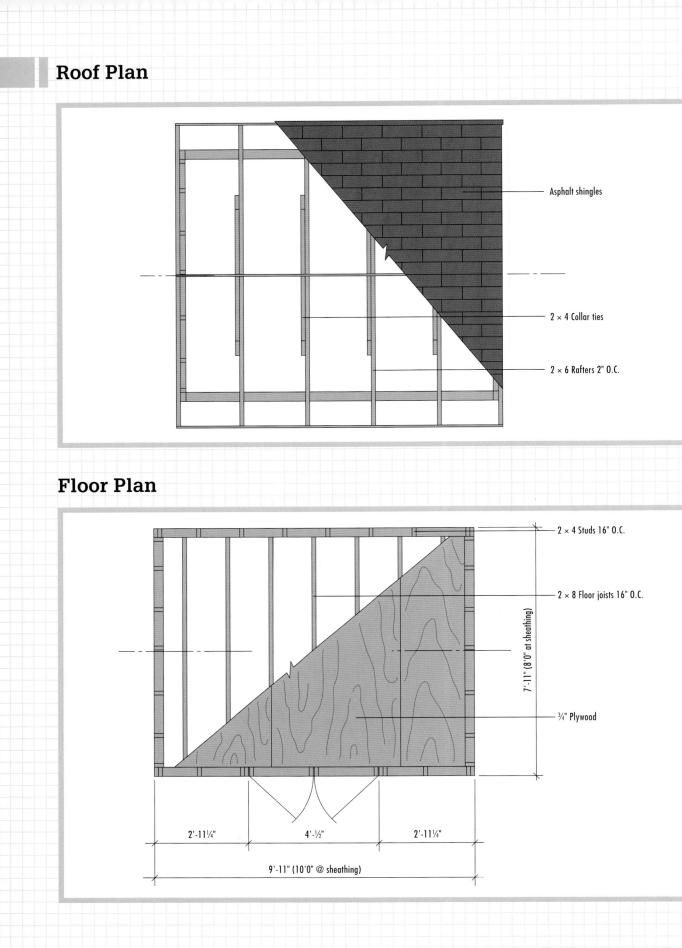

Asphalt shingles

2 × 4 Collar ties

2 × 6 Rafters 2" O.C.

Floor Plan

2 × 4 Studs 16" O.C.

2 × 8 Floor joists 16" O.C.

7'-11" (8'0" at sheathing)

¾" Plywood

2'-11¼"

4'-½"

2'-11¼"

9'-11" (10'0" @ sheathing)

Rafter Template

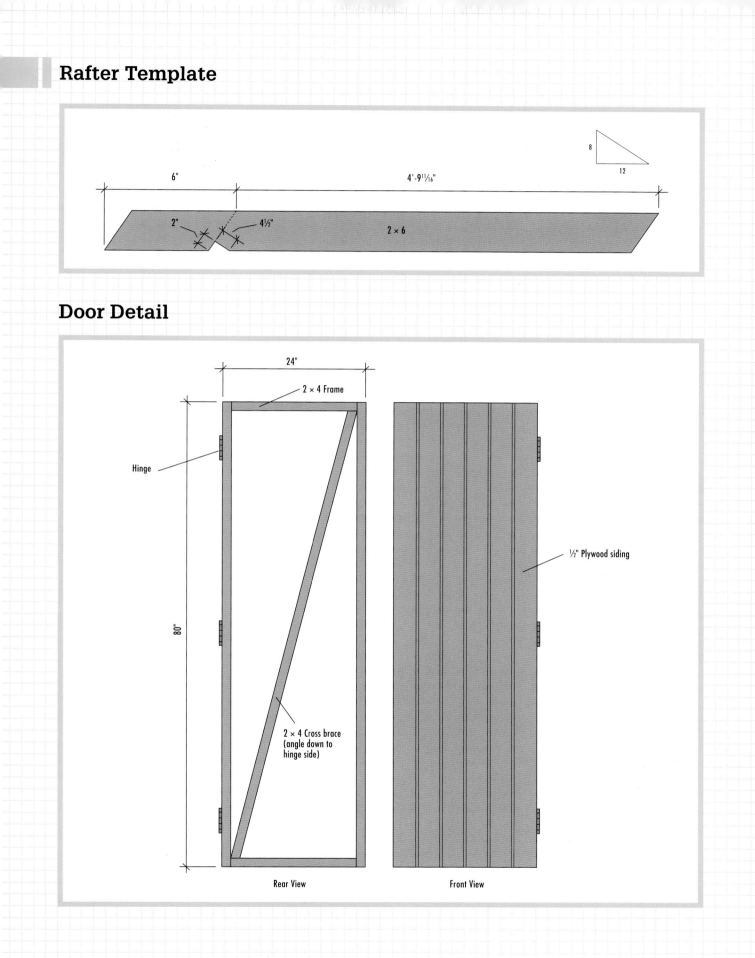

6"

4'-9¹¹⁄₁₆"

8

12

2"

4½"

2 × 6

Door Detail

24"

2 × 4 Frame

Hinge

80"

2 × 4 Cross brace
(angle down to
hinge side)

½" Plywood siding

Rear View

Front View

How to Build the Simple Storage Shed

Prepare the foundation site with a 4" layer of compacted gravel where the skids will be located. Cut the two 4 × 6 timber skids at 119". Position the skids on the gravel beds so their outside edges are 95" apart, making sure they are level and parallel.

Cut two 2 × 8 rim joists at 119". Cut nine 2 × 8 joists at 92". Assemble the floor frame following the FLOOR FRAMING (page 63), then set it on the skids and measure the diagonals to make sure the frame is square. Fasten the joists to the skids with 16d galvanized common nails.

Attach tongue-and-groove plywood flooring to the floor frame, starting at the left front corner of the shed. Begin the second row of plywood with a full sheet in the right rear corner to stagger end joints. Make sure the tongues are fully seated in the mating grooves. Fasten the sheathing with 8d galvanized common nails.

Frame the rear wall: Cut one 2 × 4 bottom plate and one top plate at 119". Cut ten 2 × 4 studs at 92⅜". Assemble the wall using 16" on-center spacing, as shown in the REAR FRAMING (page 63). Raise the wall and fasten it flush to the rear edge of the floor, then brace the wall in position with 2 × 4 braces.

Build the side walls following the SIDE FRAMING (page 62). The two side walls are identical. Each has a bottom and top plate at 88" and seven studs at 92⅜". Assemble each wall, then install it and brace it in position.

Frame the front wall following the FRONT FRAMING (page 63): Cut two plates at 119", cut eight studs at 92⅜", and cut two jack studs at 79". Install the 2 × 6 built-up header (add a layer of ½" plywood as a spacer between the 2 × 6s), then add three cripple studs. Raise and fasten the front wall, then install the double top plates along all four walls.

Cut two 2 × 6 pattern rafters following the RAFTER TEMPLATE (page 65). Test-fit the rafters and make any necessary adjustments. Use one of the patterns to mark and cut the remaining 10 rafters. Cut the 1 × 8 ridge board at 119". Mark the rafter layout onto the ridge and the front and rear wall plates following the ROOF PLAN (page 64). *Note: Before installing the rafters on the long sides of the shed (door face and wall parallel to door), first install siding. The rafters overhang the siding on the long sides, therefore the siding (at least on those sides) needs to be in place before the rafters are installed.*

Cover the shed exterior with ½" siding, starting at the left end of the rear wall. Butt full sheets up against the rafters, letting the bottom edges overhang the floor frame by at least 1". Complete the front wall, and then the side walls, keeping the bottom edges even with the sheets on the front and side walls. Add Z-flashing, and continue the siding to the tops of the end rafters.

(continued)

9

Install the rafters and ridge board. Cut four 2 × 4 collar ties at 64", mitering the ends at 33.5°. Fasten the collar ties between each set of the four inner rafters, using 10d common nails. Make sure the ties are level and extend close to but not above the top edges of the rafters. *Note: Do not install collar ties if you're building an attic floor.*

10

Mark the gable wall stud layout onto the sidewall top plates. Use a level to transfer the marks to the end rafters. Cut each of the 10 2 × 4 studs to fit, mitering the top ends at 33.5°. Install the studs. *Note: The center stud on each wall is located to the rear side of the ridge board. If desired, frame in the attic floor at this time (see Adding an Attic, below).*

Adding an Attic or Loft ▸

To build an attic floor for storage, cut six 2 × 4 or 2 × 6 floor joists at 95" (use 2 × 6s if you plan to store heavy items in the attic). If necessary, clip the top corners of the joists so they won't extend above the tops of the rafters. Fasten the joists to the rafters and wall plates with 10d common nails (photo 1). At the end rafters, install 2" blocking against the rafters, then attach the joists to the blocking and gable wall studs.

Frame access openings with two header joists spanning neighboring floor joists (photo 2). For heavier storage, double up the floor joists on either side of the opening, then use doubled headers to frame the opening. Join doubled members with pairs of 10d common nails every 16". Cover the joists with ½" plywood fastened with 8d nails to complete the attic floor.

1

2

Enclose the rafter bays over the walls with 2 × 6 blocking. Bevel the top edge of the blocking at 33.5° so it will be flush with the rafters. Cut the blocks to fit snugly between pairs of rafters and install them. Install 1 × 8 fascia boards at the ends of the rafters along the eaves, and over the siding on the gable ends. Keep the fascia ½" above the tops of the rafters.

Apply ½" roof sheathing, starting at the bottom corner of either roof plane. The sheathing should be flush with the tops of the fascia boards. Add the metal drip edge, building paper, and asphalt shingle roofing.

Construct the two doors from 2 × 4 bracing and ½" siding, as shown in the DOOR DETAIL (page 65). The doors are identical. Each measures 48½" × 80½". Mortise the butt hinges into the door brace and wall frame, and install the doors leaving a ¼" gap between the doors and along the top and bottom.

Trim the corners of the shed with 1 × 2s. Also add a piece of 1 × 2 trim on one of the doors to cover the gap between the doors. Install 1 × 4 trim horizontally to cover the Z-flashing at the side walls. Install door locks and hardware as desired.

Modern Utility Shed

As its name suggests, this is a useful shed that is well suited to serve many purposes. It's a do-all shed. The 8 × 12 ft. footprint provides plenty of room for storage, work space or a little of both. The 60-inch-wide double doors are wide enough to provide access for a larger lawn tool, such as a riding lawn mower or they can simply be left open to let in lots of natural light. A 30 × 30 inch window is positioned to the right of the door and is installed high enough to leave room for a workbench to fit below—the perfect place to work on small projects.

This shed features basic wall framing construction. The roof is a classic single-sloped roof. The siding material that we used on this shed is a shiplap 4 × 8 panel called LP SmartSide. These panels are approved to serve as both the sheathing and siding. This type of siding is typically installed with the grooves running vertically, but we choose to install them with the grooves running horizontally. The panels are installed so that the lower panels are overlapped by the shiplap or overlapping edge of the upper panels. The horizontal grooves give this shed a more unique and modern style.

One of the best aspects of this design is that it is easy to modify. If you like the basic design but want a more refined or finished space, there are several ways you could upgrade this shed. For example, you could build it on an elevated framed floor with a wood subfloor so that you could install just about any flooring material. Another option is to replace the plastic window with a manufactured operable window. You could also install just about any finished interior wall covering. The level of finish is limited only by your imagination and your budget.

Work. Store. Play. This shed does it all—and in a sleek, modern form that will delight everyone.

Cutting List

DESCRIPTION	QTY./SIZE	MATERIAL
Foundation		
Skids	2 × 4 × 12 ft. (3), 2 × 4 × 10 ft. (10)	Pressure treated
Floor Deck	¾ × 4 × 8" (3)	Exterior plywood
Wall Framing		
Bottom plates	2 × 4 × 8 (3), 2 × 4 × 12 (1)	Pressure treated
Top plates	2 × 4 × 8 (2), 2 × 4 × 12 (2)	
Front and back beams	4 × 4 × 14 (2)	Cedar
Studs	2 × 4 × 8 (20), 2 × 4 × 12 (6)	
Door and window headers, jack studs, cripple studs	2 × 4 × 8 (4)	
Roof Framing		
Rafters and blocking	2 × 8 × 10 (12)	Cedar
Exterior Finishes		
Fascia	1 × 8 × 14 (2)	
Siding	⅜ × 4 × 8 (10)	LP Smart Side panels
Windows trim	1 × 2 × 8 (2)	
Corner Trim	1 × 4 × 8 (6), 1 × 4 × 10 (2), 1 × 4 × 12 (1)	

DESCRIPTION	QTY./SIZE	MATERIAL
Roofing		
Roofing sheathing	¾ × 4 × 8 (5)	
15# building paper		
Drip edge	50 linear ft.	
Asphalt shingles	5 bundles	
Windows and Screens		
¼"-thick polycarbonate glazing	31¼ × 31¼ (1), 5¾ × 15¾ (3)	
Clear exterior caulk	(1 tube)	
Window screen	(1 roll)	
Frames	1 × 2 × 8 (9)	
Fasteners and Hardware		
J-bolts	½"-dia. (12)	
16d common framing nails		
10d common nails		
Box/siding/utility nails 6d × 2"		
Galvanized casing (finish) nails 8d × 2		
1" galvanized roofing nails		
1½" joist hanger nails		
Galvanized rafter (hurricane) straps	14	

Shed Final

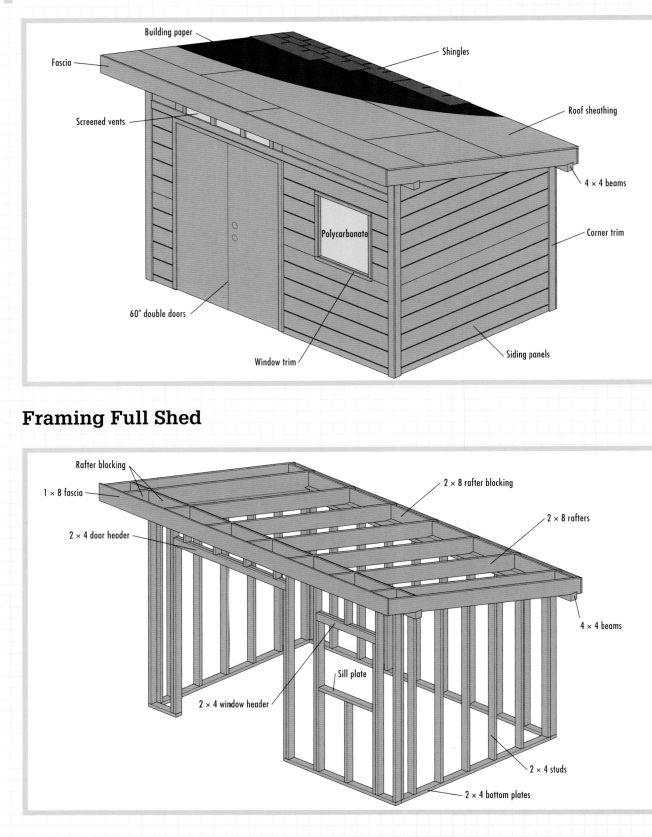

Building paper

Fascia

Shingles

Screened vents

Roof sheathing

4 × 4 beams

Corner trim

Polycarbonate

60" double doors

Window trim

Siding panels

Framing Full Shed

Rafter blocking

1 × 8 fascia

2 × 8 rafter blocking

2 × 8 rafters

2 × 4 door header

4 × 4 beams

2 × 4 window header

Sill plate

2 × 4 studs

2 × 4 bottom plates

Front Wall Framing

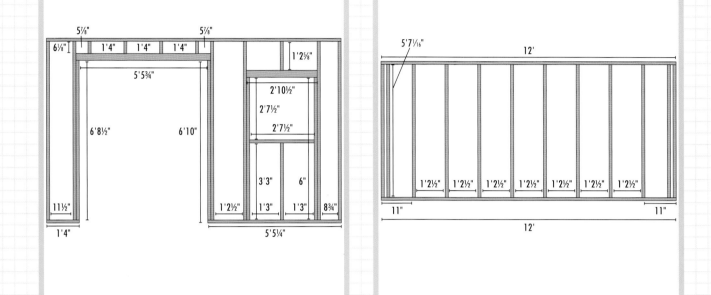

Back Wall Framing

Side Wall Framing

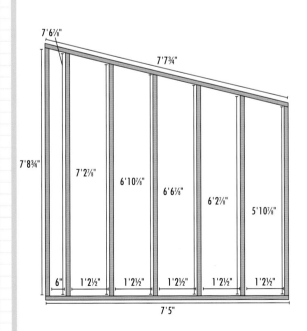

Roof Wall Framing

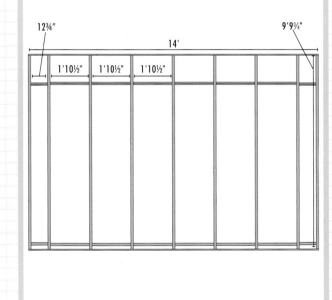

Front Sheathing

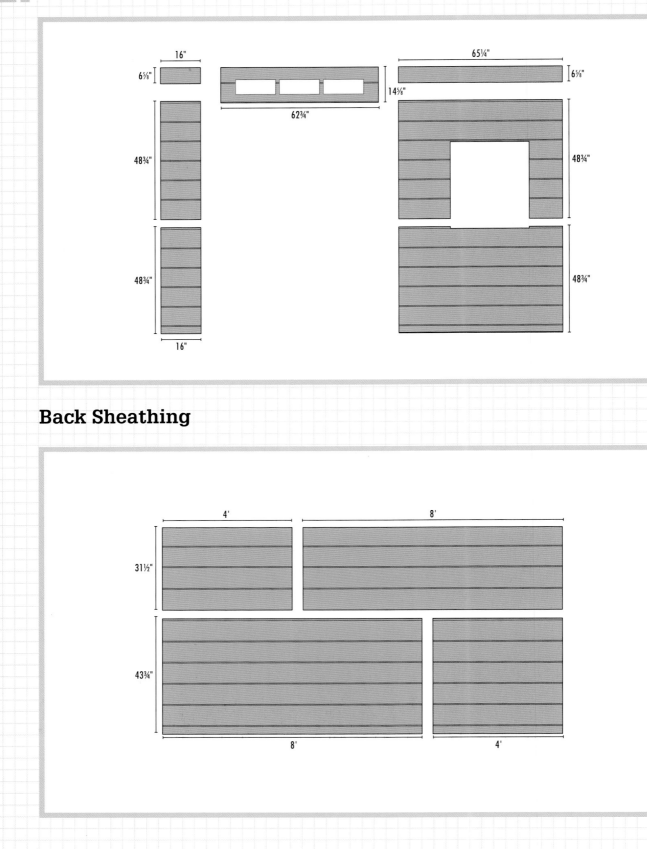

Back Sheathing

Siding Sheathing

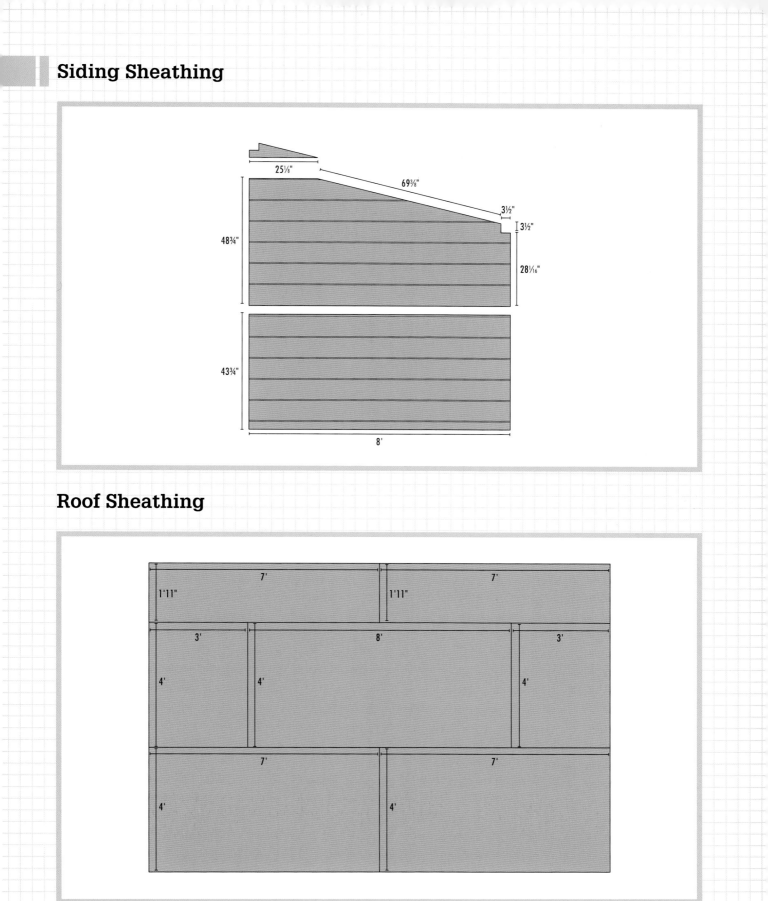

Roof Sheathing

Front Elevation

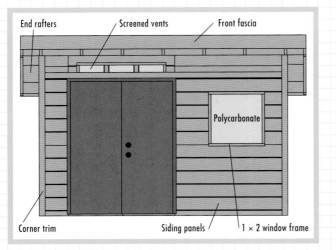

End rafters — Screened vents — Front fascia

Polycarbonate

Corner trim — Siding panels — 1 × 2 window frame

Side Elevation

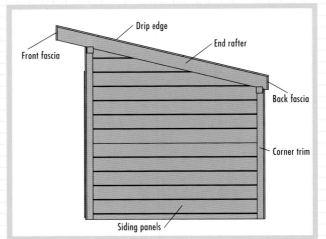

Drip edge

Front fascia — End rafter

Back fascia

Corner trim

Siding panels

Back Elevation

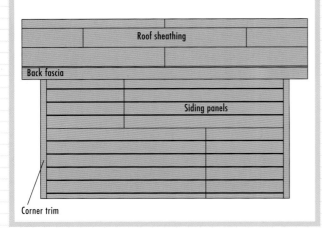

Roof sheathing

Back fascia

Siding panels

Corner trim

Front Trim Dimension

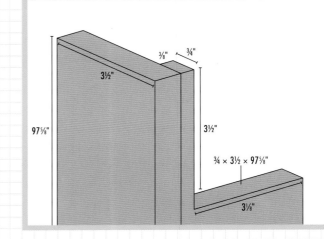

3/8" — 3/4"

3½"

97⅝"

3½"

¾ × 3½ × 97⅝"

3⅛"

Back Trim Dimension

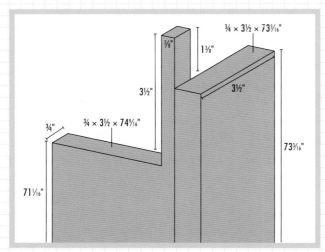

¾ × 3½ × 73³⁄₁₆"

3/8"

1⅜"

3½" — 3½"

¾ × 3½ × 74⁹⁄₁₆"

¾"

73³⁄₁₆"

71¹⁄₁₆"

Side Siding Top Piece Dimension

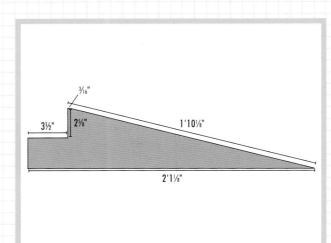

³⁄₁₆"

3½" — 2⅝"

1'10⅛"

2'1⅛"

Window Frames

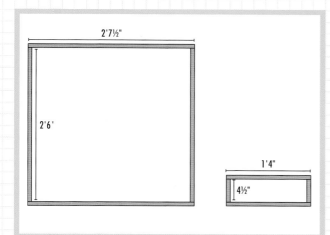

2'7½"

2'6'

1'4"

4½"

Front Corner Trim Detail

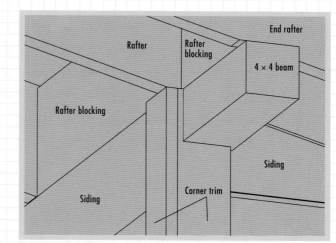

End rafter

Rafter

Rafter blocking

4 × 4 beam

Rafter blocking

Siding

Siding

Corner trim

Rafter Blocking

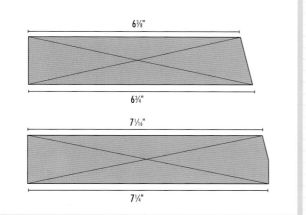

6⅜"

6¾"

7¹⁄₁₆"

7¼"

Floor Framing

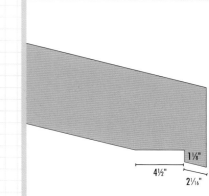

¾ Exterior plywood, typ.

4 × 4 ft.

4 × 8 ft.

4 × 8 ft.

4 × 4 ft.

Rafter Top Notch

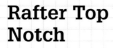

1'4⅜"

1"

3¹⁵⁄₁₆"

End Bottom Rafter Notch

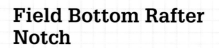

1"

4⅛"

2⁷⁄₁₆"

Field Bottom Rafter Notch

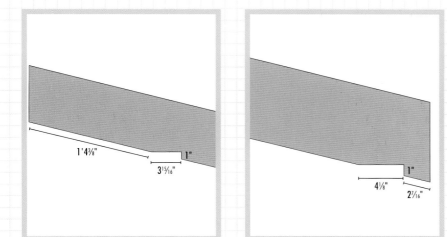

1⅛"

4½"

2⁷⁄₁₆"

How to Build the Utility Shed

Build the foundation. Prepare foundation base by digging a hole matching shed dimensions, and fill using a 4" layer of compacted gravel. Construct a 2 × 4 or 2 × 6 floor frame using the FLOOR FRAMING on page 77. Install frame on gravel and check for level, using more gravel under frame if appropriate.

Attach the sheathing using deck screws, alternating the seams when possible. Try and leave a gap not more than 1¼" between sheets and make sure seams fall above the floor framing members.

Build the back wall using the BACK WALL FRAMING on page 73. Raise the framed wall into position using a helper. The edges of the sole plate should be flush with the floor sheathing. Level and plumb the frame, and then tack into position using temporary 2 × 4 braces.

Frame both side walls by following the SIDE WALL FRAMING illustration on page 73. Lay out the stud locations on the bottom plate. Cut the studs to length, cutting the top at a 14° angle. Then nail the bottom and top plate to the studs with 16d common nails. Keep the studs perpendicular to the bottom plate and maintain the stud spacing for the full length of each stud.

Attach the side walls to the back wall using 16d common nails, keeping the outside edges of the walls flush. Plumb the front end of each side wall and then brace them with temporary 2 × 4s attached to the floor foundation.

Frame the front wall by following the FRONT WALL FRAMING illustration on page 73. Attach front wall to side walls with 16d common nails. Leave the side wall bracing in place until you are ready to attach the siding panels.

The side wall roof overhang is supported by 4 × 4 beams. Attach these beams to the top plate with framing nails. Drive the fasteners up through the top plate and into the beam. If you are not using a pneumatic framing nail gun, then consider attaching the beams with 3" deck screws.

Use a straight edge as a guide and cut the siding panels with a circular saw. The siding panels serve as both the sheathing and siding. These panels are typically used with the long seams running vertically, but in this case we chose to run the long seams horizontally. It is important to orient each panel so that the top piece overlaps the bottom piece. Follow the SIDING SHEATHING illustration on page 73 to cut each piece to the proper width and length.

(continued)

Attach the siding panels with 6d × 2" ring shank nails. Space nails every six inches around the perimeter and every 12 inches along studs in the field. Carefully align the shiplap evenly with each panel. The vertical edges do not overlap. If you are concerned about water penetration in the vertical seam, then install a piece of double channel (a metal flashing that looks like two pieces of j-channel back-to-back). We chose to leave a ¹⁄₁₆" gap between the pieces and fill that gap with exterior-paintable caulk. Though not an acceptable system for a house, but it should be sufficient for this shed.

Draw the top angle on the back of a top siding piece with the aid of a helper. Use this same scribing method to mark the irregular pieces that fit around the door and window. Cut along the lines with a circular saw or jigsaw. Paint the shed after all the siding pieces are attached.

Use a carpenter's square and refer to the RAFTER LAYOUT illustrations on page 77 to lay out the rafter notches. There are two different rafter layouts, one for the end rafters and one for the inside (or field) rafters. Use a jigsaw to cut out the rafter notches.

Install blocking pieces on top of the beams between each rafter. *Note: Two of the openings between the rafters on the front side do not get blocking because the two screen frames are attached in those openings.* See the RAFTER BLOCKING illustration on page 77 to cut the rafter blocking to length with a miter saw or circular saw. Then tilt the table saw blade to 14° and bevel cut the top edges. Set the table saw fence to trim ³⁄₁₆" off the front wall blocking. Set the fence to rip the back wall blocking to 6¾" wide.

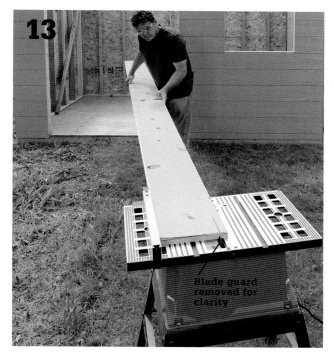

Use a table saw to rip the front fascia board to a width of 8¼". The roof sheathing rests on top of the back fascia board and butts into the front fascia board. The back fascia board is a full-width 1 × 10, but the front fascia is wider and must be ripped down from a piece of 1 × 10.

Stain everything at once. Stain the fascia boards, rafters, rafter blocking and all of the stock that you will use for the window/screen frames and trim boards. Stain all sides of each piece. *Note: This is also a good time to stain the bottom sides of the plywood that will be used for the roof sheathing.*

Attach the rafters by referring to the RAFTER FRAMING illustration on page 77 to place and tack each rafter in place by toe nailing it with 16d common nails. Then secure each rafter with galvanized rafter ties (sometimes referred to as hurricane straps). Attach the rafter ties with galvanized joist hanger nails.

Install the rafter blocking between the rafters. Attach one end of the blocking by driving 10d common nails through the adjacent rafter and into the end of the blocking. Then toenail the other end of the blocking to the next rafter.

(continued)

Make 1 × 2 frames to fit the two openings left between the rafters on the front wall. Then use a staple gun to attach window screen to the back edges of the frames. Trim the excess screen and install the screen frames between the rafters with 2" deck screws. Drill pilot holes through the frame for each screw to prevent splitting the wood.

Attach the front and back fascia boards to the rafter ends with 8d galvanized casing nails. Then cut the roof sheathing to size using the ROOF SHEATHING LAYOUT illustration on page 75. Stain the underside of the roof sheathing panels if you haven't already. Once the stain is dry, attach the roof sheathing to the rafters with 8d box nails or 2" deck screws. Leave a ⅛" space between each sheet.

Attach the roofing materials. First attach the drip edge along the back edge of the roof. Then attach overlapping layers of building paper to the sheathing with staples. Next, attach drip edge along the side edges and front edge of the roof. Then shingle the roof. Use ⅞" roofing nails so that the nails do not break through the inside face of the sheathing.

Use a circular saw or table saw to cut the plastic for the windows. The best way to cut plastic with a circular saw is to place the sheet of plastic on a large piece of plywood. The plywood supports the plastic and helps prevent it from vibrating during the cut. You will cut into the plywood as you are cutting the plastic. Install a triple-chip tooth blade or plywood blade in your saw and set the blade to a 1" cutting depth. Apply a piece of masking tape over the general cutting line, then mark the actual cutting line on the tape. Clamp a straight piece of wood on the plastic to act as a guide.

21

The windows are held in place between two frames. Cut the 1 × 2 frame pieces to length following WINDOW FRAME illustrations on page 77. Attach the outside window frame flush with the outside face of the siding with 2" deck screws. Drill pilot holes through the frame for each screw. Deck screws are used to attach the window frames so that they can easily be removed if the window is ever damaged.

22

Apply a bead of clear exterior caulk along the inside edge of the outside window frame. Set the window in place. Then install the inside window frame pieces. Repeat the window installation process for the three windows above the door. Next, install the door.

23

Install the door. For security and ease of access, an outswinging double door made of steel is used in this shed.

24

Attach the window trim pieces. Measure and cut each piece so that it is flush with the inside edge of the window frames. Attach the trim pieces with 8d galvanized casing nails or pneumatic finish nails.

25

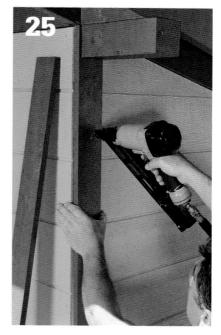

The side corner trim pieces must be notched to fit around the beam. Follow the CORNER TRIM illustration on pages 76-77. Use a jigsaw to cut the notches. Then attach the corner trim pieces with 8d galvanized casing nails.

Service Shed

This versatile shelter structure is actually two projects in one. Using the same primary design, you can build an open-sided firewood shelter, or you can add doors and a shelf and create a secured shed that's perfect for trash cans or recyclables. Both projects have four vertical corner posts, a rectangular floor frame decked with 2 × 6s, and gapped side slats that provide cross ventilation. The plywood, shed-style roof is covered with cedar shingles, but you can substitute with any type of roofing.

To adapt the service shed for use as a closed storage shed, you can add a center post (mostly to function as a nailer) and attach slats to create a rear wall. With two more posts in the front, you may define door openings. The adapted shed won't offer secure storage for valuable items like tools, but it will prevent dogs, squirrels, raccoons and other pests from getting into your trashcans.

As for materials, you can save a lot of money by building this project with pressure-treated lumber. Stain or paint the greenish lumber to change its coloring or leave it bare and allow it to weather to a silvery gray. If you prefer the look of cedar lumber, use it for everything but the shelter's floor frame and decking. Also, you might want to set the corner posts on concrete blocks or stones to prevent the cedar from rotting prematurely due to ground contact.

The service shed can be fitted with slatted walls and doors for secure, well-ventilated storage.

If you leave out the doors and back wall, the shed becomes a charming and very practical firewood shelter.

Seasoning Firewood ▸

Proper seasoning, or drying, of firewood takes time. After freshly cut logs are split, the drying process can take six to 12 months, given the right conditions. Stacking split wood under a shelter with one or more open sides is ideal because it protects the wood from rain and snow moisture while letting airflow through the stack to hasten drying.

You can test wood for seasoning by its look and feel and by how it burns. The ends of dry logs show cracks and typically have a grayish color, while unseasoned wood still looks freshly cut and may be moist to the touch. Fresher wood also makes a heavy, dull thud when pieces are knocked together. When it comes to burning, dry wood lights easily and burns consistently, while wet wood tends to burn out if unattended and often smokes excessively as the internal moisture turns to steam.

If you order split firewood from a supplier and can't guarantee how well seasoned it is, have it delivered at least six months before the start of the burning season. This gives the wood plenty of time to dry out. Regarding quantity, a "cord" of neatly stacked split logs measures 128 cubic feet—a stack that's 4 ft. high, 4 ft. deep, and 8 ft. long. A "half cord" measures 64 cubic feet.

Cutting List

PART	QTY./SIZE Firewood Shed	QTY./SIZE Garbage Shed	MATERIAL
Side & end floor supports	2 @ 10'	2 @ 10'	2 × 4 pressure-treated
Center floor support	1 @ 8'	1 @ 8'	2 × 4 pressure-treated
Floor boards	3 @ 10'	3 @ 10'	2 × 6 pressure-treated
Corner posts	4 @ 8'	4 @ 8'	2 × 4 cedar
Headers	2 @ 8'	2 @ 3'	2 × 4 cedar
Rafters	1 @ 8' 1 @ 4'	1 @ 8' 1 @ 4'	2 × 4 cedar
Rear center post		1 @ 4'	2 × 4 cedar
Door posts		1 @ 8'	2 × 4 cedar
Door ledger		1 @ 8'	2 × 4 cedar
Slats			
End slats	5 @ 8'	5 @ 8'	1 × 6 cedar
Back slats		5 @ 8'	1 × 6 cedar
Roofing			
Sheathing	1 sheet @ 4 × 8'	1 sheet @ 4 × 8'	¾" CDX plywood
Roof edging	2 @ 10'	2 @ 10'	1 × 2 T
15# building paper	37 sq. ft.	37 sq. ft.	
Shingles	25 sq. ft	25 sq. ft.	18" cedar shingles
Roof cap	1 @ 8' 1 @ 8'	1 @ 8' 1 @ 8'	1 × 4 cedar 1 × 3 cedar

PART	QTY./SIZE Firewood Shed	QTY./SIZE Garbage Shed	MATERIAL
Shelf & Doors			
Shelf		1 @ 24⅝ × 28⅛"	¾" ext.-grade plywood
Shelf cleats		1 @ 6'	1 × 3 cedar
Door panels		1 sheet @ 4 × 8'	¾" ext.-grade plywood
Stiles		3 @ 8' (wide doors) 1 @ 10' (narrow door)	1 × 4 cedar
Hinges		6	Exterior hinges
Door handles		3	Exterior handles
Fasteners			
¼" × 3" lag screws	8, with washers	10, with washers	
Deck Screws			
3½"	12	12	
3"	62	62	
2½"	36	48	
2"	50	62	
1⅝"	100	160	
1¼"		116	
6d galvanized finish nails	30	30	
3d galvanized roofing nails	1 lb.	1 lb.	

Floor Framing Plan

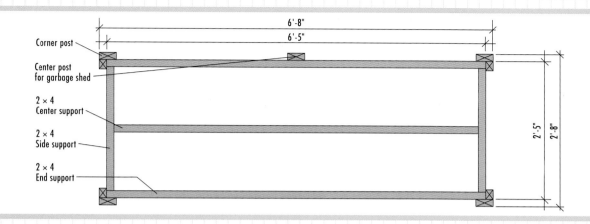

6'-8"

6'-5"

Corner post

Center post
for garbage shed

2 × 4
Center support

2 × 4
Side support

2 × 4
End support

2'-5"

2'-8"

Roof Framing Plan

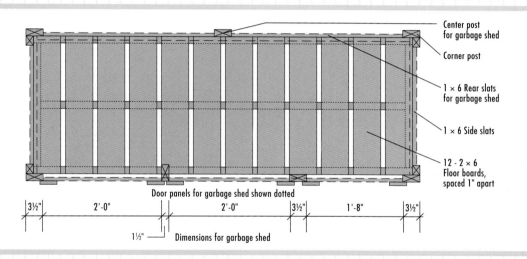

Center post
for garbage shed

Corner post

1 × 6 Rear slats
for garbage shed

1 × 6 Side slats

12 - 2 × 6
Floor boards,
spaced 1" apart

Door panels for garbage shed shown dotted

3½"   2'-0"   2'-0"   3½"   1'-8"   3½"

1½"   Dimensions for garbage shed

Floor Plan

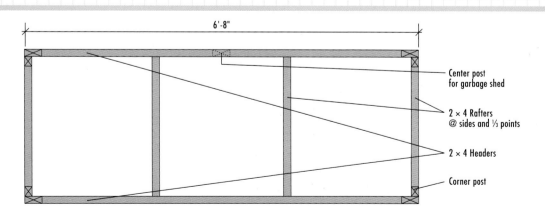

6'-8"

Center post
for garbage shed

2 × 4 Rafters
@ sides and ⅓ points

2 × 4 Headers

Corner post

Building Section

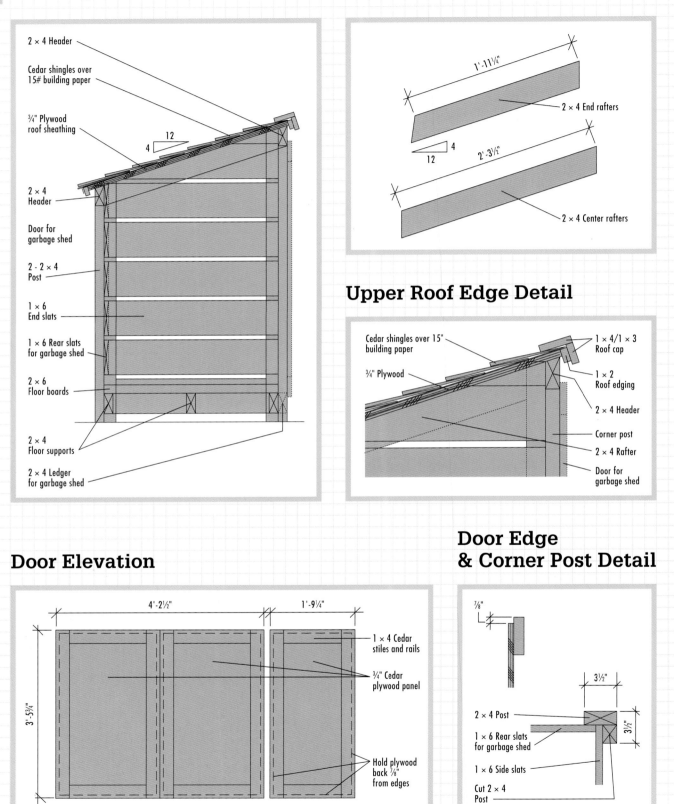

2 × 4 Header

Cedar shingles over
15# building paper

¾" Plywood
roof sheathing

2 × 4
Header

Door for
garbage shed

2 - 2 × 4
Post

1 × 6
End slats

1 × 6 Rear slats
for garbage shed

2 × 6
Floor boards

2 × 4
Floor supports

2 × 4 Ledger
for garbage shed

Rafter Templates

1'-11¼"

2 × 4 End rafters

4
12

2'-3½"

2 × 4 Center rafters

Upper Roof Edge Detail

Cedar shingles over 15"
building paper

¾" Plywood

1 × 4/1 × 3
Roof cap

1 × 2
Roof edging

2 × 4 Header

Corner post

2 × 4 Rafter

Door for
garbage shed

Door Elevation

4'-2½"   1'-9¼"

3'-5¾"

1 × 4 Cedar
stiles and rails

¾" Cedar
plywood panel

Hold plywood
back ⅞"
from edges

Door Edge
& Corner Post Detail

⅞"

3½"

2 × 4 Post

1 × 6 Rear slats
for garbage shed

3½"

1 × 6 Side slats

Cut 2 × 4
Post

Front Elevation

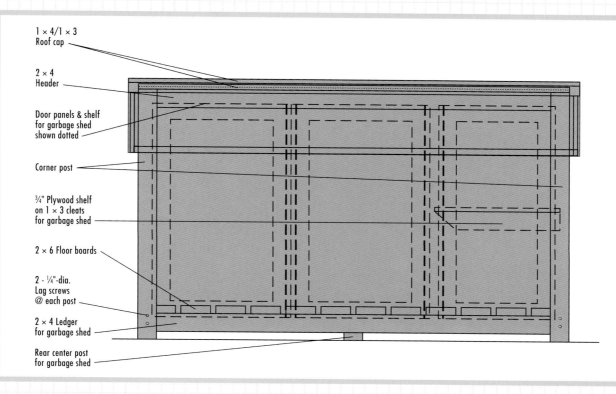

1 × 4/1 × 3
Roof cap

2 × 4
Header

Door panels & shelf
for garbage shed
shown dotted

Corner post

¾" Plywood shelf
on 1 × 3 cleats
for garbage shed

2 × 6 Floor boards

2 - ¼"-dia.
Lag screws
@ each post

2 × 4 Ledger
for garbage shed

Rear center post
for garbage shed

Rear Elevation

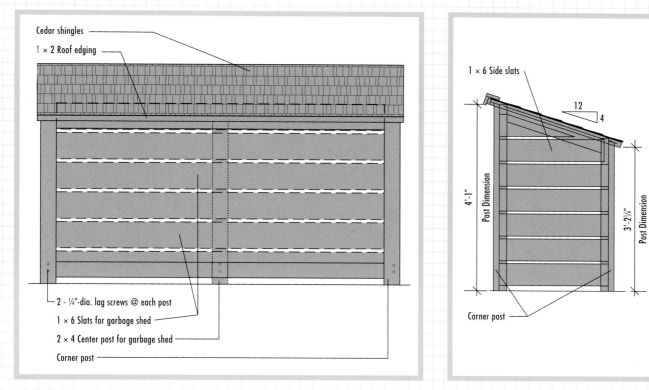

Cedar shingles

1 × 2 Roof edging

2 - ¼"-dia. lag screws @ each post

1 × 6 Slats for garbage shed

2 × 4 Center post for garbage shed

Corner post

Side Elevation

1 × 6 Side slats

12
4

4'-1"
Post Dimension

3'-2¼"
Post Dimension

Corner post

How to Build the Service Shed

Construct the floor frame: Cut the side supports, end supports, and one center support. Fasten the end supports between the sides with 3½" deck screws, as shown in the FLOOR FRAMING PLAN (page 87); locate the screws where they won't interfere with the corner post lag screws (see Step 4). Fasten the center support between the end supports, centered between the side supports.

Cut twelve 2 × 6 floorboards to length. Make sure the floor frame is square, then install the first board at one end, flush with the outsides of the frame, using 3" deck screws. Use 1" spacers to set the gaps as you install the remaining boards. Rip the last board as needed. (For the closed shed, create a 1½" × 2" notch for the left door post, starting 26" from the left end of the floor frame).

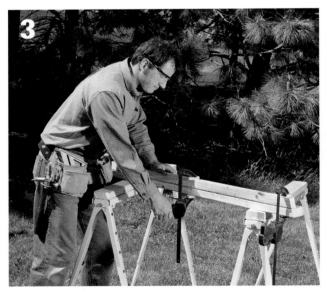

Build the corner posts: Rip two 8-ft. 2 × 4s to 2" in width. Make an 18° cut at about 53", leaving a 43' piece from each board. Cut two full-width 2 × 4 pieces at 53" and two at 43", beveling the top ends at 18°. Assemble each front post to form an "L", using the 53" pieces and keeping the angled ends flush; use 2½" deck screws. Assemble the rear posts the same way, using the 43" pieces.

Trim the corner posts to length: First, cut the front posts at 49", measuring from the longest point of the angled ends. Cut the rear posts at 38¼", measuring from the shortest point of the angled ends. Mark the insides of the posts 1½" from the bottom ends. Set each post on the floor frame so the mark is aligned with the bottom of the frame, then anchor the post with two 3" lag screws and washers, driven through counterbored pilot holes.

To begin framing the roof, cut two 2 × 4 roof headers at 73". Bevel the top edges of the headers at 18° using a circular saw and cutting guide or a tablesaw (the broad face of the header should still measure 3½"). Position the headers between the corner posts, flush with the outsides of the posts. Also, the beveled edges should be flush with the post tops. Fasten the headers to the posts with 2½" deck screws.

Cut two upper and two lower rafters, following the RAFTER TEMPLATES (page 88). Install the end rafters between the corner posts, flush with the tops of the posts, using 2½" deck screws. Install the two center rafters between the headers, 25" in from the end rafters. For the closed shed, cut the 2 × 4 rear center post to run from the bottom of the rear header down to 1½" below the bottom of the floor frame (as shown). Install the center post centered between the corner posts.

Plan the layout of the 1 × 6 slats, gapping the slats as desired. On each side, the bottom slat mounts to the outside of the floor, covering the floor from view. The remaining slats mount to the insides of the corner posts. Cut the side slats to fit and install them with 1⅝" deck screws. For the closed shed, cover the rear side with slats, using the same techniques.

(continued)

Sheath the roof with a piece of ¾" exterior plywood cut to 35½" × 81½". Overhang the posts by ¾" on all sides, and fasten the sheathing to the posts, headers, and rafters with 2" deck screws. Add 1 × 2 trim along all edges of the sheathing, mitering the ends at the corners. Fasten the trim with 6d galvanized finish nails so the top edges are flush with the sheathing.

Apply building paper over the sheathing and trim, overhanging the bottom roof edge by 1" and the sides by ½". Install the cedar shingles. Construct the roof cap with 1 × 3 and 1 × 4 trim boards. Join the boards to form an "L" using 6d finish nails. Fasten the cap along the top edge of the roof with 6d nails.

For the closed shed only, complete the following four steps

Cut the 2 × 2 door ledger at 73". Install the ledger flush with the top of the floor frame, screwing through the back of the side support with 2½" screws. Cut the 2 × 4 door posts to fit between the ledger and door header, as shown in the FLOOR PLAN (page 87). *Note: The left post is on edge, and the right post is flat. Make sure the posts are plumb, and fasten them with 2½" screws.*

Install 1 × 3 shelf cleats at the desired height, fastening them to the rear and side slats and the right doorpost. Cut the ¾" plywood shelf to fit the space and install it with 1⅝" deck screws.

For the door trim, cut four stiles at 41¾" and four rails at 18¼" from three 8-ft. 1 × 4s. Cut two stiles at 41¾" and two rails at 14¼" from one 10-ft. 1 × 4. Cut two ¾" plywood panels at 23½ × 40" and one panel at 19½ × 40".

Fasten the rails and stiles to the door panels with 1¼" deck screws, following the DOOR ELEVATION (page 88). Screw through the backsides of the panels. Install the doors with two hinges each. Use offset sash hinges mounted to the shed posts, or use standard strap hinges mounted to ¾"-thick blocks.

Timber-frame Shed

Timber-framing is a traditional style of building that uses a simple framework of heavy timber posts and beams connected with hand-carved joints. From the outside, a timber-frame building looks like a standard stick-frame structure, but on the inside, the stout, rough-sawn framing members evoke the look and feel of an 18th-century workshop. This 8 × 10-ft. shed has the same basic design used in traditional timber-frame structures but with joints that are easy to make.

In addition to the framing, some notable features of this shed are its simplicity and proportions. It's a nicely symmetrical building with full-height walls and an attractively steep-pitched roof, something you seldom find on manufactured kit sheds. The clean styling gives it a traditional, rustic look, but also makes the shed ideal for adding custom details. Install a skylight or windows to brighten the interior, or perhaps cut a crescent moon into the door in the style of old-fashioned backyard privies.

The materials for this project were carefully chosen to enhance the traditional styling. The 1 × 8 tongue-and-groove siding and all exterior trim boards are made from rough-sawn cedar, giving the shed a natural, rustic quality. The door is hand-built from rough cedar boards and includes exposed Z-bracing, a classic outbuilding detail. As shown here, the roof frame is made with standard 2 × 4s, but if you're willing to pay a little more to improve the appearance, you can use rough-cut 2 × 4s or 4 × 4s for the roof framing.

Another option to consider is traditional spaced sheathing instead of plywood for the roof deck. Spaced sheathing consists of 1 × 4 boards nailed perpendicular to the roof frame, with a 1½" gap between boards. The roof shingles are nailed directly to the sheathing without building paper in between, creating an attractive ceiling of exposed boards and shingles inside the shed.

The timber-frame shed evokes an old-world appeal by using rough-sawn cedar and heavy timber posts.

Cutting List

DESCRIPTION	QTY./SIZE	MATERIAL
Foundation		
Drainage material	1 cu. yard	Compactible gravel
Skids	3 @ 10'	6 × 6 treated timbers
Floor Framing		
Rim joists	2 @ 10'	2 × 6 pressure-treated
Joists	9 @ 8'	2 × 6 pressure-treated
Joist clip angles	18	3 × 3 × 3" × 18-gauge galvanized
Floor sheathing	3 sheets @ 4 × 8'	¾" tongue-&-groove ext.-grade plywood
Wall Framing		
Posts	6 @ 8'	4 × 4 rough-sawn cedar
Window posts	2 @ 4'	4 × 4 rough-sawn cedar
Girts	2 @ 10' 2 @ 8'	4 × 4 rough-sawn cedar
Beams	2 @ 10' 2 @ 8'	4 × 6 rough-sawn cedar
Braces	8 @ 2'	4 × 4 rough-sawn cedar
Post bases	6, with nails	Simpson BC40
Post-beam connectors	8 pieces, with nails	Simpson LCE
L-connectors	4, with nails	Simpson A34
Additional posts	6 @ 8'	4 × 4 rough-sawn cedar
Roof Framing		
Rafters	12 @ 7'	2 × 4
Collar ties	2 @ 10'	2 × 4
Ridge board	1 @ 10'	2 × 6
Metal anchors — rafters	8, with nails	Simpson H1
Gable-end blocking	4 @ 7'	2 × 2
Exterior Finishes		
Siding	2 @ 14', 8 @ 12' 10 @ 10', 29 @ 9'	1 × 8 V-joint rough-sawn cedar
Corner trim	8 @ 9'	1 × 4 rough-sawn cedar
Fascia	4 @ 7', 2 @ 12'	1 × 6 rough-sawn cedar
Fascia trim	4 @ 7', 2 @ 12'	1 × 2 rough-sawn cedar
Subfascia	2 @ 12'	1 × 4 pine
Plywood soffits	1 sheet 4 × 8'	⅜" cedar or fir plywood
Soffit vents (optional)	4 @ 4 × 12"	Louver with bug screen
Flashing (door)	4 linear ft.	Galvanized — 18 gauge

DESCRIPTION	QTY./SIZE	MATERIAL
Roofing		
Roof sheathing	6 sheets @ 4 × 8'	½" ext.-grade plywood
Cedar shingles	1.7 squares	
15# building paper	140 sq. ft.	
Roof vents (optional)	2 units	
Door		
Frame	2 @ 7', 1 @ 4'	¾ × 4¼" (actual) S4S cedar
Stops	2 @ 7', 1 @ 4'	1 × 2 S4S cedar
Panel material	7 @ 7'	1 × 6 T&G V-joint rough-sawn cedar
Z-brace	1 @ 8' to 2 @ 8'	1 × 6 rough-sawn cedar
Strap hinges	3	
Trim	5 @ 7'	1 × 3 rough-sawn cedar
Flashing	42" metal flashing	
Fasteners		
60d common nails	16 nails	
20d common nails	32 nails	
16d galvanized common nails	3½ lbs.	
10d common nails	1 lb.	
10d galvanized casing nails	½ lb.	
8d galvanized box nails	1½ lbs.	
8d galvanized finish nails	7 lbs.	
8d box nails	¼ lb.	
6d galvanized finish nails	40 nails	
3d galvanized finish nails	50 nails	
1½" joist hanger nails	72 nails	
2½" deck screws	25 screws	
1½" wood screws	50 screws	
⅞" galvanized roofing nails	2 lbs.	
⅜" × 6" lag screws, w/washers	16 screws	
¼" × 6" lag screws, w/washers		
Construction adhesive	4 tubes	

Note: Additional posts may be added as a safety precaution to prevent eave beam deflection.

Front Framing Elevation

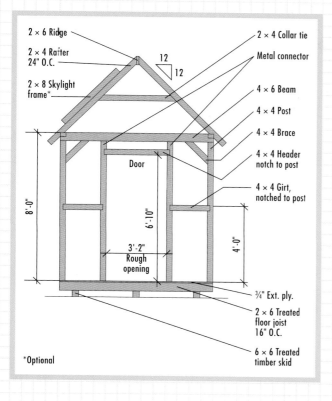

2 × 6 Ridge

2 × 4 Rafter 24" O.C.

2 × 8 Skylight frame*

2 × 4 Collar tie

Metal connector

4 × 6 Beam

4 × 4 Post

4 × 4 Brace

4 × 4 Header notch to post

4 × 4 Girt, notched to post

Door

8'-0"

6'-10"

3'-2" Rough opening

4'-0"

¾" Ext. ply.

2 × 6 Treated floor joist 16" O.C.

6 × 6 Treated timber skid

*Optional

Left Side Framing Elevation

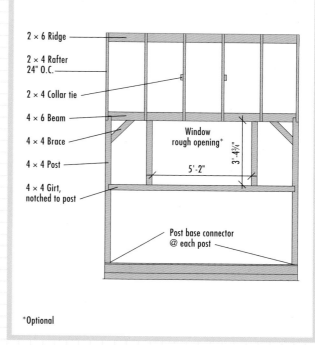

2 × 6 Ridge

2 × 4 Rafter 24" O.C.

2 × 4 Collar tie

4 × 6 Beam

4 × 4 Post

4 × 4 Brace

4 × 4 Girt, notched to post

Rear Framing Elevation

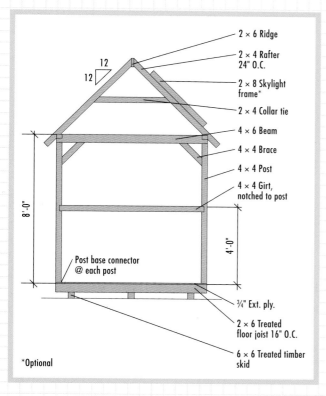

2 × 6 Ridge

2 × 4 Rafter 24" O.C.

2 × 8 Skylight frame*

2 × 4 Collar tie

4 × 6 Beam

4 × 4 Brace

4 × 4 Post

4 × 4 Girt, notched to post

8'-0"

4'-0"

Post base connector @ each post

¾" Ext. ply.

2 × 6 Treated floor joist 16" O.C.

6 × 6 Treated timber skid

*Optional

Right Side Framing Elevation

2 × 6 Ridge

2 × 4 Rafter 24" O.C.

2 × 4 Collar tie

4 × 6 Beam

4 × 4 Brace

4 × 4 Post

4 × 4 Girt, notched to post

Window rough opening*

3'-4¾"

5'-2"

Post base connector @ each post

*Optional

Building Section

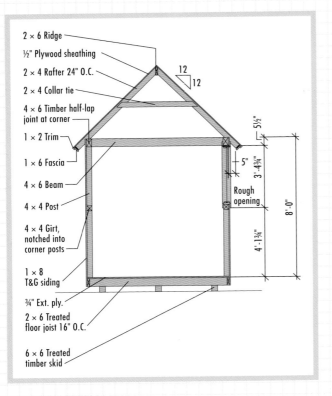

- 2 × 6 Ridge
- ½" Plywood sheathing
- 2 × 4 Rafter 24" O.C.
- 2 × 4 Collar tie
- 4 × 6 Timber half-lap joint at corner
- 1 × 2 Trim
- 1 × 6 Fascia
- 4 × 6 Beam
- 4 × 4 Post
- 4 × 4 Girt, notched into corner posts
- 1 × 8 T&G siding
- ¾" Ext. ply.
- 2 × 6 Treated floor joist 16" O.C.
- 6 × 6 Treated timber skid

5½"
5"
3'-4¾"
Rough opening
8'-0"
4'-1¾"

Rafter Template

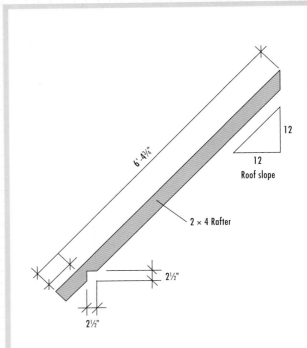

6'-4¾"
12
12
Roof slope
2 × 4 Rafter
2½"
2½"

Floor Framing Plan

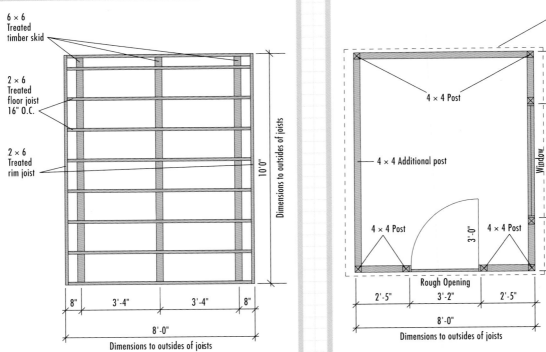

- 6 × 6 Treated timber skid
- 2 × 6 Treated floor joist 16" O.C.
- 2 × 6 Treated rim joist

10'0"
Dimensions to outsides of joists

8" 3'-4" 3'-4" 8"
8'-0"
Dimensions to outsides of joists

Floor Plan

Roof lines shown dashed

4 × 4 Post
4 × 4 Additional post
4 × 4 Post
4 × 4 Post
Window
Rough Opening

2'-5"
5'-2"
Rough Opening 10'-0"
Dimensions to outsides of joists
2'-5"
3'-0"

2'-5" 3'-2" 2'-5"
Rough Opening
8'-0"
Dimensions to outsides of joists

Front Elevation

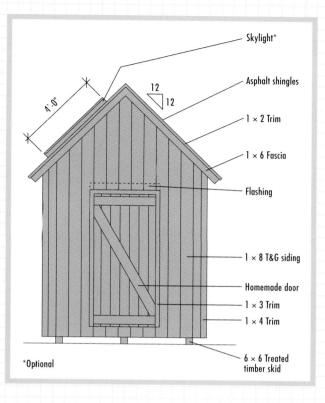

Skylight*

Asphalt shingles

1 × 2 Trim

1 × 6 Fascia

Flashing

1 × 8 T&G siding

Homemade door

1 × 3 Trim

1 × 4 Trim

6 × 6 Treated timber skid

4'-0"

12 / 12

*Optional

Left Side Elevation

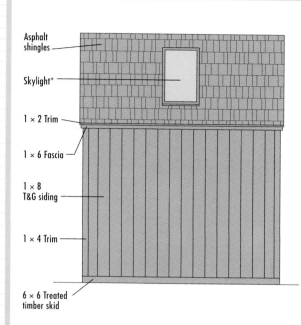

Asphalt shingles

Skylight*

1 × 2 Trim

1 × 6 Fascia

1 × 8 T&G siding

1 × 4 Trim

6 × 6 Treated timber skid

*Optional

Rear Elevation

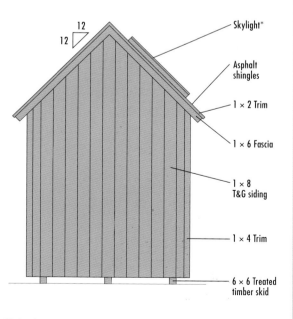

Skylight*

Asphalt shingles

1 × 2 Trim

1 × 6 Fascia

1 × 8 T&G siding

1 × 4 Trim

6 × 6 Treated timber skid

12 / 12

*Optional

Right Side Elevation

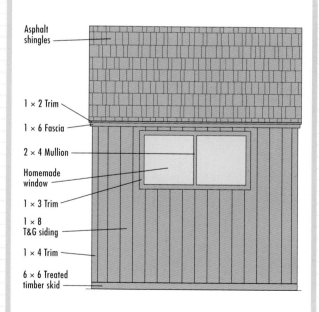

Asphalt shingles

1 × 2 Trim

1 × 6 Fascia

2 × 4 Mullion

Homemade window

1 × 3 Trim

1 × 8 T&G siding

1 × 4 Trim

6 × 6 Treated timber skid

Gable Overhang Detail

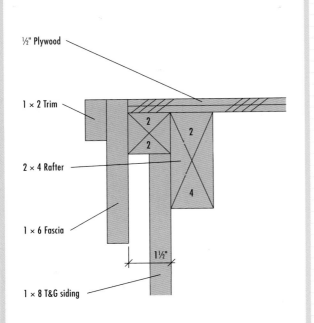

½" Plywood

1 × 2 Trim

2 × 4 Rafter

1 × 6 Fascia

1½"

1 × 8 T&G siding

Eave Detail

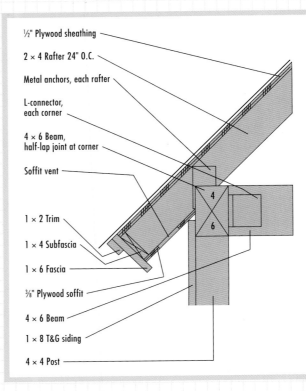

½" Plywood sheathing

2 × 4 Rafter 24" O.C.

Metal anchors, each rafter

L-connector, each corner

4 × 6 Beam, half-lap joint at corner

Soffit vent

1 × 2 Trim

1 × 4 Subfascia

1 × 6 Fascia

⅜" Plywood soffit

4 × 6 Beam

1 × 8 T&G siding

4 × 4 Post

Door Jamb Detail

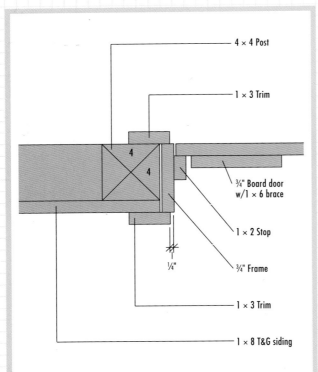

4 × 4 Post

1 × 3 Trim

¾" Board door w/1 × 6 brace

1 × 2 Stop

¾" Frame

1 × 3 Trim

1 × 8 T&G siding

¼"

Door Detail

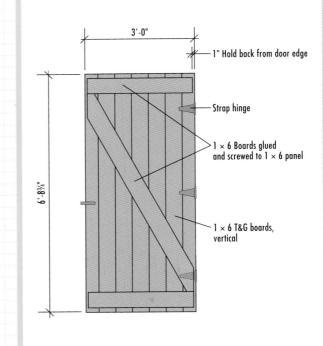

3'-0"

1" Hold back from door edge

Strap hinge

1 × 6 Boards glued and screwed to 1 × 6 panel

1 × 6 T&G boards, vertical

6'-8¾"

How to Build the Timber-frame Shed

Prepare the foundation site with a 4"-deep layer of compacted and leveled gravel. Cut three 6 × 6 treated timber skids (120"). Place the skids following the FLOOR FRAMING PLAN (page 98). Lay a straight 2 × 4 across the skids and test with a level.

Cut two 2 × 6 rim joists (120") and nine joists (93"). Assemble the floor frame with galvanized nails, as shown in the FLOOR FRAMING PLAN. Check the frame to make sure it is square by measuring the diagonals.

Position the floor frame on top of the skids and measure the diagonals to make sure it's square. Install joist clip angles at each joist along the two outer skids with galvanized nails. Toenail each joist to the center skid.

Install the tongue-and-groove plywood floor sheathing, starting with a full sheet at one corner of the frame. The flooring should extend all the way to the outside edges of the floor frame.

(continued)

To prepare the wall posts, cut six 4 × 4 posts (90½"), making sure both ends are square. On the four corner posts, mark for 3½"-long × 1½"-deep notches (to accept the girts) on the two adjacent inside faces of each post. Start the notches 46¼" from the bottom ends of the posts.

Mark the door frame posts for notches to receive a girt at 46¼" and for the door header at 82"; see the FRONT FRAMING ELEVATION (page 97). Remove the waste from the notch areas with a circular saw and clean up with a broad wood chisel. Test-fit the notches to make sure the 4 × 4 girts will fit snugly.

Position the post bases so the posts will be flush with the outsides of the shed floor. Install the bases with 16d galvanized common nails. The insides of the door posts should be 29" from the floor sides. Brace each post so it is perfectly plumb, and then fasten it to its base using the base manufacturer's recommended fasteners.

Cut two 4 × 6 beams at 10 ft. and two at 8 ft. Notch the ends of the beams for half-lap joints: Measure the width and depth of the beams and mark notches equal to the width × ½ the depth. Orient the notches as shown in the FRAMING ELEVATIONS (page 97). Cut the notches with a handsaw, then test-fit the joints, and make fine adjustments with a chisel.

Set an 8-ft. beam onto the front wall posts and tack it in place with a 16d nail at each end. Tack the other 8-ft. beam to the back posts. Then, position the 10 ft. beams on top of the short beam ends, forming the half-lap joints. Measure the diagonals of the front wall frame to make sure it's square, and then anchor the beams with two 60d galvanized nails at each corner (drill pilot holes for the nails).

Reinforce the beam connections with a metal post-beam connector on the outside of each corner and on both sides of the door posts, using the recommended fasteners. Install an L-connector on the inside of the beam-to-beam joints; see the EAVE DETAIL (page 100).

Cut eight 4 × 4 corner braces (20"), mitering the ends at 45°. Install the braces flush with the outsides of the beams and corner posts, using two ⅜ × 6" lag screws (with washers) driven through counterbored pilot holes.

Measure between the posts at the notches, and cut the 4 × 4 girts to fit. To allow the girts to meet at the corner posts, make a 1½ × 1½" notch at both ends of the rear wall girts and the outside ends of the front wall girts. Install the girts with construction adhesive and two 20d nails driven through the outsides of the posts (make pilot holes). Cut and install the 4 × 4 door header in the same fashion.

(continued)

Frame the roof: Cut two pattern rafters using the RAFTER TEMPLATE (page 98). Test-fit the patterns, and then cut the remaining ten rafters. Cut the 2 × 6 ridge (120"). Install the rafters and ridge using 24" on-center spacing. Cut four 2 × 2s to extend from the roof peak to the rafter ends, and install them flush with the tops of the rafters; see the GABLE OVERHANG DETAIL (page 100). Add framing connectors at the rafter-beam connections (except the outer rafters). *Note: If desired, you can add framing for a skylight.*

Cut four **2 × 4 collar ties** (58"), mitering the tops of the ends at 45°. Install the ties ½" below the tops of the rafters, as shown in the FRAMING ELEVATIONS.

Install the 1 × 8 siding on the front and rear walls so it runs from the 2 × 2s down to ¾" below the bottom of the floor frame. Fasten the siding with 8d corrosion-resistant finish nails or siding nails. Don't nail the siding to the door header in this step.

Cover the rafter ends along the eaves with 1 × 4 subfascia, flush with the tops of the rafters; see the EAVE DETAIL. Install the 1 × 6 fascia and 1 × 2 trim at the gable ends, then along the eaves, mitering the corner joints. Keep the fascia and trim ½" above the rafters so it will be flush with the roof sheathing.

17

Rip the plywood soffit panels to fit between the wall framing and the fascia, and install them with 3d galvanized box nails; see the EAVE DETAIL.

18

Deck the roof with ½" plywood sheathing, starting at the bottom corners. Cover the sheathing with building paper, overhanging the 1 × 2 fascia trim by ¾". Install the cedar shingle roofing or asphalt shingles. Include roof vents, if desired (they're a good idea). Finish the roof at the peak with a 1× ridge cap.

19

Construct the door frame from ¾" × 4¼" stock. Cut the head jamb at 37¾" and the side jambs at 81". Fasten the head jamb over the ends of the side jambs with 2½" deck screws. Install the frame in the door opening, using shims and 10d galvanized casing nails. Add 1 × 2 stops to the jambs, ¾" from the outside edges.

20

Build the door with seven pieces of 1 × 6 siding cut at 80¾". Fit the boards together, then mark and trim the outer pieces so the door is 36" wide. Install the 1 × 6 Z-bracing with adhesive and 1¼" wood screws, as shown in the DOOR DETAIL (page 100). Install flashing over the outside of the door, then add 1 × 3 trim around both sides of the door opening, as shown in the DOOR JAMB DETAIL (page 100). Hang the door with three strap hinges.

Salt Box Storage Shed

The asymmetrical roofline of this shed, taller in front than in back, resembles the salt box house, a classic of colonial American architecture. Here is a great basic shed that offers lots of storage space with a slightly lower elevation than the Simple Storage Shed. At 77 inches, the doors are still plenty tall enough for almost everyone to enter easily, but the shallow peaked roof and 66 inch rear wall means the overall building height is just under eight feet. The gravel base and 4 × 4 joists (no skids needed) also keep this building close to the ground. These factors all create a smaller visual impact and a pleasing proportional look.

The 8 × 12-foot floor plan and the 6-foot-wide double doors give it excellent versatility and access. The sturdy ¾" floor will support a riding mower or other heavy equipment. The centered doors create two feet of space around all sides of parked equipment; however, you could position the doors off center to suit your storage needs.

The construction is quite simple stick framing. Additional features include enclosed soffits to keep out bugs and birds, and a roof vent to prevent overheating. Clapboard style siding would enhance the colonial look of this shed, if you wanted to move away from the standard vertically grooved plywood siding.

The width of this shed can be easily adjusted from 12 feet down to 8 feet or up to 16 feet. The top and bottom plates for the front and rear walls and the ridge board would be shorter or longer, and you would need to subtract or add more studs, joists, and rafters, but the height and depth measurements remain the same.

Examine the plans carefully before you start, as the joists and front and rear wall studs have different spacing on the left side versus the right.

The salt box storage shed draws on classic American architecture to create a space that's as simple on the inside as it is beautiful on the outside.

Cutting List

DESCRIPTION	QTY./SIZE	MATERIAL
Foundation/Floor		
Drainage material	1.25 cu. yd.	Compactible gravel
Skids	7 @ 8'	4 × 4 pressure treated
Rim joists	2 @ 12'	2 × 4 pressure treated
Floor sheathing	3 sheets @ 4 × 8'	¾" exterior grade plywood
Wall Framing		
Bottom plate, front & rear	2 @ 12'	2 × 4
Bottom plate, sides	2 @ 8'	2 × 4
Top plates, front & rear	2 @ 12	2 × 4
Top plates, sides	2 @ 8'	2 × 4
Studs, wall (cut in two pieces)	10 @ 12'	2 × 4
Studs, front	10 @ 7	2 × 4
Studs, gable	2 @ 12	2 × 4
Door header	1 @ 14'	2 × 6
Roof Framing		
Rafters	7 @ 10'	2 × 4
Ridge board	1 @ 12'	2 × 6
Rafter tie	1 @ 12'	2 × 4
Exterior Finishes		
Siding	11 sheets @ 4 × 8'	⅝" plywood siding
Eave fascia	2 @ 14'	1 × 6 cedar
Gable fascia	2 @ 10'	1 × 4 cedar
Eave soffit	2 @ 12'	1 × 4 cedar
Frieze, rear	1 @ 12'	1 × 4 cedar

DESCRIPTION	QTY./SIZE	MATERIAL
Frieze, front ripped	1 @ 12'	1 × 6 cedar
Wall corner trim	4 @ 14'	1 × 4 cedar
Roofing		
Sheathing	4 sheets @ 4 × 8'	½" exterior grade plywood roof sheathing
Drip edge	50 linear ft.	Metal drip edge
15# building paper	1 roll	
Shingles	1⅔ squares	Asphalt shingles
Door		
Door stop	3 @ 8'	1 × 2 cedar
Door trim & casing	10 @ 8'	1 × 4 cedar
Fasteners & Hardware		
16d galvanized common nails	1 lb.	
16d coated common nails	4 lbs.	
8d coated plywood nails	3 lbs.	
8d galvanized siding nails	5 lbs.	
1¼" galvanized roofing nails	3 lbs.	
8d galvanized casing nails	2 lbs.	
Hinges	6	6" T-strap
3d galvanized door nails	1 lb.	
Exterior caulk	1 tube	
Glue	1 tube	Exterior wood glue
Roof vent	1	

Overview of Framing

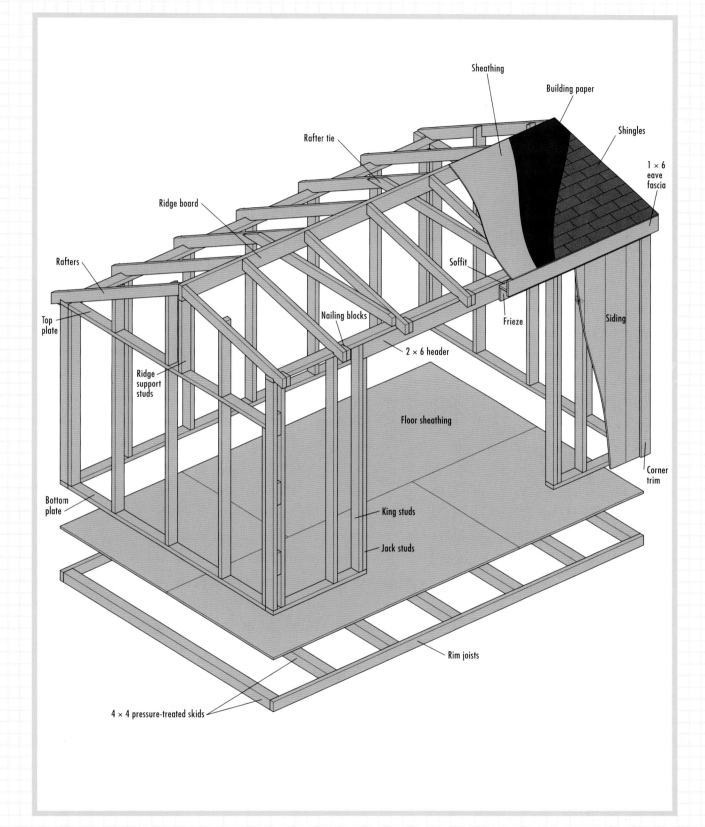

Sheathing

Building paper

Shingles

Rafter tie

1 × 6 eave fascia

Ridge board

Soffit

Rafters

Frieze

Siding

Top plate

Nailing blocks

2 × 6 header

Ridge support studs

Floor sheathing

Corner trim

Bottom plate

King studs

Jack studs

Rim joists

4 × 4 pressure-treated skids

Sideview of Framing Section

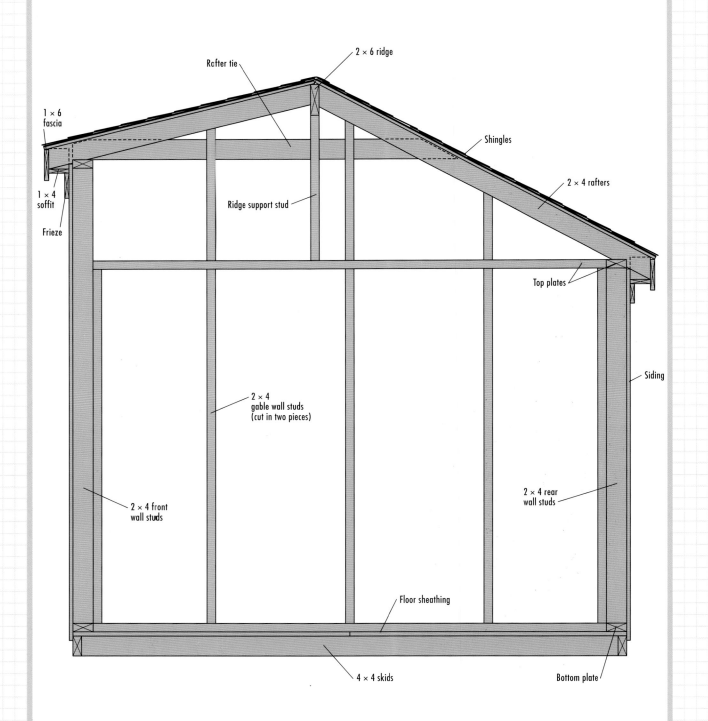

Rafter tie

2 × 6 ridge

1 × 6 fascia

Shingles

1 × 4 soffit

2 × 4 rafters

Frieze

Ridge support stud

Top plates

Siding

2 × 4 gable wall studs (cut in two pieces)

2 × 4 rear wall studs

2 × 4 front wall studs

Floor sheathing

4 × 4 skids

Bottom plate

Front Elevation

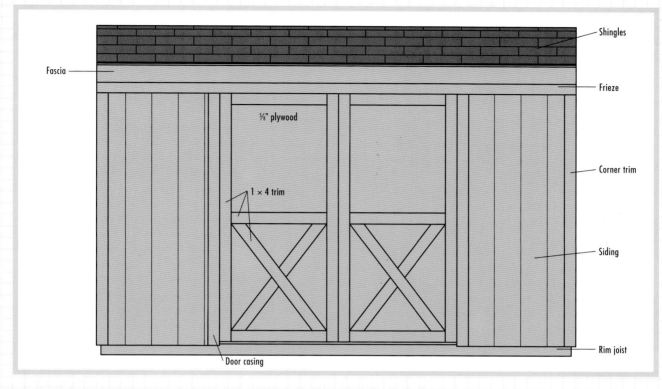

Shingles

Fascia

Frieze

⅝" plywood

Corner trim

1 × 4 trim

Siding

Door casing

Rim joist

Rear Elevation

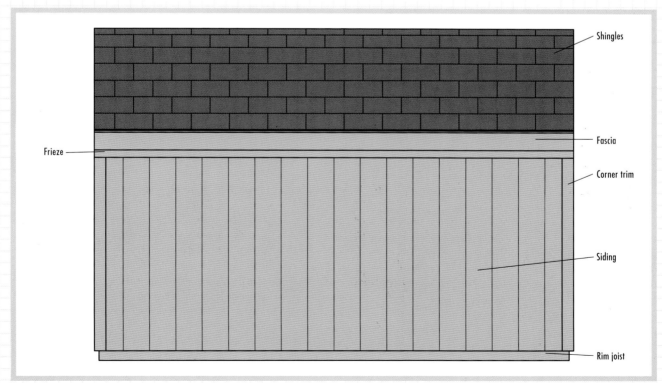

Shingles

Fascia

Frieze

Corner trim

⅝" plywood

Siding

Rim joist

Left Side Elevation

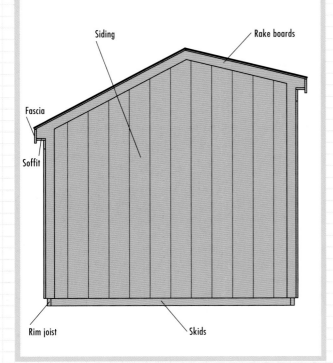

Siding

Rake boards

Fascia

Soffit

Rim joist

Skids

Right Side Elevation

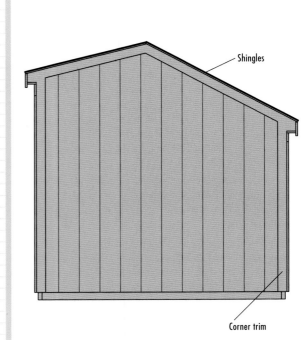

Shingles

Corner trim

Front Wall Framing

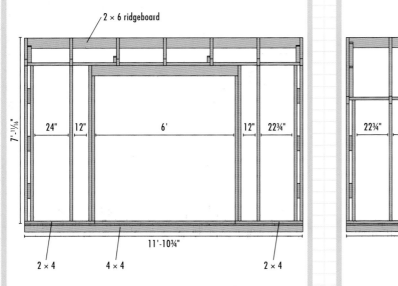

2 × 6 ridgeboard

7'-1¹¹/₁₆"

24" 12" 6' 12" 22¾"

11'-10¾"

2 × 4

4 × 4

2 × 4

Rear Wall Framing

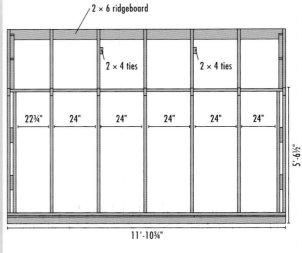

2 × 6 ridgeboard

2 × 4 ties

2 × 4 ties

22¾" 24" 24" 24" 24" 24"

5'-6½"

11'-10¾"

Right Side Framing

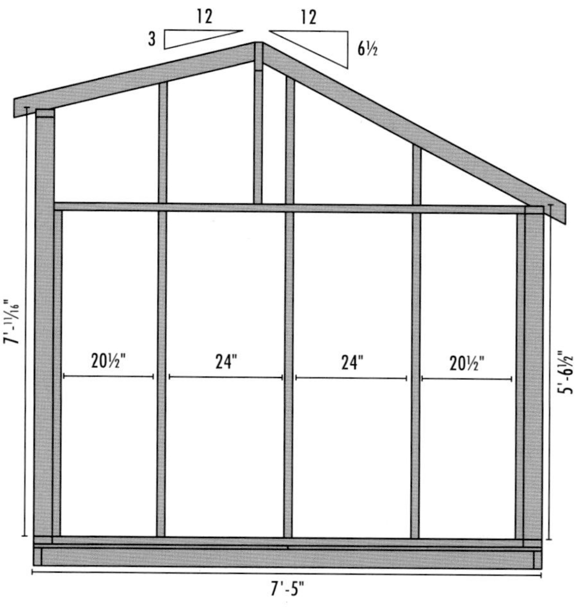

12
3
12
6½
7'-1¹⁄₁₆"
20½"
24"
24"
20½"
5'-6½"
7'-5"

Left Side Framing

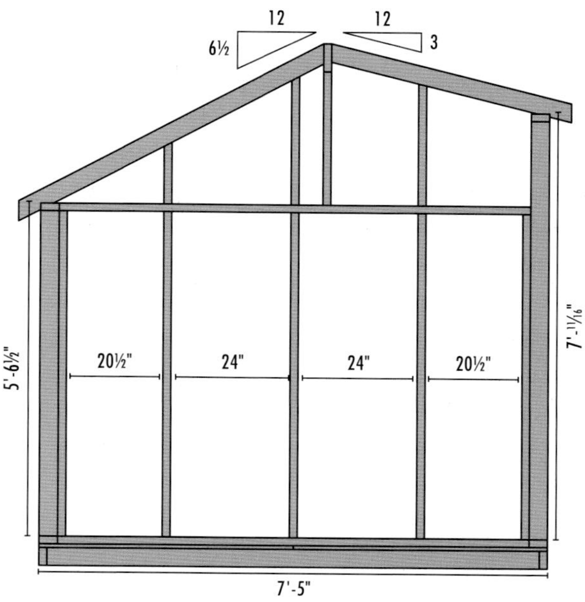

12
6½
12
3
5'-6½"
20½"
24"
24"
20½"
7'-1¹⁄₁₆"
7'-5"

Floor Framing

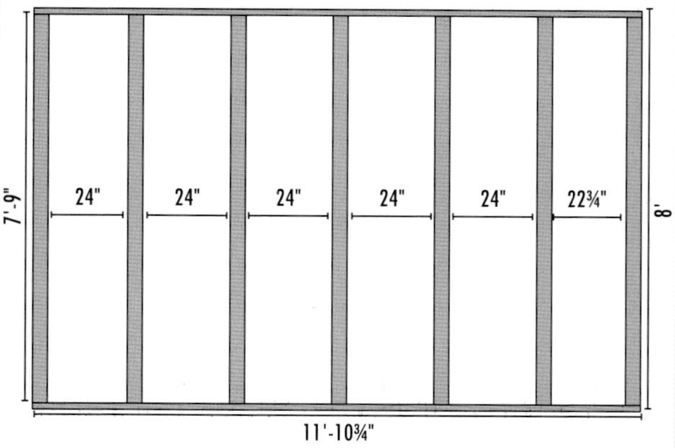

7'-9"
24"
24"
24"
24"
24"
22¾"
8'
11'-10¾"

Head Detail

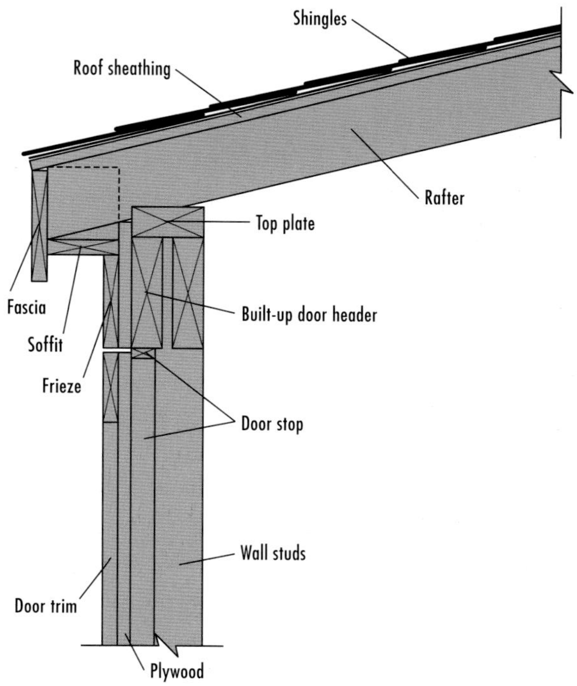

Shingles
Roof sheathing
Rafter
Top plate
Fascia
Soffit
Frieze
Built-up door header
Door stop
Wall studs
Door trim
Plywood

Rake Detail

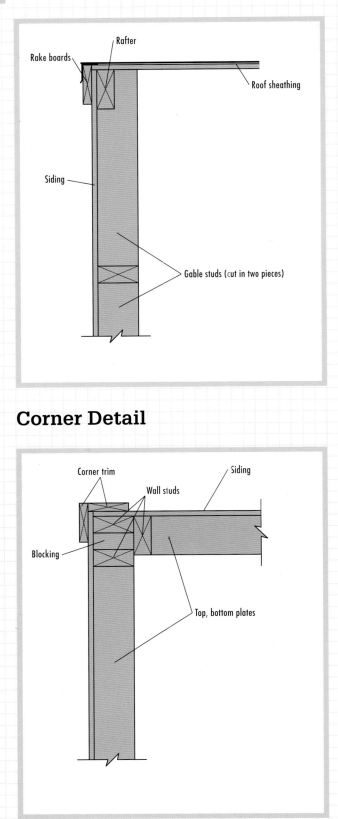

Rake boards

Rafter

Roof sheathing

Siding

Gable studs (cut in two pieces)

Door Detail

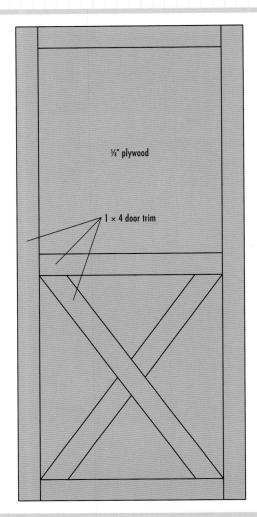

⅝" plywood

1 × 4 door trim

Corner Detail

Corner trim

Wall studs

Siding

Blocking

Top, bottom plates

Door Jamb Detail

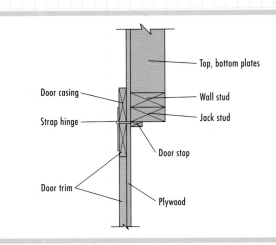

Top, bottom plates

Door casing

Wall stud

Strap hinge

Jack stud

Door stop

Door trim

Plywood

How to Build the Salt Box Shed

Prepare the foundation by following the steps for a simple skid foundation. First, prepare a bed of compacted gravel. Make sure the bed is flat and level. Cut seven 4 × 4" × 8 ft. pressure-treated posts to 93" to serve as skids. Position the joists as shown in the FLOOR FRAMING PLAN on page 113. Note that the right end of the shed is spaced at 21" on center, not 24" on center, as is the rest of the shed. Cut two 12-ft. pressure-treated 2 × 4s to 142¾" for rim joists and fasten to the ends of the 4 × 4 joists using 16d galvanized nails. Measure the diagonals of the foundation to make sure the frame is square.

Install the floor sheathing onto the floor frame. Begin at the left front end of the shed with a full 4 × 8 ft. sheet of ¾" plywood. Attach the plywood with 8d plywood nails, 6" on center around the edges and 10" on center in the field. Cut another 4 × 8 ft. sheet of ¾" plywood into two 4-ft. pieces. Attach one piece at the back left end of the shed. Cut the second full 4 × 8 ft. sheet to fit the back right end and attach. Cut the half sheet to fit the front right end.

Begin assembling the rear wall panel by cutting two 2 × 4s at 142¾" for the bottom and top plates. Cut nine 2 × 4s at 63½" for the rear wall studs. Assemble the rear wall according to the REAR WALL FRAMING PLAN on page 112. Nail through the top and bottom plates using two 16d nails at the top and the bottom. Note in the CORNER DETAIL on page 114 that the doubled end studs are spaced 1½" apart with three 6" lengths of 2 × 4 blocking.

Begin assembling the front wall panel by cutting two 2 × 4s at 142¾" for the bottom and top plates. Cut eight 2 × 4s at 81¹¹⁄₁₆" for the wall studs. Assemble the front wall according to the FRONT WALL FRAMING PLAN on page 112.

(continued)

Cut two 2 × 4s at 76³⁄₁₆" for jack studs. Create the built-up door header by sandwiching a piece of 5½" × 75" piece of ½" plywood between two 2 × 6s cut to 75". Apply construction adhesive to both sides of the plywood. Nail together on both sides with 8d coated common nails or screw together with deck screws. Attach the jack studs and header to the king studs and top and bottom plates.

Begin assembling the side wall panels by cutting four 2 × 4s at 89" for the side wall top and bottom plates. Cut ten 2 × 4s at 63½" for the side wall studs. Assemble the side walls according to the RIGHT SIDE FRAMING and LEFT SIDE FRAMING on page 113. Note that the three middle studs are 24" on center, and the two end studs are spaced 20½" on center.

Tilt the rear wall panel into place. Make sure that the narrow stud spacing is at the right end of the shed. Attach the bottom plate to the rim joist with 16d nails. Plumb the wall and brace into place.

Tilt the side wall panels into place. Attach the bottom plate to the joists with 16d nails. Check for plumb and nail the panels together at the corners.

Tilt the front panel into place. Attach the bottom plate, except for the portion in the doorway, to the rim joist with 16d nails. Check for plumb and attach the panels at the corners.

Install the plywood siding on the front and rear walls. Start on the left hand end of the shed. Cut the siding to length so it is flush with the top of the top plate and overlaps the top of the floor joists by ½". The siding should not extend to the ground as it is not rated for ground contact. Make sure all vertical seams fall on the studs. Attach the siding to the studs with 8d galvanized nails 6" on center at edges and 12" on center in the field.

Cut two 2 × 4 ridge support studs at 26". Center the studs 42" back from the outside face of the front wall stud at each end of the shed. Toenail the studs into place.

Create the ridge board by cutting the 2 × 6 ridge board to 142¾". Set it on top of the ridge support studs and toenail into place. You may need to add braces to hold the ridge support studs plumb while you cut and fit the rafters.

(continued)

Build the rafters as described in the CUTTING LIST on page 108. Cut one pair of rafters from a 10-ft. long 2 × 4. Set the rafters in place, making sure that the ridge support studs are plumb. If the rafters fit well, use them as patterns for cutting the remaining six pairs of rafters. Attach the rafters aligned with the spacing of the wall studs. On the third and fifth rafter pairs, attach 2 × 4 ties. Cut the ties to fit so that they rest atop the front top plate and are level. Attach the ties with 16d nails.

Cut 2 × 4 rake support studs to fit in the gable ends, aligned with the side wall studs to act as siding nailers. Toenail into place. Measure the side wall elevation at the middle siding nailer and at the corners, allowing for ½" overlap over the joist. Cut plywood siding to size and apply siding to the side walls.

Cut fourteen 4" long nailing blocks from scrap 2 × 4s. Attach the nailing blocks to the rafters so that they are flush with the bottom point of the rafter as shown on the HEAD DETAIL, page 113.

Attach the plywood sheathing to the rafters using 8d nails 6" on center on the edges and 12" on center in the field. Make sure all seams fall on rafters. Cut to fit and attach the 1 × 4 cedar rake boards on the gable ends.

To install the roof vent, cut a hole one foot down from the peak of the roof in the middle of the rear roof. Apply roofing felt. Cut the felt away from the vent hole and install the vent. Install the metal drip edging and shingle the roof as shown on pages 56 and 57.

Attach the 1 × 6 cedar fascia to the rafter ends using 8d galvanized trim nails. Attach the 1 × 4 cedar soffit to the nailing blocks. Attach the 1 × 4 cedar frieze board under the soffit as shown on the HEAD DETAIL. Attach the 1 × 4 cedar corner trim and 1 × 4 cedar doorway trim.

Cut out the bottom plate in the door opening, using a reciprocating saw or a back saw. Measure the door opening and adjust door dimensions if necessary. Cut two doors from the plywood siding at 36 × 77½". Attach 1 × 4 cedar trim around the edges of the plywood door blanks with exterior wood glue and 1¼" deck screws. Attach screws from the front and back. Apply decorative X to bottom, or top and bottom of each door panel. Install door casing.

Attach three exterior strap hinges to each door, taking care to make them square to the door edge. With a helper, place a door in the opening, flush with the door trim. Use shims to create a ¼" gap at the side and top. Attach the hinges. Repeat for the second door. Install 1 × 2 cedar door stops around the inside of the door frame. Attach a cedar 1 × 4 on the reverse of the left door with a 2" overhang to act as a stop. Attach desired handles and hasp to the doors. Paint or seal the shed.

Mini Garden Shed

Whether you are working in a garden or on a construction site, getting the job done is always more efficient when your tools are close at hand. Offering just the right amount of on-demand storage, this mini garden shed can handle all of your gardening hand tools but with a footprint that keeps costs and labor low.

The mini shed base is built on two 2 × 8 front and back rails that raise the shed off the ground. The rails can also act as runners, making it possible to drag the shed like a sled after it is built. The exterior is clad with vertical-board-style fiber-cement siding. This type of siding not only stands up well to the weather, but it is also very stable and resists rotting and warping. It also comes preprimed and ready for painting. Fiber-cement siding is not intended to be in constant contact with moisture, so the manufacturer recommends installing it at least 6" above the ground. You can paint the trim and siding any color you like. You might choose to coordinate the colors to match your house, or you might prefer a unique color scheme so that the shed stands out as a garden feature.

The roof is made with corrugated fiberglass roof panels. These panels are easy to install and are available in a variety of colors, including clear, which will let more light into the shed. An alternative to the panels is to attach plywood sheathing and then attach any roofing material you like over the sheathing. These plans show how to build the basic shed, but you can customize the interior with hanging hooks and shelves to suit your needs.

Working with Fiber-cement Siding ▶

Fiber-cement siding is sold in ¼"-thick, 4 × 8-ft. sheets at many home centers. There are specially designed shearing tools that contractors use to cut this material, but you can also cut it by scoring it with a utility knife and snapping it—just like cement tile backer board or drywall board. You can also cut cementboard with a circular saw, but you must take special precautions. Cementboard contains silica. Silica dust is a respiratory hazard. If you choose to cut it with a power saw, then minimize your dust exposure by using a manufacturer-designated saw blade designed to create less fine dust and by wearing a NIOSH/MSHA-approved respirator with a rating of N95 or better.

This scaled-down garden shed is just small enough to be transportable. Locate it near gardens or remote areas of your yard where on-demand tool storage is useful.

Cutting List

KEY	PART	DIMENSION	PCS.	MAT.
Lumber				
A	Front/back base rails	1½ × 7¼ × 55"	2	Treated pine
B	Base crosspieces	1½ × 3½ × 27"	4	Treated pine
C	Base platform	¾ × 30 × 55"	1	Ext. plywood
D	Front/back plates	1½ × 3½ × 48"	2	SPF
E	Front studs	1½ × 3½ × 81"	4	SPF
F	Door header	1½ × 3½ × 30"	1	SPF
G	Back studs	1½ × 3½ × 75"	4	SPF
H	Side bottom plate	1½ × 3½ × 30"	2	SPF
I	Top plate	1½ × 3½ × 55"	2	SPF
J	Side front stud	1½ × 3½ × 81"	2	SPF
K	Side middle stud	1½ × 3½ × 71"	2	SPF
L	Side back stud*	1½ × 3½ × 75¼"	2	SPF
M	Side crosspiece	1½ × 3½ × 27"	2	SPF
N	Door rail (narrow)	¾ × 3½ × 29¾"	1	SPF
O	Door rail (wide)	¾ × 5½ × 23"	2	SPF
P	Door stiles	¾ × 3½ × 71"	2	SPF
Q	Rafters	1½ × 3½ × 44"	4	SPF
R	Outside rafter blocking*	1½ × 3½ × 15¼"	4	SPF
S	Inside rafter blocking*	1½ × 3½ × 18¾"	2	SPF
Siding & Trim				
T	Front left panel	¼ × 20 × 85"	1	Siding
U	Front top panel	¼ × 7½ × 30"	1	Siding
V	Front right panel	¼ × 5 × 85"	1	Siding

KEY	PART	DIMENSION	PCS.	MAT.
W	Side panels	¼ × 30½ × 74½"	2	Siding
X	Back panel	¼ × 48 × 79"	1	Siding
Y	Door panel	¾ × 29¾ × 74"	1	Ext. plywood
Z	Front corner trim	¾ × 3½ × 85"	2	SPF
AA	Front top trim	¾ × 3½ × 50½"	1	SPF
BB	Side casing	¾ × 1½ × 81½"	2	SPF
CC	Top casing	¾ × 1½ × 30"	1	SPF
DD	Bottom casing	¾ × 2½ × 30"	1	SPF
EE	Trim rail (narrow)	¾ × 1½ × 16½"	3	SPF
FF	Trim rail (wide)	¾ × 3½ × 16½"	1	SPF
GG	Side trim	¾ × 2½ × 27"	2	SPF
HH	Side trim	¾ × 2½ × 27¾"	2	SPF
II	Side corner trim (long)	¾ × 1¾ × 85¼"	2	SPF
JJ	Side corner trim (short)	¾ × 1¾ × 79½"	2	SPF
KK	Side trim (wide)	¾ × 3½ × 27"	2	SPF
LL	Side trim (narrow)	¾ × 1½ × 69"	2	SPF
MM	Back corner trim	¾ × 3½ × 79"	2	SPF
NN	Back trim (wide)	¾ × 3½ × 50½"	2	SPF
OO	Back trim (narrow)	¾ × 1½ × 72"	2	SPF
PP	Side windows	¼ × 10 × 28"	2	Acrylic
Roof				
QQ	Purlins	1½ × 1½ × 61½"	5	
RR	Corrugated closure strips	61½" L	5	
SS	Corrugated roof panels	24 × 46"	3	

Not shown

Mini Garden Shed

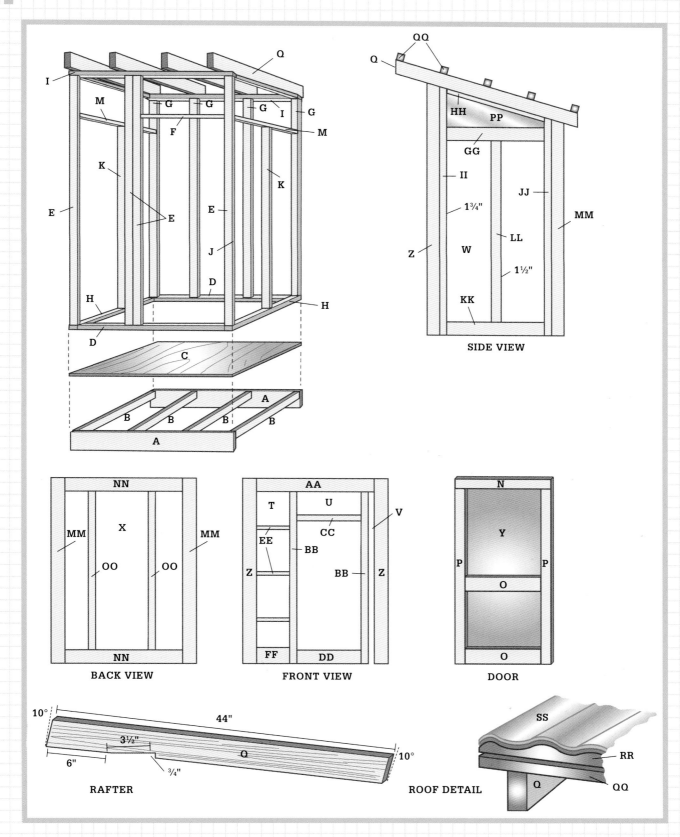

Q

QQ

I

M

G G G I G

F

M

K

K

E

E E

E

J

D

H H

D

C

A

B B B B

A

SIDE VIEW

Q

HH

PP

GG

II

JJ

Z

W

LL

KK

MM

1³⁄₄"

1¹⁄₂"

BACK VIEW

NN

MM

X

MM

OO OO

NN

FRONT VIEW

AA

T

U

CC

EE

BB

Z

BB

Z

FF

DD

V

DOOR

N

Y

P

O

O

P

RAFTER

10°

44"

3¹⁄₂"

6"

³⁄₄"

Q

10°

ROOF DETAIL

SS

RR

Q

QQ

How to Build a Mini Garden Shed

BUILD THE BASE

Even though moving it is possible, this shed is rather heavy and will require several people or a vehicle to drag it if you build it in your workshop or garage. When possible, determine where you want the shed located and build it in place. Level a 3 × 5-ft. area of ground. The shed base is made of treated lumber, so you can place it directly on the ground. If you desire a harder, more solid foundation, dig down 6" and fill the area with tamped compactible gravel.

Cut the front and back base rails and base crosspieces to length. Place the base parts upside-down on a flat surface and attach the crosspieces to the rails with 2½" deck screws. Working with the parts upside-down makes it easy to align the top edges flush. Cut the base platform to size. Flip the base frame over and attach the base platform (functionally, the floor) with 1½" screws. Set and level the base in position where the shed will be built.

FRAME THE SHED

Cut the front wall framing members to size, including the top and bottom plates, the front studs, and the door header. Lay out the front wall on a flat section of ground, such as a driveway or garage floor. Join the wall framing components with 16d common nails (photo 1). Then, cut the back-wall top and bottom plates and studs to length. Lay out the back wall on flat ground and assemble the back wall frame.

Cut both sidewall top and bottom plates to length, and then cut the studs and crosspiece. Miter-cut the ends of the top plate to 10°. Miter-cut the top of the front and back studs at 10° as well. Lay out and assemble the side walls on the ground. Place one of the side walls on the base platform. Align the outside edge of the wall so it is flush with the outside edge of the base platform. Get a helper to hold the wall plumb while you position the back wall. If you're working alone, attach a brace to the side of the wall and the platform to hold the wall plumb (photo 2).

Place the back wall on the platform and attach it to the side wall with 2½" deck screws (photo 3). Align the outside edge of the back wall with the edge of the platform. Place the front wall on the platform and attach it to the side wall with 2½" screws. Place the

Build the wall frames. For the front wall, attach the plates to the outside studs first and then attach the inside studs using the door header as a spacer to position the inside studs.

Raise the walls. Use a scrap of wood as a brace to keep the wall plumb. Attach the brace to the side-wall frame and to the base platform once you have established that the wall is plumb.

Fasten the wall frames. Attach the shed walls to one another and to the base platform with 2½" screws. Use a square and level to check that the walls are plumb and square.

Make the rafters. Cut the workpieces to length, then lay out and cut a birdsmouth notch in the bottom of the two inside rafters. These notches will keep the tops of the inside rafters in line with the outside rafters. The ends shou'd be plumb-cut at 10°.

Install rafter blocking. Some of the rafter blocking must be attached to the rafters by toe-screwing (driving screws at an angle). If you own a pocket screw jig you can use it to drill angled clearance holes for the deck screw heads.

Install the roofing. Attach the corrugated roof panels with 1" neoprene gasket screws (sometimes called pole barn screws) driven through the panels at closure strip locations. Drill slightly oversized pilot holes for each screw and do not overdrive screws—it will compress the closure strips or even cause the panels to crack.

second side wall on the platform and attach it to the front and back walls with 2½" screws.

Cut the rafters to length, then miter-cut each end to 10° for making a plumb cut (this way the rafter ends will be perpendicular to the ground). A notch, referred to as a "birdsmouth," must be cut into the bottom edge of the inside rafters so the tops of these rafters align with the outside rafter tops while resting solidly on the wall top plates. Mark the birdsmouth on the inside rafters (see Diagram, page 123) and cut them out with a jigsaw (photo 4). Cut the rafter blocking to length; these parts fit between the rafters at the front and back of the shed to close off the area above the top plates. Attach the rafters to the rafter blocking and to the top plates. Use the blocking as spacers to position the rafters and then drive 2½" screws up through the top plates and into the rafters. Then, drive 2½" screws through the rafters and into the blocking (photo 5). Toe-screw any rafter blocking that you can't access to fasten through a rafter. Finally, cut the door rails and stiles to length. Attach the rails to the stiles with 2½" screws.

INSTALL THE ROOFING

This shed features 24"-wide corrugated roofing panels. The panels are installed over wood or foam closure strips that are attached to the tops of 2 × 2 purlins running perpendicular to the rafters. Position the purlins so the end ones are flush with the ends of the rafters and the inner ones are evenly spaced. The overhang beyond the rafters should be equal on the purlin ends.

Cut five 61½"-long closure strips. If the closure strips are wood, drill countersunk pilot holes through the closure strips and attach them to the purlins with 1½" screws. Some closure strips are made of foam with a self-adhesive backing. Simply peel off the paper backing and press them in place. If you are installing foam strips that do not have adhesive backing, tack them down with a few pieces of double-sided carpet tape so they don't shift around.

Cut three 44"-long pieces of corrugated roofing panel. Use a jigsaw with a fine-tooth blade or a circular saw with a fine-tooth plywood blade to cut fiberglass or plastic panels. Clamp the panels

(continued)

Cut the wall panels. Use a utility knife to score the fiber-cement panel along a straightedge. Place a board under the scored line and then press down on the panel to break the panel as you would with drywall.

Attach siding panels. Attach the fiber-cement siding with 1½" siding nails driven through pilot holes. Space the nails 8 to 12" apart. Drive the nails a minimum ⅜" away from the panel edges and 2" from the corners.

Cut the acrylic window material to size. One way to accomplish this is to sandwich the acrylic between two sheets of scrap plywood and cut all three layers at once with a circular saw (straight cuts) or jigsaw.

together between scrap boards to minimize vibration while they're being cut (but don't clamp down so hard that you damage the panels). Position the panels over the closure strips, overlapping roughly 4" of each panel and leaving a 1" overhang in the front and back.

Drill pilot holes 12" apart in the field of panels and along the overlapping panel seams. Fasten only in the valleys of the corrugation. The pilot hole diameter should be slightly larger than the diameter of the screw shanks. Fasten the panels to the closure strips and rafters with hex-head screws that are pre-fitted with neoprene gaskets (photo 6, page 125).

ATTACH THE SIDING

Cut the siding panels to size by scoring them with a utility knife blade designated for scoring concrete and then snapping them along the scored line (photo 7). Or, use a rented cementboard saw (see page 120). Drill pilot holes in the siding and attach the siding

to the framing with 1½" siding nails spaced at 8 to 12" intervals (photo 8). (You can rent a cementboard coil nailer instead.) Cut the plywood door panel to size. Paint the siding and door before you install the windows and attach the wall and door trim. Apply two coats of exterior latex paint.

INSTALL THE WINDOWS

The windows are fabricated from ¼"-thick sheets of clear plastic or acrylic. To cut the individual windows to size, first mark the cut lines on the sheet. To cut acrylic with a circular saw, secure the sheet so that it can't vibrate during cutting. The best way to secure it is to sandwich it between a couple of pieces of scrap plywood and cut through all three sheets (photo 9). Drill ¼"-dia. pilot holes around the perimeter of the window pieces. Position the holes ½" from the edges and 6" apart. Attach the windows to the side wall framing on the exterior side using 1½" screws (photo 10).

ATTACH THE TRIM

Cut the wall and door trim pieces to length. Miter-cut the top end of the side front and back trim pieces to 10°. Attach the trim to the shed with 2" galvanized finish nails (photo 11). The horizontal side trim overlaps the window and the side siding panel. Be careful not to drive any nails through the plastic window panels. Attach the door trim to the door with 1¼" exterior screws.

HANG THE DOOR

Make the door and fasten a utility handle or gate handle to it. Fasten three door hinges to the door and then fasten the hinges to a stud on the edge of the door opening (photo 12). Use a scrap piece of siding as a spacer under the door to determine the proper door height in the opening. Add hooks and hangers inside the shed as needed to accommodate the items you'll be storing. If you have security concerns, install a hasp and padlock on the mini shed door.

Attach the window panels. Drill a ¼"-dia. pilot hole for each screw that fastens the window panels. These oversized holes give the plastic panel room to expand and contract. The edges of the windows (and the fasteners) will be covered by trim.

Attach the trim boards with 2" galvanized finish nails. In the areas around windows, predrill for the nails so you don't crack the acrylic.

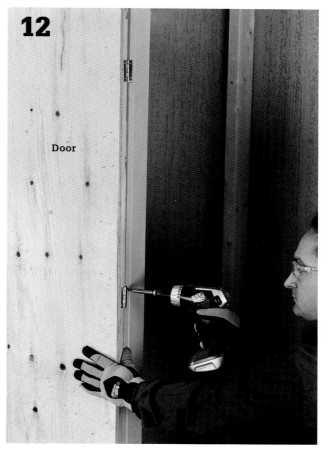

Hang the door using three exterior-rated door hinges. Slip a scrap of ¼"-thick siding underneath the door to raise it off the bottom plate while you install it.

Clerestory Studio

This easy-to-build shed is made distinctive by its three clerestory windows on the front side. In addition to their unique architectural effect, clerestory windows offer some practical advantages over standard windows. First, their position at the top of the building allows sunlight to spread downward over the interior space to maximize illumination. Most of the light is indirect, creating a soft glow without the harsh glare of direct sunlight. Clerestories also save on wall space and offer more privacy and security than windows at eye level. These characteristics make this shed design a great choice for a backyard office, artist's studio or even a remote spot for the musically inclined to get together and jam.

As shown, the Clerestory Studio has a 10 × 10-ft. floorplan. It can be outfitted with double doors that open up to a 5 ft.-wide opening, as seen here. But if you don't need a door that large, you can pick up about 2½ ft. of additional (and highly prized) wall space by framing the opening for a 30" wide door. The studio's striking roofline is created by two shed-style roof planes, which makes for deceptively easy construction.

The shed's walls and floor follow standard stick-frame construction. For simplicity, you can frame the square portions of the lower walls first, then piece in the framing for the four "rake," or angled, wall sections. To support the roof rafters, the clerestory wall has two large headers (beams) that run the full length of the building. These and the door header are all made with standard 2× lumber and a ½" plywood spacer.

You can increase the natural light in your studio—and add some passive solar heating—by including the two optional skylights. To prevent leaks, be sure to carefully seal around the glazing and the skylight frame. Flashing around the frame will provide an extra measure of protection.

The clerestory windows on this sunlight-filled shed introduce natural light without introducing a security risk.

Cutting List

DESCRIPTION	QTY./SIZE	MATERIAL
Foundation		
Drainage material	1.5 cu. yd.	Compactible gravel
Skids	2 @ 10'	4 × 6 pressure-treated landscape timbers
Floor		
Rim joists	2 @ 10'	2 × 6 pressure-treated
Joists	9 @ 10'	2 × 6 pressure-treated
Floor sheathing	4 sheets, 4 × 8'	¾" tongue-&-groove ext.-grade plywood
Wall Framing		
Bottom plates	4 @ 10'	2 × 4
Top plates, front walls	5 @ 10'	2 × 4
Top plates, rear wall	2 @ 10'	2 × 4
Top plates, side walls	6 @ 10'	2 × 4
Studs, rear wall	11 @ 8'	2 × 4
Studs, front wall (& clerestory wall)	11 @ 8'	2 × 4
Studs, side walls	26 @ 8'	2 × 4
Header, above windows	2 @ 10'	2 × 6
Header, below windows	2 @ 10'	2 × 10
Header, door	2 @ 8'	2 × 6
Header & post spacers		See Sheathing, below
Roof Framing		
Rafters (& blocking)	20 @ 8'	2 × 6
Exterior Finishes		
Side wall fascia	4 @ 8'	2 × 6
Eave fascia	3 @ 12'	2 × 6
Fascia drip edge	8 @ 8'	1 × 2
Siding	10 sheets @ 4 × 8'	⅝" Texture 1-11 plywood siding
Corner trim	10 @ 8'	1 × 4 cedar
Bottom siding trim	5 @ 12'	1 × 4 cedar
Vents	8	2"-dia. round metal vents
Roofing		
Sheathing (& header/post spacers)	6 sheets @ 4 × 8'	½" exterior-grade plywood roof sheathing
15# building paper	1 roll	

DESCRIPTION	QTY./SIZE	MATERIAL
Shingles	1⅔ squares	Asphalt shingles — 250# per sq. min.
Roof flashing	10'-6"	Aluminum
Windows		
Glazing	3 pieces @ 21 × 36"	¼"-thick acrylic or polycarbonate glazing
Window stops	5 @ 8'	1 × 2 cedar
Glazing tape	60 linear ft.	
Clear exterior caulk	1 tube	
Door		
Panels	2 sheets @ 4 × 8'	¾" exterior-grade plywood
Panel trim	8 @ 8'	1 × 4 cedar
Stops	3 @ 8'	1 × 2 cedar
Flashing	6 linear ft.	Aluminum
Skylights (optional)		
Glazing	2 pieces @ 13 × 22½"	¼"-thick plastic or polycarbonate glazing
Frame	2 @ 8'	1 × 4 cedar
Stops	2 @ 8'	1 × 2 cedar
Glazing tape	25 linear ft.	
Fasteners & Hardware		
16d galvanized common nails	4 lbs.	
16d common nails	16½ lbs.	
10d common nails	1 lb.	
8d galvanized common nails	3 lbs.	
8d box nails	3½ lbs.	
8d galvanized siding nails	7 lbs.	
1" galvanized roofing nails	5 lbs.	
8d galvanized casing nails	2 lbs.	
1¼" galvanized screws	1 lb.	
2" galvanized screws	1 lb.	
Door hinges with screws	6 @ 3½"	
Door handle	2	
Door lock (optional)	1	

10 × 10 Front Elevation

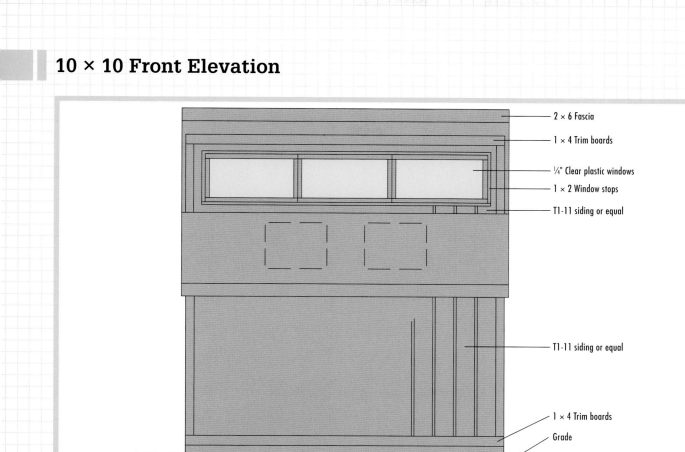

2 × 6 Fascia

1 × 4 Trim boards

¼" Clear plastic windows

1 × 2 Window stops

T1-11 siding or equal

T1-11 siding or equal

1 × 4 Trim boards

Grade

10 × 10 Rear Elevation

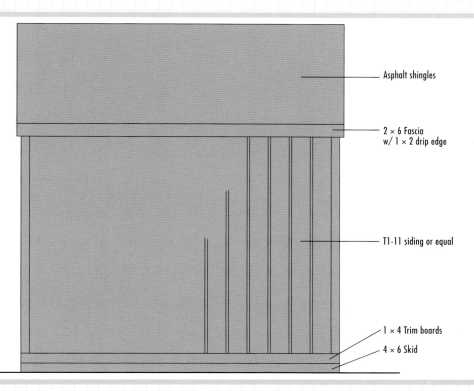

Asphalt shingles

2 × 6 Fascia
w/ 1 × 2 drip edge

T1-11 siding or equal

1 × 4 Trim boards

4 × 6 Skid

Building Section

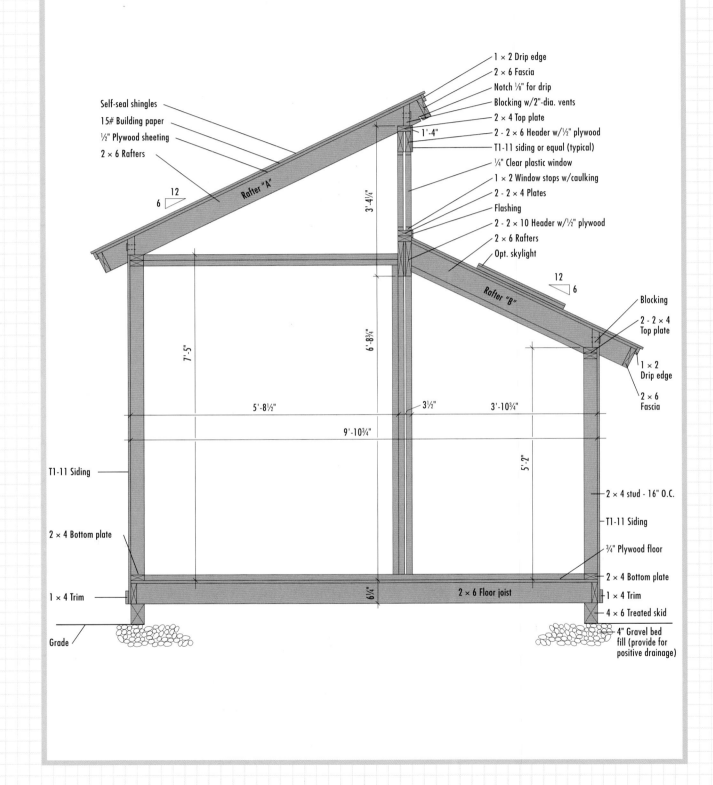

Self-seal shingles
15# Building paper
½" Plywood sheeting
2 × 6 Rafters

Rafter "A"

12
6

1 × 2 Drip edge
2 × 6 Fascia
Notch ⅛" for drip
Blocking w/2"-dia. vents
2 × 4 Top plate
2 - 2 × 6 Header w/½" plywood
T1-11 siding or equal (typical)
¼" Clear plastic window
1 × 2 Window stops w/caulking
2 - 2 × 4 Plates
Flashing
2 - 2 × 10 Header w/½" plywood
2 × 6 Rafters
Opt. skylight

1'-4"

3'-4¼"

Rafter "B"

12
6

Blocking
2 - 2 × 4 Top plate
1 × 2 Drip edge
2 × 6 Fascia

7'-5"

6'-8¾"

5'-2"

5'-8½"

3½"

3'-10¾"

9'-10¾"

T1-11 Siding

2 × 4 Bottom plate

1 × 4 Trim

Grade

6¼"

2 × 6 Floor joist

2 × 4 stud - 16" O.C.
T1-11 Siding
¾" Plywood floor
2 × 4 Bottom plate
1 × 4 Trim
4 × 6 Treated skid
4" Gravel bed fill (provide for positive drainage)

Front Framing

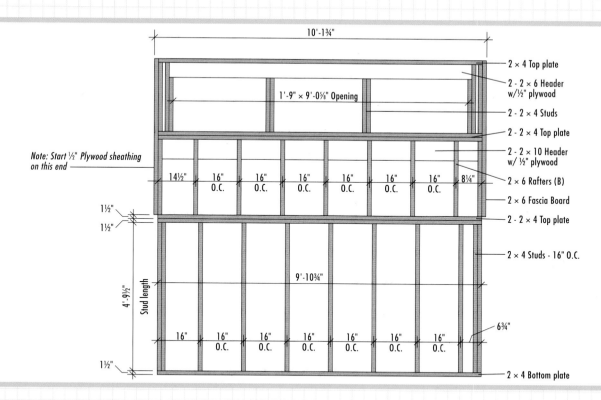

10'-1¾"

2 × 4 Top plate

2 - 2 × 6 Header
w/½" plywood

1'-9" × 9'-0⅝" Opening

2 - 2 × 4 Studs

2 - 2 × 4 Top plate

Note: Start ½" Plywood sheathing
on this end

2 - 2 × 10 Header
w/ ½" plywood

14½"   16"   16"   16"   16"   16"   16"   8¼"
       O.C. O.C. O.C. O.C. O.C. O.C.

2 × 6 Rafters (B)

2 × 6 Fascia Board

1½"

1½"

2 - 2 × 4 Top plate

2 × 4 Studs - 16" O.C.

4'-9½"

Stud length

9'-10¾"

6¾"

16"   16"   16"   16"   16"   16"   16"
      O.C. O.C. O.C. O.C. O.C. O.C.

1½"

2 × 4 Bottom plate

Rear Framing

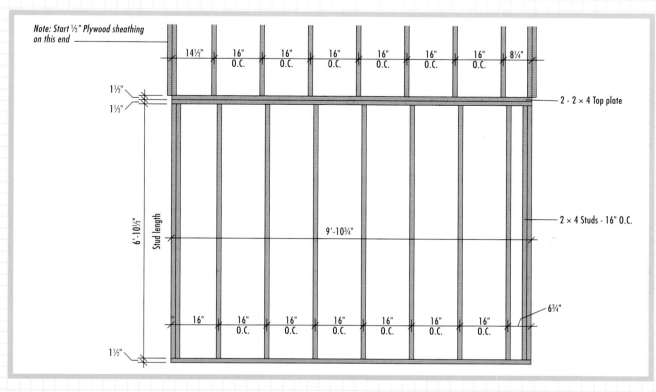

Note: Start ½" Plywood sheathing
on this end

14½"   16"   16"   16"   16"   16"   16"   8¼"
       O.C. O.C. O.C. O.C. O.C. O.C.

1½"

1½"

2 - 2 × 4 Top plate

6'-10½"

Stud length

9'-10¾"

2 × 4 Studs - 16" O.C.

6¾"

16"   16"   16"   16"   16"   16"   16"
      O.C. O.C. O.C. O.C. O.C. O.C.

1½"

Left Side Wall Framing

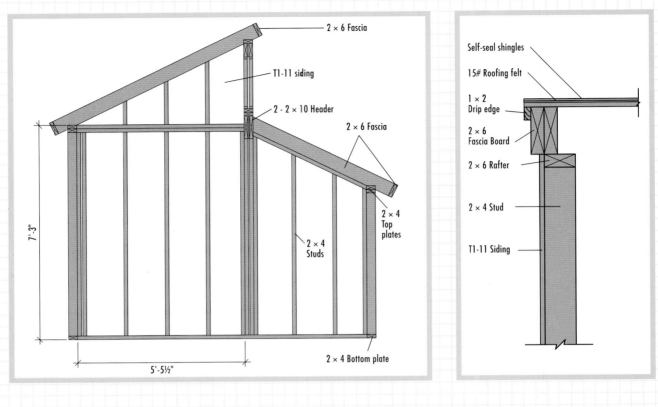

- 2 × 6 Fascia
- T1-11 siding
- 2 - 2 × 10 Header
- 2 × 6 Fascia
- 2 × 4 Top plates
- 2 × 4 Studs
- 2 × 4 Bottom plate
- 7'-3"
- 5'-5½"

Rake Detail

- Self-seal shingles
- 15# Roofing felt
- 1 × 2 Drip edge
- 2 × 6 Fascia Board
- 2 × 6 Rafter
- 2 × 4 Stud
- T1-11 Siding

Door Detail

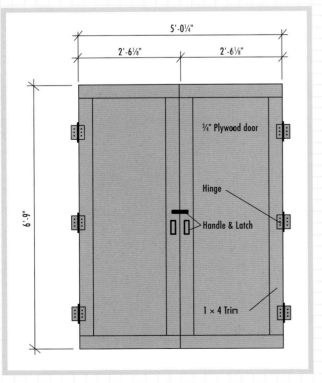

- 5'-0¼"
- 2'-6⅛"
- 2'-6⅛"
- ¾" Plywood door
- Hinge
- Handle & Latch
- 1 × 4 Trim
- 6'-9"

Jamb/Corner Detail

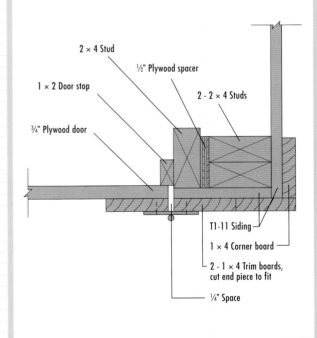

- 2 × 4 Stud
- ½" Plywood spacer
- 1 × 2 Door stop
- 2 - 2 × 4 Studs
- ¾" Plywood door
- T1-11 Siding
- 1 × 4 Corner board
- 2 - 1 × 4 Trim boards, cut end piece to fit
- ¼" Space

Right Side Elevation

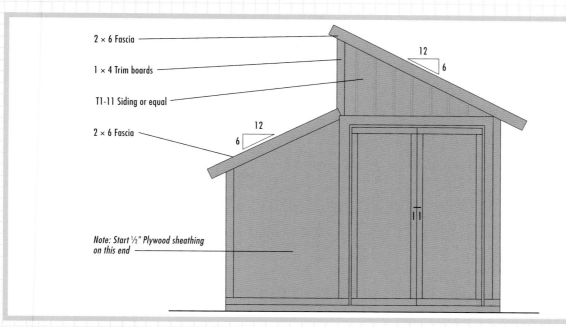

2 × 6 Fascia

1 × 4 Trim boards

T1-11 Siding or equal

2 × 6 Fascia

12 / 6

6 / 12

Note: Start ½" Plywood sheathing on this end

Floor Plan

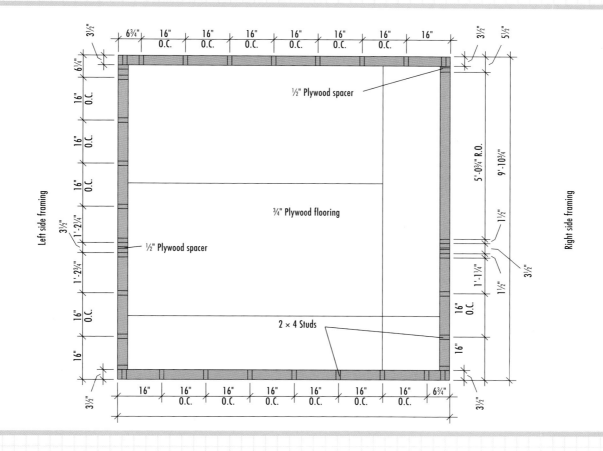

3½"

6¾" | 16" O.C. | 16" O.C. | 16" O.C. | 16" O.C. | 16" O.C. | 16" O.C. | 16"

3½"

5½"

6¼"

Left side framing

16" O.C.

16" O.C.

16" O.C.

3½"

1'-2¼"

1'-2¾"

16" O.C.

16"

½" Plywood spacer

¾" Plywood flooring

½" Plywood spacer

2 × 4 Studs

5'-0¾" R.O.

9'-10¾"

1½"

1'-1¼"

1½"

3½"

16" O.C.

16"

Right side framing

3½" | 16" O.C. | 16" O.C. | 16" O.C. | 16" O.C. | 16" O.C. | 16" O.C. | 16" O.C. | 6¾"

3½"

Rafter Template (A)

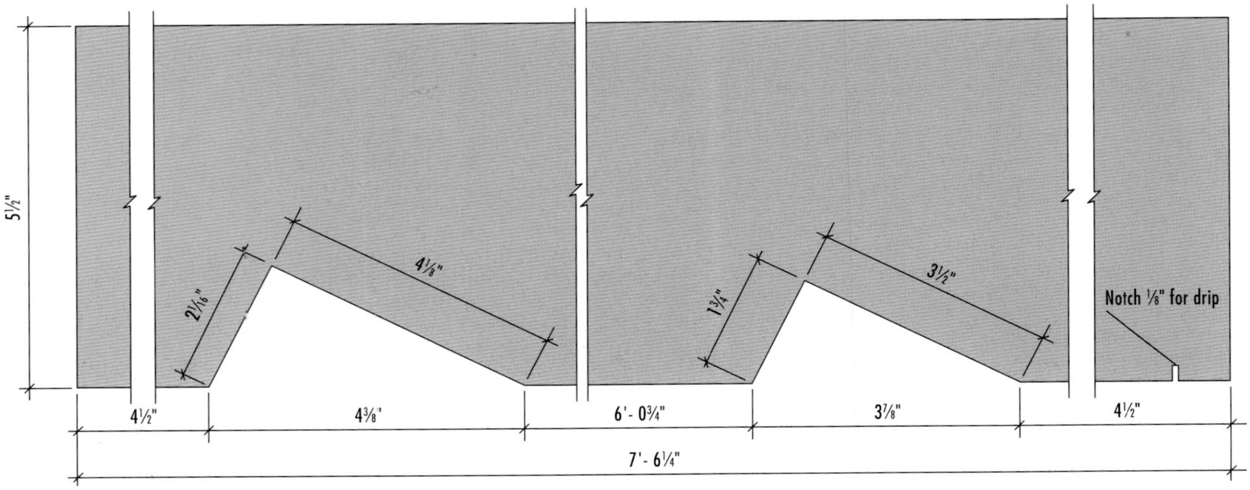

5½"
2 1/16"
4⅛"
1¾"
3½"
Notch ⅛" for drip
4½"
4⅜'
6'- 0¾"
3⅞"
4½"
7'- 6¼"

Rafter Template (B)

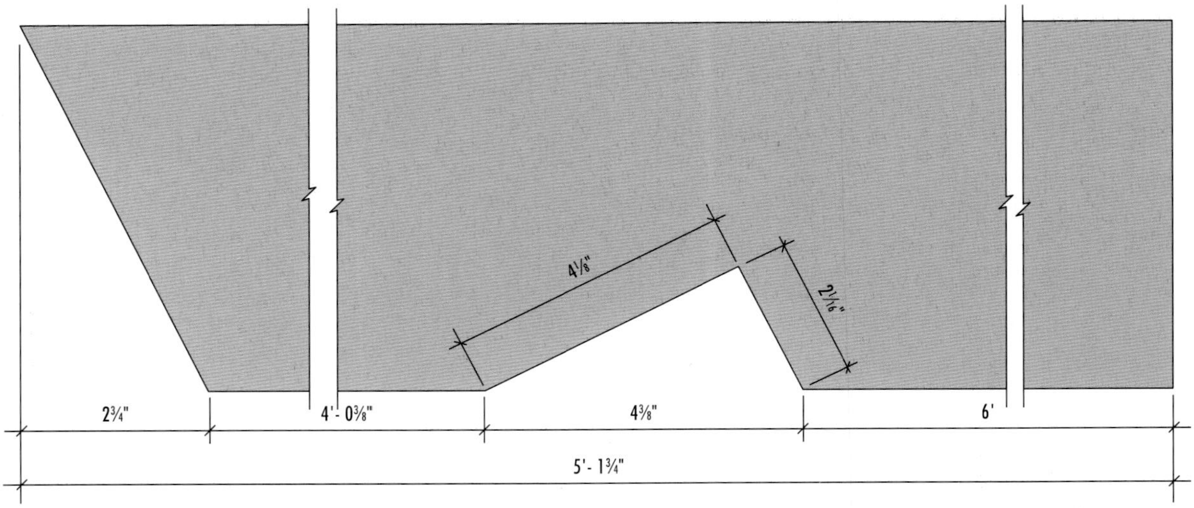

4⅛"
2 1/16"
2¾"
4'- 0⅜"
4⅜"
6'
5'- 1¾"

How to Build the Clerestory Studio

Prepare the foundation site with a 4"-deep layer of compacted gravel. Cut the two 4 × 6 timber skids at 118¾". Position the skids on the gravel bed so their outside edges are 118¾' apart, making sure they are level and parallel with one another.

Cut two 2 × 6 rim joists at 118¾". Cut nine 2 × 6 joists at 115¾". Build the floor frame on the skids and measure the diagonals to make sure the frame is square. Fasten the rim joists to the skids with 16d galvanized common nails driven toenail style through the joists and into the skids.

Install floor sheathing onto the floor frame, starting at the left rear corner of the shed, as shown in the FLOOR PLAN (page 135). Rip the two outer pieces and final corner piece so their outside edges are flush with the sides of the foundation skids.

Cut the studs and top and bottom plates for the front wall and nail together with 8d common nails. Position the wall on the floor deck and raise it. Fasten it by driving 16d common nails through the sole plate and into the floor deck and frame.

(continued)

Assemble the back wall framing with a bottom plate and double top plate at 118¾" and 82½" studs 16" O.C. Assemble the square portions of the left and right side walls. Attach the back wall and nail the side walls in place.

Take measurements to confirm the dimensions for the clerestory wall frame. Build the clerestory frame wall to match the dimensions.

Construct the sloped portions of the side walls. Install them by nailing them to the floor deck with 16d common nails. Also nail the corners to the front wall.

Create the headers by sandwiching a ½" plywood strip between two 2× dimensional framing members. Assemble the header with deck screws driven through both faces.

Set the main header on top of the sidewall posts and toenail it in place with 16d common nails. The main header ends should be flush with the outsides of the side walls.

Lift the clerestory wall frame onto the main header. Orient the wall so it is flush in front and on the ends and then attach it to the main header with 16d nails.

Install T1-11 siding on the front wall, starting at the left side (when facing the front of the shed). Cut the siding to length so it's flush with the top of the top plate and the bottom of the floor joists. Make sure any vertical seams fall at stud locations. Add strips of siding to cover the framing on the clerestory wall. Install siding on the rear wall, starting at the left side (when facing the rear side of the shed).

Cut one of each "A" and "B" pattern rafters from a single 16-ft. 2 × 6, using the RAFTER TEMPLATES (page 136). Both roof planes have a 6-in-12 slope. Test-fit the rafters and make any necessary adjustments, then use the patterns to cut eight more rafters of each type. Install the rafters as shown in the REAR FRAMING and FRONT FRAMING (page 133). Toenail the top ends of the "B" rafters to the main header.

(continued)

Frame each of the upper rake walls following the same technique used for gable walls. Cut the top plate to fit between the clerestory header and the door header (on the right side wall) or the top plate (on the left side wall). Install four studs in each wall using 16" on-center spacing.

Install 2 × 6 fascia boards flush with the top edges and ends of the rafters. The upper roof gets fascia on all four sides; the lower roof on three sides. Miter the corner joints if desired. Install siding on the side walls, flush with the bottom of the fascia; see the RAKE DETAIL (page 134.)

Install ½" plywood roof sheathing, starting at the bottom left side of the roof on both sides of the shed. Run the sheathing to the outside edge of the fascia. Add 1 × 2 trim to serve as a drip edge along all fascia boards, flush with the top of the sheathing.

Fasten 1 × 2 stops inside the window rough openings, flush with the inside edges of the framing, using 2" screws. Set each window panel into its opening, using glazing tape as a sealant. Install the outer stops; see the BUILDING SECTION (page 132). Caulk around the windows and the bottom outside stops to prevent leaks. Add 2 × 6 blocking (and vents) or screen to enclose the rafter bays above the walls.

Add vertical trim at the wall corners. Trim and flash around the door opening and windows. Install flashing—and trim, if desired—along the joint where the lower roof plane meets the clerestory wall.

Add 15# building paper and install the asphalt shingle roofing. The shingles should overhang the fascia drip edge by ½" along the bottom of the roof and by ⅜" along the sides. Install 1 × 4 horizontal trim boards flush with the bottom of the siding on all four walls.

Cut out the bottom plate inside the door's rough opening. Cut the two door panels at 30⅛ × 81". Install 1 × 4 trim around the panels, as shown in the DOOR DETAIL (page 134), using exterior wood glue and 1¼" screws or nails. Add 1 × 2 stops at the sides and top of the rough opening; see the JAMB DETAIL (page 134). Also add a 1 × 4 stop to the back side of one of the doors. Hang the doors with galvanized hinges, leaving a ¼" gap all around.

Finish the interior to your desired level. If you will be occupying the shed for activities, adding some wall covering, such as paneling, makes the interior much more pleasant. If you add wiring and wall insulation, the Clerestory Studio can function as a 3-season studio in practically any climate.

Sunlight Garden Shed

This unique outbuilding is part greenhouse and part shed, making it perfect for a year-round garden space or backyard sunroom, or even an artist's studio. The front facade is dominated by windows—four 29 × 72" windows on the roof, plus four 29 × 18" windows on the front wall. When appointed as a greenhouse, two long planting tables inside the shed let you water and tend to plants without flooding the floor. If gardening isn't in your plans, you can omit the tables and cover the entire floor with plywood, or perhaps fill in between the floor timbers with pavers or stones.

Some other details that make this 10 × 12-ft. shed stand out are the homemade Dutch door, with top and bottom halves that you can open together or independently, and its traditional saltbox shape. The roof covering shown here consists of standard asphalt shingles, but cedar shingles make for a nice upgrade.

Because sunlight plays a central role in this shed design, consider the location and orientation carefully. To avoid shadows from nearby structures, maintain a distance between the shed and any structure that's at least 2½ times the height of the obstruction. With all of that sunlight, the temperature inside the shed is another important consideration. You may want to install some roof vents (see page 119) to release hot air and water vapor.

Building the Sunlight Garden Shed involves a few unconventional construction steps. First, the side walls are framed in two parts: You build the square portion of the end walls first, then move onto the roof framing. After the rafters are up, you complete the "rake," or angled, sections of the side walls. This makes it easy to measure for each wall stud, rather than having to calculate the lengths beforehand. Second, the shed's 4 × 4 floor structure also serves as its foundation. The plywood floor decking goes on after the walls are installed, rather than before.

Enjoy your hobbies or your plants in the attractive sunlight garden shed.

Cutting List

DESCRIPTION	QTY./SIZE	MATERIAL
Foundation/Floor		
Foundation base & interior drainage beds	5 cu. yds.	Compactible gravel
Floor joists & blocking	7 @ 10'	4 × 4 pressure-treated landscape timbers
4 × 4 blocking	1 @ 10' / 1 @ 8'	4 × 4 pressure-treated landscape timbers
Box sills (rim joists)	2 @ 12'	2 × 4 pressure-treated
Nailing cleats & 2 × 4 blocking	2 @ 8'	2 × 4 pressure-treated
Floor sheathing	2 sheets @ 4 × 8'	¾" ext.-grade plywood
Wall Framing		
Bottom plates	2 @ 12', 2 @ 10'	2 × 4 pressure-treated
Top plates	4 @ 12', 2 @ 10'	2 × 4
Studs	43 @ 8'	2 × 4
Door header & jack studs	3 @ 8'	2 × 4
Rafter header	2 @ 12'	2 × 8
Roof Framing		
Rafters—A & C, & nailers	10 @ 12'	2 × 4
Rafters—B & lookouts	10 @ 10'	2 × 4
Ridge board	1 @ 14'	2 × 6
Exterior Finishes		
Rear fascia	1 @ 14'	1 × 6 cedar
Rear soffit	1 @ 14'	1 × 8 cedar
Gable fascia (rake board) & soffit	4 @ 16'	1 × 6 cedar
Siding	10 sheets @ 4 × 8'	⅝" Texture 1-11 plywood siding
Siding flashing	10 linear ft.	Metal Z-flashing
Trim*	4 @ 12' / 1 @ 12'	1 × 4 cedar / 1 × 2 cedar
Wall corner trim	6 @ 8'	1 × 4 cedar
Roofing		
Sheathing	5 sheets @ 4 × 8'	½" exterior-grade plywood roof sheathing
15# building paper	1 roll	
Drip edge	72 linear ft.	Metal drip edge
Shingles	2⅔ squares	Asphalt shingles — 250# per sq. min.

DESCRIPTION	QTY./SIZE	MATERIAL
Windows		
Glazing	4 pieces @ 31¼ × 76½" / 4 pieces @ 31¼ × 20¾"	¼"-thick clear plastic glazing
Window stops	12 @ 10'	2 × 4
Glazing tape	60 linear ft.	
Clear exterior caulk	5 tubes	
Door		
Trim & stops	3 @ 8'	1 × 2 cedar
Surround	4 @ 8'	2 × 2 cedar
Z-flashing	3 linear ft.	
Plant Tables (optional)		
Front table, top & trim	6 @ 12'	1 × 6 cedar or pressure-treated
Front table, plates & legs	4 @ 12'	2 × 4 pressure-treated
Rear table, top & trim	6 @ 8'	1 × 6 cedar or pressure-treated
Rear table, plates & legs	4 @ 8'	2 × 4 pressure-treated
Fasteners & Hardware		
16d galvanized common nails	5 lbs.	
16d common nails	16 lbs.	
10d common nails	1½ lbs.	
8d galvanized common nails	2 lbs.	
8d galvanized box nails	3 lbs.	
10d galvanized finish nails	2½ lbs.	
8d galvanized siding nails	8 lbs.	
1" galvanized roofing nails	7 lbs.	
8d galvanized casing nails	3 lbs.	
6d galvanized casing nails	2 lbs.	
Door hinges with screws	4 @ 3½"	Corrosion-resistant hinges
Door handle	1	
Sliding bolt latch	1	
Construction adhesive	1 tube	
2" galvanized screws	1 lb.	
Door hinges with screws	6 @ 3½"	
Door handle	2	
Door lock (optional)	1	

*Note: The 1 × 4 trim bevel at the bottom of the sloped windows can be steeper (45° or more) so the trim slopes away from the window if there is concern that the trim may capture water running down the glazing (see WINDOW DETAIL, page 150).

Building Section

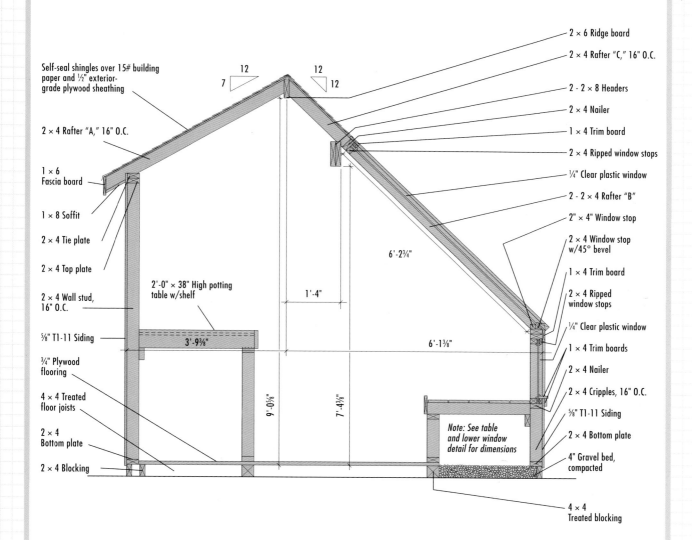

Self-seal shingles over 15# building paper and ½" exterior-grade plywood sheathing

2 × 4 Rafter "A," 16" O.C.

1 × 6 Fascia board

1 × 8 Soffit

2 × 4 Tie plate

2 × 4 Top plate

2 × 4 Wall stud, 16" O.C.

⅝" T1-11 Siding

¾" Plywood flooring

4 × 4 Treated floor joists

2 × 4 Bottom plate

2 × 4 Blocking

2'-0" × 38" High potting table w/shelf

3'-9⅜"

9'-0⅝"

7'-4⅜"

1'-4"

6'-2¾"

6'-1⅜"

Note: See table and lower window detail for dimensions

2 × 6 Ridge board

2 × 4 Rafter "C," 16" O.C.

2 - 2 × 8 Headers

2 × 4 Nailer

1 × 4 Trim board

2 × 4 Ripped window stops

¼" Clear plastic window

2 - 2 × 4 Rafter "B"

2" × 4" Window stop

2 × 4 Window stop w/45° bevel

1 × 4 Trim board

2 × 4 Ripped window stops

¼" Clear plastic window

1 × 4 Trim boards

2 × 4 Nailer

2 × 4 Cripples, 16" O.C.

⅝" T1-11 Siding

2 × 4 Bottom plate

4" Gravel bed, compacted

4 × 4 Treated blocking

Floor Framing Plan

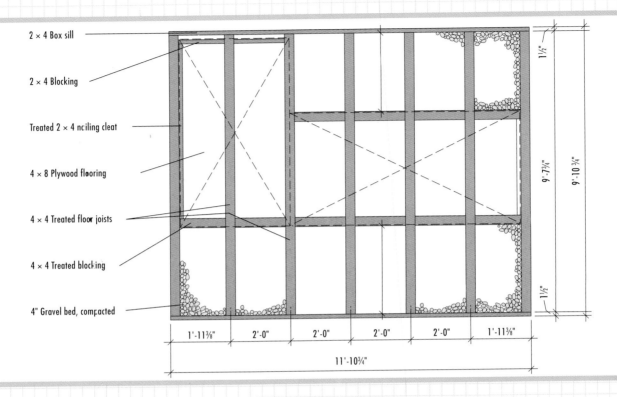

2 × 4 Box sill

2 × 4 Blocking

Treated 2 × 4 nciling cleat

4 × 8 Plywood flooring

4 × 4 Treated floor joists

4 × 4 Treated blocking

4" Gravel bed, compacted

1'-11⅜" 2'-0" 2'-0" 2'-0" 2'-0" 1'-11⅜"

11'-10¾"

1½"

9'-7¾"

9'-10¾"

1½"

Left Side Framing

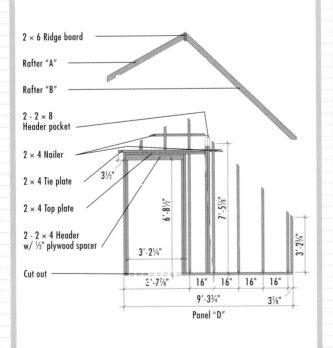

2 × 6 Ridge board

Rafter "A"

Rafter "B"

2 - 2 × 8 Header pocket

2 × 4 Nailer

2 × 4 Tie plate

2 × 4 Top plate

2 - 2 × 4 Header w/ ½" plywood spacer

Cut out

3½"

6'-8½"

7'-5⅝"

3'-2¼"

3'-2¾"

3'-7⅞" 16" 16" 16" 16"

9'-3¾" 3⅞"

Panel "D"

Right Side Framing

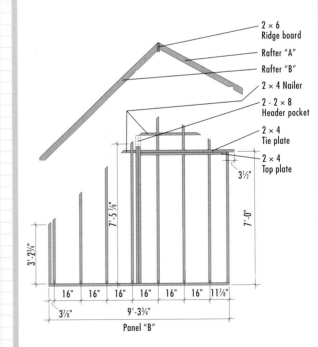

2 × 6 Ridge board

Rafter "A"

Rafter "B"

2 × 4 Nailer

2 - 2 × 8 Header pocket

2 × 4 Tie plate

2 × 4 Top plate

3½"

7'-0"

7'-5⅝"

3'-2¾"

16" 16" 16" 16" 16" 16" 11⅞"

3⅞" 9'-3¾"

Panel "B"

Front Framing

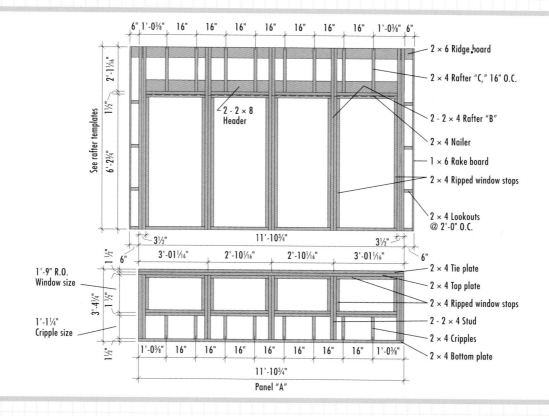

6" 1'-0⅜" 16" 16" 16" 16" 16" 16" 1'-0⅜" 6"

2 × 6 Ridge board

2 × 4 Rafter "C," 16" O.C.

2 - 2 × 4 Rafter "B"

2 × 4 Nailer

1 × 6 Rake board

2 × 4 Ripped window stops

2 × 4 Lookouts @ 2'-0" O.C.

See rafter templates

2'-1¹⁄₁₆"

1½"

6'-2¾"

2 - 2 × 8 Header

3½" 11'-10¾" 3½"

1½" 6" 3'-01¹⁄₁₆" 2'-10¹⁄₁₆" 2'-10¹⁄₁₆" 3'-01¹⁄₁₆" 6"

1½"

1'-9" R.O. Window size

3'-4¼"

1'-1¼" Cripple size

1½"

2 × 4 Tie plate

2 × 4 Top plate

2 × 4 Ripped window stops

2 - 2 × 4 Stud

2 × 4 Cripples

2 × 4 Bottom plate

1'-0⅜" 16" 16" 16" 16" 16" 16" 16" 1'-0⅜"

11'-10¾"

Panel "A"

Rear Framing

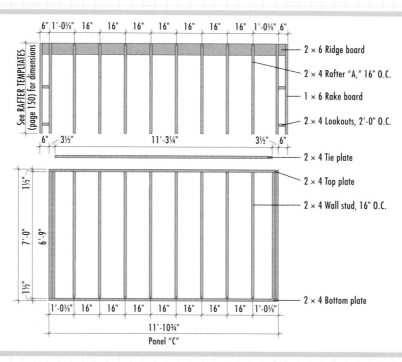

6" 1'-0⅜" 16" 16" 16" 16" 16" 16" 1'-0⅜" 6"

2 × 6 Ridge board

2 × 4 Rafter "A," 16" O.C.

1 × 6 Rake board

2 × 4 Lookouts, 2'-0" O.C.

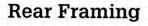

See RAFTER TEMPLATES (page 150) for dimensions

6" 3½" 11'-3¼" 3½" 6"

2 × 4 Tie plate

2 × 4 Top plate

1½"

7'-0" 6'-9"

2 × 4 Wall stud, 16" O.C.

1½"

2 × 4 Bottom plate

1'-0⅜" 16" 16" 16" 16" 16" 16" 16" 1'-0⅜"

11'-10¾"

Panel "C"

Front Elevation

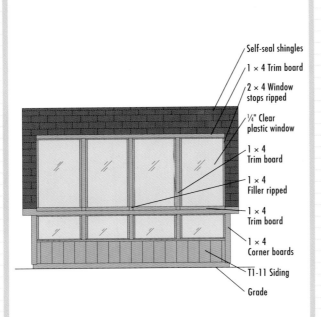

Self-seal shingles

1 × 4 Trim board

2 × 4 Window stops ripped

¼" Clear plastic window

1 × 4 Trim board

1 × 4 Filler ripped

1 × 4 Trim board

1 × 4 Corner boards

T1-11 Siding

Grade

Rear Elevation

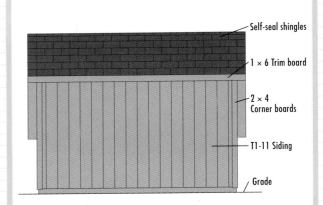

Self-seal shingles

1 × 6 Trim board

2 × 4 Corner boards

T1-11 Siding

Grade

Right Side Elevation

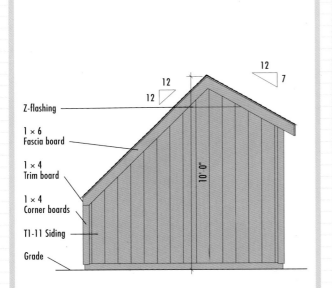

12
12

12
7

Z-flashing

1 × 6 Fascia board

1 × 4 Trim board

1 × 4 Corner boards

T1-11 Siding

Grade

10' 0"

Soffit Detail

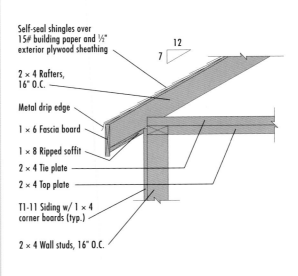

12
7

Self-seal shingles over 15# building paper and ½" exterior plywood sheathing

2 × 4 Rafters, 16" O.C.

Metal drip edge

1 × 6 Fascia board

1 × 8 Ripped soffit

2 × 4 Tie plate

2 × 4 Top plate

T1-11 Siding w/ 1 × 4 corner boards (typ.)

2 × 4 Wall studs, 16" O.C.

Front & Side Door Construction

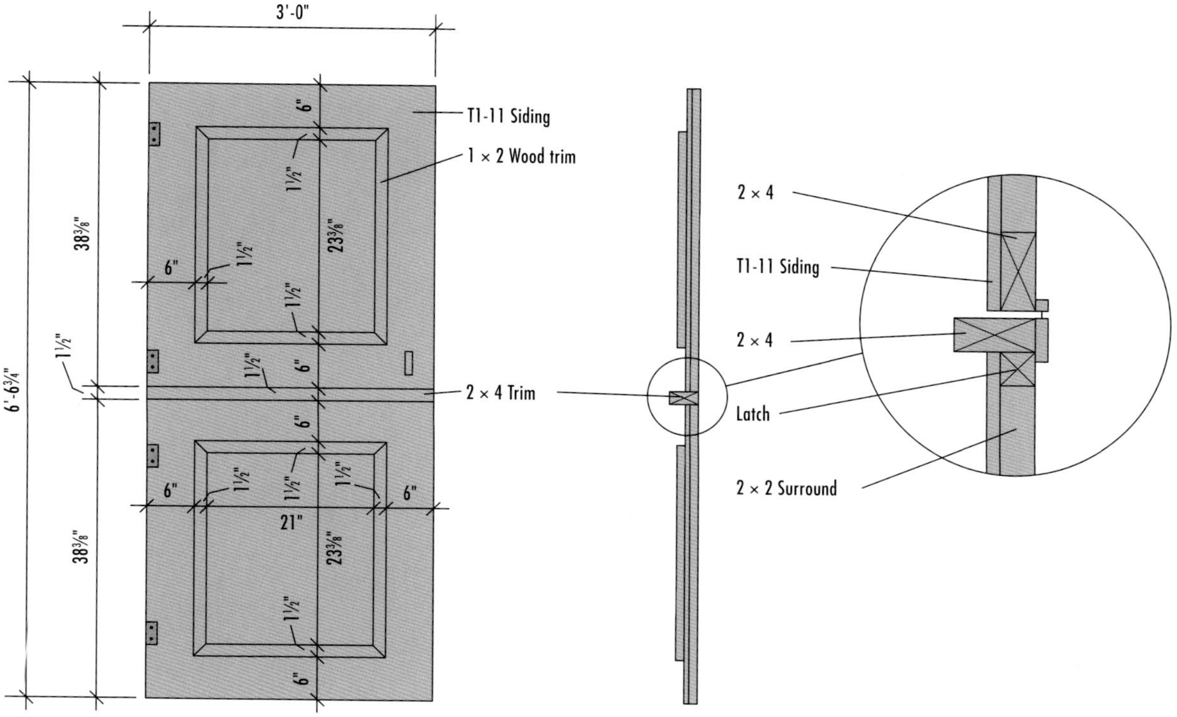
3'-0"
T1-11 Siding
1 × 2 Wood trim
6'-6¾"
38⅜"
38⅜"
1½"
6"
1½"
23⅜"
2 × 4 Trim
21"
2 × 4
T1-11 Siding
2 × 4
Latch
2 × 2 Surround

Front & Side Door Construction (Door Jamb, Rear, Door Header)

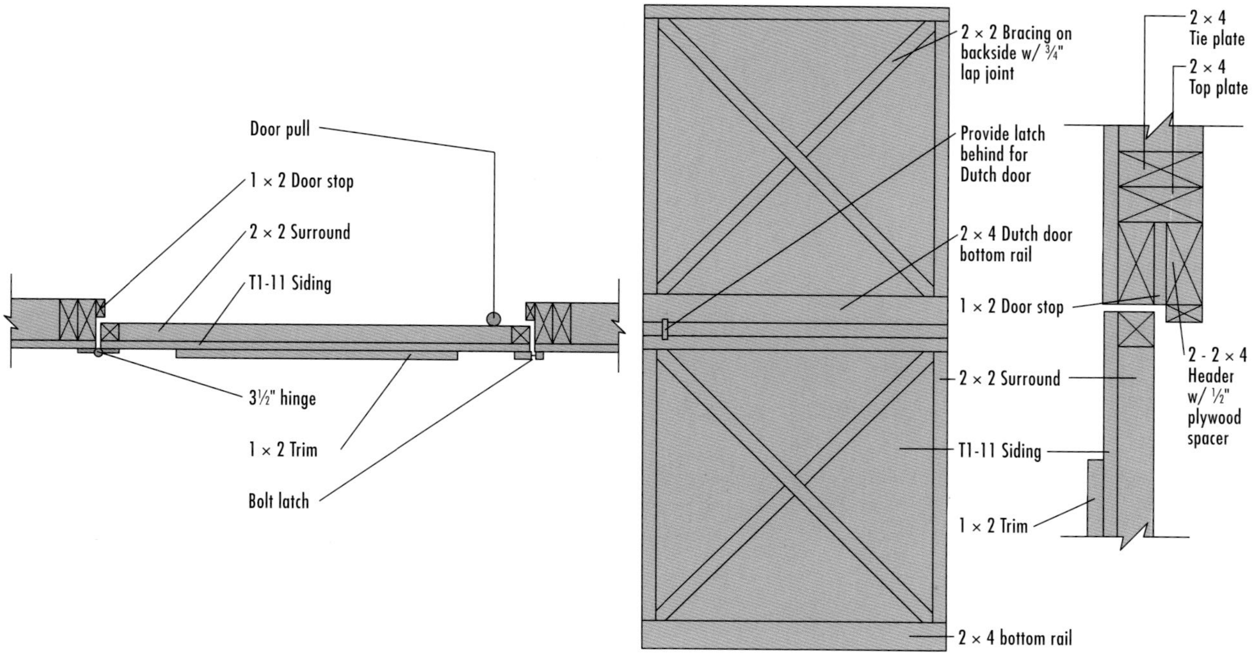
Door pull
1 × 2 Door stop
2 × 2 Surround
T1-11 Siding
3½" hinge
1 × 2 Trim
Bolt latch
2 × 2 Bracing on backside w/ ¾" lap joint
Provide latch behind for Dutch door
2 × 4 Dutch door bottom rail
1 × 2 Door stop
2 × 2 Surround
T1-11 Siding
1 × 2 Trim
2 × 4 bottom rail
2 × 4 Tie plate
2 × 4 Top plate
2 - 2 × 4 Header w/ ½" plywood spacer

Header & Window Detail

2 - 2 × 4 Rafters

Self-seal shingles
over 15# building
paper and ½" exterior
plywood sheathing

Z-flashing

1 × 4 Trim board

2 × 4 Nailer

2 - 2 × 8 Header
glued and nailed

2 × 4 Ripped window stop

¼" Clear plastic window panel

2 × 4 Ripped window stop with caulking

12
12

Window Section

¼" Clear plastic window panel

2 - 2 × 4 Rafters

2 × 4
Ripped window
stops with caulking
(typ.)

1 × 4 Trim board

1½"
1½"
2¼"
2'-10¹¹⁄₁₆"
1"
¼"
3½"

Window Detail

¼" Clear plastic
window panel

2 - 2 × 4 Rafters

2 × 4 Ripped window stop
w/ 45° bevel and caulking

Caulking (typical)

2 × 2 Window stop
with caulking

2 × 4 Tie plate

1 × 4 Trim board

2 × 4 Top plate

2 × 4 Ripped window stops
with caulking (typical)

2 - 2 × 4 Wall stud

12
12

Table & Lower Window Detail

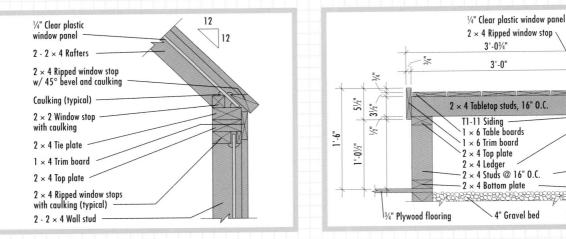

¼" Clear plastic window panel
2 × 4 Ripped window stop
3'-0¾"
3'-0"
¾"
¾"
5½"
3½"
½"
1'-0½"
1'-6"
2 × 4 Tabletop studs, 16" O.C.
T1-11 Siding
1 × 6 Table boards
1 × 6 Trim board
2 × 4 Top plate
2 × 4 Ledger
2 × 4 Studs @ 16" O.C.
2 × 4 Bottom plate
¾" Plywood flooring
4" Gravel bed
1 × 4 Ripped

Rafter Templates

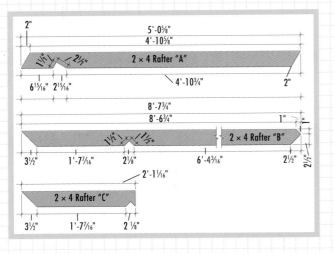

2"
5'-0⅝"
4'-10⅝"
1½"
2½"
2 × 4 Rafter "A"
6¹⁵⁄₁₆"
2¹⁵⁄₁₆"
4'-10¾"
2"

8'-7¾"
8'-6¾"
1"
1"
1½"
1½"
2 × 4 Rafter "B"
3½"
1'-7⁷⁄₁₆"
2⅛"
6'-4³⁄₁₆"
2½"
2½"

2'-1¹⁄₁₆"
2 × 4 Rafter "C"
3½"
1'-7⁷⁄₁₆"
2⅛"

Rake Board Detail

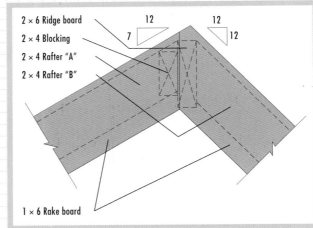

2 × 6 Ridge board
2 × 4 Blocking
2 × 4 Rafter "A"
2 × 4 Rafter "B"
12
7
12
12
1 × 6 Rake board

How to Build the Sunlight Garden Shed

Build the foundation, following the basic steps used for a wooden skid foundation (page 28). First, prepare a bed of compacted gravel. Make sure the bed is flat and level. Cut seven 4 × 4" × 10 ft. pressure-treated posts down to 115¾" to serve as floor joists. Position the joists as shown in the FLOOR FRAMING PLAN. Level each joist, and make sure all are level with one another and the ends are flush. Add rim joists and blocking: Cut two 12-ft. 2 × 4s (142¾") for rim joists. Fasten the rim joists to the ends of the 4 × 4 joists (see the FLOOR FRAMING PLAN) with 16d galvanized common nails.

Cut ten 4 × 4 blocks to fit between the joists. Install six blocks 34½" from the front rim joist, and install four blocks 31½" from the rear. Toenail the blocks to the joists. All blocks, joists, and sills must be flush at the top.

To frame the rear wall, cut one top plate and one pressure-treated bottom plate (142¾"). Cut twelve studs (81"). Assemble the wall following the layout in the REAR FRAMING (page 147). Raise the wall and fasten it to the rear rim joist and the intermediate joists, using 16d galvanized common nails. Brace the wall in position with 2 × 4 braces staked to the ground.

For the front wall, cut two top plates and one treated bottom plate (142¾"). Cut ten studs (35¾") and eight cripple studs (13¼"). Cut four 2 × 4 window sills (311⁄16"). Assemble the wall following the layout in the FRONT FRAMING (page 147). Add the double top plate, but do not install the window stops at this time. Raise, attach, and brace the front wall.

(continued)

Cut lumber for the right side wall: one top plate (54⅞"), one treated bottom plate (111¾"), four studs (81"), and two header post studs (86⅞"); and for the left side wall: top plate (54⅞"), bottom plate (111¾"), three studs (81"), two jack studs (77½"), two posts (86⅞"), and a built-up 2 × 4 header (39¼"). Assemble and install the walls as shown in the RIGHT SIDE FRAMING and LEFT SIDE FRAMING (page 146). Add the doubled top plates along the rear and side walls. Install treated 2 × 4 nailing cleats to the joists and blocking as shown in the FLOOR FRAMING PLAN (page 146) and BUILDING SECTION (page 145).

Trim two sheets of ¾" plywood as needed and install them over the joists and blocking as shown in the FLOOR FRAMING PLAN, leaving open cavities along the front of the shed and a portion of the rear. Fasten the sheets with 8d galvanized common nails driven every 6" along the edges and 8" in the field. Fill the exposed foundation cavities with 4" of gravel and compact it thoroughly.

Construct the rafter header from two 2 × 8s cut to 142¾". Join the pieces with construction adhesive and pairs of 10d common nails driven every 24" on both sides. Set the header on top of the side wall posts, and toenail it to the posts with four 16d common nails at each end.

Cut one of each "A" and "B" pattern rafters using the RAFTER TEMPLATES (page 150). Test-fit the rafters. The B rafter should rest squarely on the rafter header, and its bottom end should sit flush with outside of the front wall. Adjust the rafter cuts as needed, then use the pattern rafters to mark and cut the remaining A and B rafters.

Cut the 2 × 6 ridge board (154¾"). Mark the rafter layout onto the ridge and front and rear wall plates following the FRONT FRAMING and REAR FRAMING. Install the A and B rafters and ridge. Make sure the B rafters are spaced accurately so the windows will fit properly into their frames; see the WINDOW SECTION (page 150).

Cut a pattern "C" rafter, test-fit, and adjust as needed. Cut the remaining seven C rafters and install them. Measure and cut four 2 × 4 nailers (311⁄16") to fit between the sets of B rafters (as shown). Position the nailers as shown in the HEADER & WINDOW DETAIL (page 150) and toenail them to the rafters.

Complete the rake portions of each side wall. Mark the stud layouts onto the bottom plate, and onto the top plate of the square wall section; see the RIGHT and LEFT SIDE FRAMING. Use a plumb bob to transfer the layout to the rafters. Measure for each stud, cutting the top ends of the studs under the B rafters at 45° and those under the A rafters at 30°. Toenail the studs to the plates and rafters. Add horizontal 2 × 4 nailers as shown in the framing drawings.

Blade guard removed for clarity

Create the inner and outer window stops from 10-ft.-long 2 × 4s. For stops at the sides and tops of the roof windows and all sides of the front wall windows, rip the inner stops to 2¼" wide and the outer stops to 1" wide; see the WINDOW SECTION and WINDOW DETAIL (page 150). For the bottom of each roof window, rip the inner stop to 1½"; bevel the edge of the outer stop at 45°.

(continued)

Install each window as follows: Attach inner stops as shown in the drawings, using galvanized finish nails. Paint or varnish the rafters and stops for moisture protection. Apply a heavy bead of caulk at each location shown on the drawings (HEADER & WINDOW DETAIL, WINDOW SECTION/DETAIL, TABLE & LOWER WINDOW DETAIL). Set the glazing in place, add another bead of caulk, and attach the outer stops. Cover the rafters and stop edges with 1 × 4 trim.

Cover the walls with T1-11 siding, starting with the rear wall. Trim the sheets as needed so they extend from the bottom edges of the rafters down to at least 1" below the tops of the foundation timbers. On the side walls, add Z-flashing above the first row and continue the siding up to the rafters.

Install 1 × 6 fascia over the ends of the A rafters. Keep all fascia ½" above the rafters so it will be flush with the roof sheathing. Using scrap rafter material, cut the 2 × 4 lookouts (5¼"). On each outer B rafter, install one lookout at the bottom end and four more spaced 24" on center going up. On the A rafters, add a lookout at both ends and two spaced evenly in between. Install the 1 × 6 rake boards (fascia) as shown in the RAKE BOARD DETAIL (page 150).

Soffit

Rip 1 × 6 boards to 5¼" width (some may come milled to 5¼" already) for the gable soffits. Fasten the soffits to the lookouts with siding nails. Rip a 1 × 8 board for the soffit along the rear eave, beveling the edges at 30° to match the A rafter ends. Install the soffit.

Deck the roof with ½" plywood sheathing, starting at the bottom ends of the rafters. Install metal drip edge, building paper, and asphalt shingles. If desired, add one or more roof vents during the shingle installation. Be sure to overlap shingles onto the 1 × 4 trim board above the roof windows, as shown in the HEADER & WINDOW DETAIL.

Construct the planting tables from 2 × 4 lumber and 1 × 6 boards, as shown in the TABLE & LOWER WINDOW DETAIL and BUILDING SECTION. The bottom plates of the table legs should be flush with the outside edges of the foundation blocking.

Build each of the two door panels using T1-11 siding, 2 × 2 bracing, a 2 × 4 bottom rail, and 1 × 2 trim on the front side; see the DOOR CONSTRUCTION drawings (page 149). The panels are identical except for a 2 × 4 sill added to the top of the lower panel. Install 1 × 2 stops at the sides and top of the door opening. Hang the doors with four hinges, leaving even gaps all around. Install a bolt latch for locking the two panels together.

Complete the trim details with 1 × 4 vertical corner boards, 1 × 4 horizontal trim above the front wall windows, and ripped 1 × 4 trim and 1 × 2 trim at the bottom of the front wall windows (see the TABLE & LOWER WINDOW DETAIL). Paint the siding and trim, or coat with exterior wood finish.

Gambrel Garage

Following classic barn designs, this 12 × 12-ft. garage-size storage shed has several features that make it a versatile storage shed or workshop. The garage's 144-square-foot floor is a poured concrete slab with a thickened edge that allows it to serve as the building's foundation. Designed for economy and durability, the floor can easily support heavy machinery, woodworking tools, and recreational vehicles.

The garage's sectional overhead door makes for quick access to equipment and supplies and provides plenty of air and natural light for working inside. The door opening is sized for an 8-ft.-wide × 7-ft.-tall door, but you can buy any size or style of door you like—just make your door selection before you start framing the garage.

Another important design feature of this building is its gambrel roof, which maximizes the usable interior space (see Sidebar next page). Beneath the roof is a sizeable storage attic with 315 cubic feet of space and its own double doors above the garage door.

Store your toys and tools in this classic throwback to heartland American design.

The Gambrel Roof ▶

The gambrel roof is the defining feature of two structures in American architecture: the barn and the Dutch Colonial house. Adopted from earlier English buildings, the gambrel style became popular in America during the early 17th century and was used on homes and farm buildings throughout the Atlantic region. Today, the gambrel roof remains a favorite detail for designers of sheds, garages, and carriage houses.

The basic gambrel shape has two flat planes on each side, with the lower plane sloped much more steeply than the upper. More elaborate versions incorporate a flared eave, known as a "Dutch kick," that was often extended to shelter the front and rear facades of the building. Barns typically feature an extended peak at the front, sheltering the doors of the hayloft. The main advantage of the gambrel roof is the increased space underneath the roof, providing additional headroom for upper floors in homes or extra storage space in outbuildings.

Cutting List

DESCRIPTION	QTY./SIZE	MATERIAL
Foundation		
Drainage material	1.75 cu. yds.	Compactible gravel
Concrete slab	2.5 cu. yds.	3,000 psi concrete
Mesh	144 sq. ft.	6 × 6", W1.4 × W1.4 welded wire mesh
Wall Framing		
Bottom plates	4 @ 12'	2 × 4 pressure-treated
Top plates	8 @ 12'	2 × 4
Studs	47 @ 92⅝"	2 × 4
Headers	2 @ 10', 2 @ 6'	2 × 8
Header spacers	1 @ 9', 1 @ 6'	½" plywood—7" wide
Angle braces	1 @ 4'	2 × 4
Gable Wall Framing		
Plates	2 @ 10'	2 × 4
Studs	7 @ 10'	2 × 4
Header	2 @ 6'	2 × 6
Header spacer	1 @ 5'	½" plywood—5" wide
Attic Floor		
Joists	10 @ 12'	2 × 6
Floor sheathing	3 sheets @ 4 × 8'	¾" tongue-&-groove ext.-grade plywood
Kneewall Framing		
Bottom plates	2 @ 12'	2 × 4
Top plates	4 @ 12'	2 × 4
Studs	8 @ 10'	2 × 4
Nailers	2 @ 14'	2 × 8
Roof Framing		
Rafters	28 @ 10'	2 × 4
Metal anchors—rafters	20, with nails	Simpson H2.5
Collar ties	2 @ 6'	2 × 4
Ridge board	1 @ 14'	2 × 6
Lookouts	1 @ 10'	2 × 4
Soffit ledgers	2 @ 14'	2 × 4
Soffit blocking	6 @ 8'	2 × 4
Exterior Finishes		
Plywood siding	14 sheets @ 4 × 8'	⅝" Texture 1-11 plywood, grooves 8" O. C.
Z-flashing—siding	2 pieces @ 12'	Galvanized 18-gauge
Horizontal wall trim	2 @ 12'	1 × 4 cedar
Corner trim	8 @ 8'	1 × 4 cedar
Fascia	6 @ 10', 2 @ 8'	1 × 6 cedar
Subfascia	4 @ 8'	1 × 4 pine
Plywood soffits	1 sheet @ 10'	⅜" cedar or fir plywood
Soffit vents	4 @ 4 × 12"	Louver w/ bug screen
Z-flashing—garage door	1 @ 10'	Galvanized 18-gauge

DESCRIPTION	QTY./SIZE	MATERIAL
Roofing		
Roof sheathing	12 sheets @ 4 × 8'	½" plywood
Shingles	3 squares	250# per square (min.)
15# building paper	300 sq. ft.	
Metal drip edge	2 @ 14', 2 @ 12'	Galvanized metal
Roof vents (optional)	2 units	
Window		
Frame	3 @ 6'	¾ × 4" (actual) S4S cedar
Stops	4 @ 8'	1 × 2 S4S cedar
Glazing tape	30 linear ft.	
Glass	1 piece— field measure	¼" clear, tempered
Exterior trim	3 @ 6'	1 × 4 S4S cedar
Interior trim (optional)	3 @ 6'	1 × 2 S4S cedar
Door		
Frame	3 @ 8'	1 × 6 S4S cedar
Door sill	1 @ 6'	1 × 6 S4S cedar
Stops	1 @ 8', 1 @ 6'	1 × 2 S4S cedar
Panel material	4 @ 8'	1 × 8 T&G V-joint S4S cedar
Door X-brace/panel trim	4 @ 6', 2 @ 8'	1 × 4 S4S cedar
Exterior trim	1 @ 8', 1 @ 6'	1 × 4 S4S cedar
Interior trim (optional)	1 @ 8', 1 @ 6'	1 × 2 S4S cedar
Strap hinges	4	
Garage Door		
Frame	3 @ 8'	1 × 8 S4S cedar
Door	1 @ 8' × 6' - 8"	Sectional flush door w/2" track
Rails	2 @ 8'	2 × 6
Trim	3 @ 8'	1 × 4 S4S cedar
Fasteners		
Anchor bolts	16	⅜" × 8", with washers & nuts, galvanized
16d galvanized common nails	2 lbs.	
16d common nails	17 lbs.	
10d common nails	2 lbs.	
10d galvanized casing nails	1 lb.	
8d common nails	3 lbs.	
8d galvanized finish nails	6 lbs.	
8d box nails	6 lbs.	
6d galvanized finish nails	20 nails	
3d galvanized box nails	½ lb.	
⅞" galvanized roofing nails	2½ lbs.	
2½" deck screws	24 screws	
1¼" wood screws	48 screws	
Construction adhesive	2 tubes	
Silicone-latex caulk	2 tubes	

Building Section

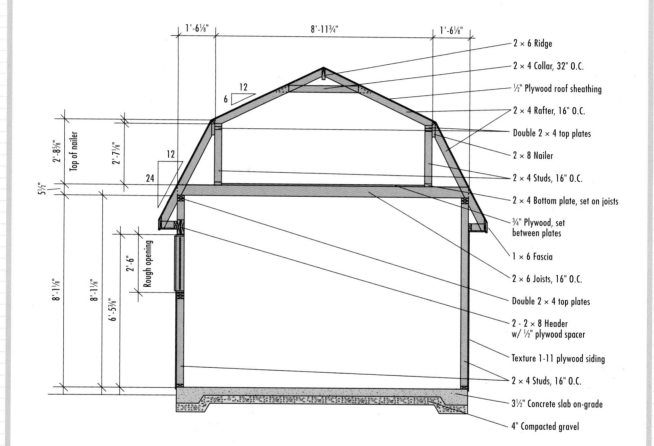

1'-6⅛" 8'-11¾" 1'-6⅛"

2 × 6 Ridge

2 × 4 Collar, 32" O.C.

½" Plywood roof sheathing

2 × 4 Rafter, 16" O.C.

Double 2 × 4 top plates

2 × 8 Nailer

2 × 4 Studs, 16" O.C.

2 × 4 Bottom plate, set on joists

¾" Plywood, set between plates

1 × 6 Fascia

2 × 6 Joists, 16" O.C.

Double 2 × 4 top plates

2 - 2 × 8 Header w/ ½" plywood spacer

Texture 1-11 plywood siding

2 × 4 Studs, 16" O.C.

3½" Concrete slab on-grade

4" Compacted gravel

12 / 6

12 / 24

Top of nailer

2'-8⅜"

2'-7⅞"

5½"

8'-1⅛"

8'-1⅛"

6'-5⅜"

2'-6"

Rough opening

Floor Plan

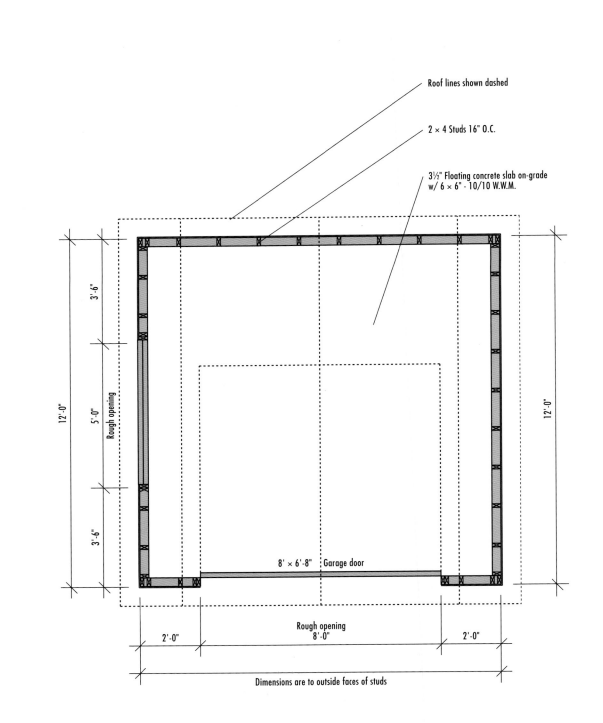

Roof lines shown dashed

2 × 4 Studs 16" O.C.

3½" Floating concrete slab on-grade
w/ 6 × 6" - 10/10 W.W.M.

12'-0"

3'-6"

5'-0"
Rough opening

3'-6"

12'-0"

8' × 6'-8"   Garage door

2'-0"

Rough opening
8'-0"

2'-0"

Dimensions are to outside faces of studs

Rafter Templates

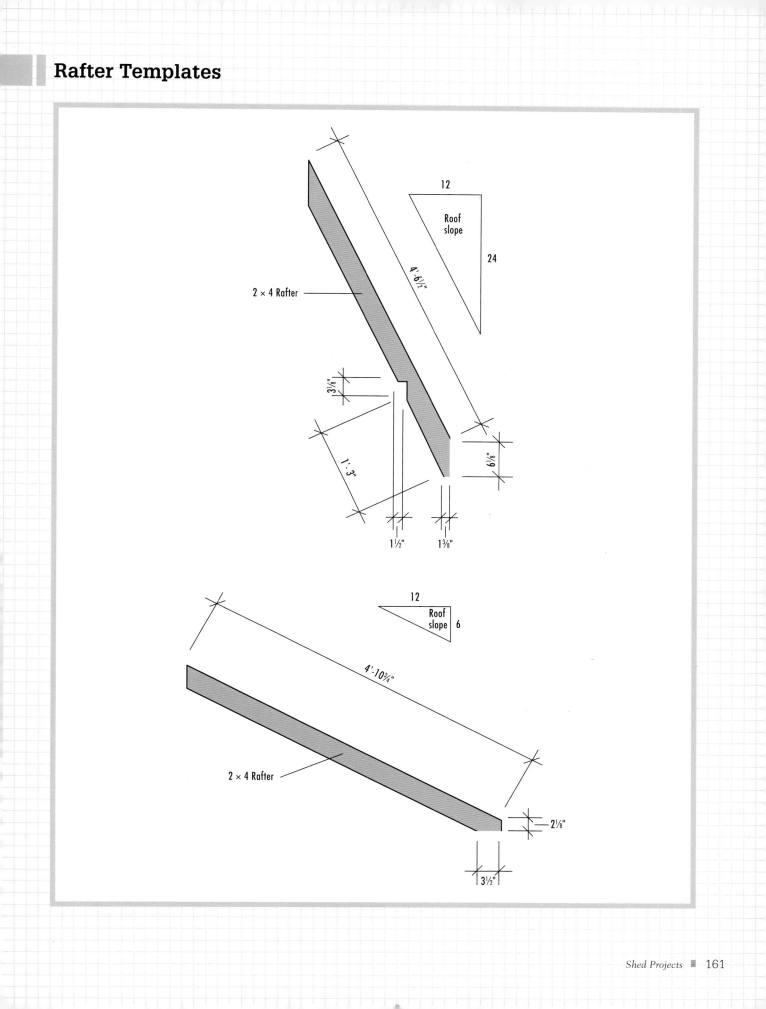

12

Roof
slope

24

2 × 4 Rafter

4'-6½"

3⅛"

1'-3"

6⅛"

1½"

1⅜"

12

Roof
slope 6

4'-10¾"

2 × 4 Rafter

2⅛"

3½"

Front Elevation

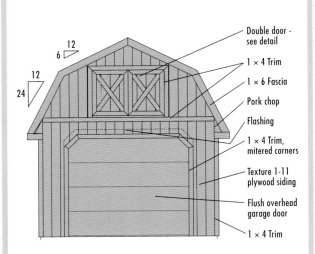

Double door -
see detail

1 × 4 Trim

1 × 6 Fascia

Pork chop

Flashing

1 × 4 Trim,
mitered corners

Texture 1-11
plywood siding

Flush overhead
garage door

1 × 4 Trim

12
6

12
24

Left Side Elevation

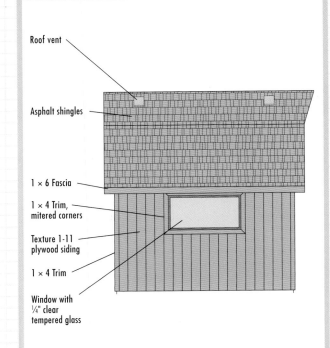

Roof vent

Asphalt shingles

1 × 6 Fascia

1 × 4 Trim,
mitered corners

Texture 1-11
plywood siding

1 × 4 Trim

Window with
¼" clear
tempered glass

Rear Elevation

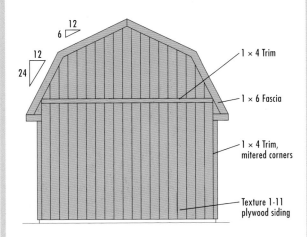

1 × 4 Trim

1 × 6 Fascia

1 × 4 Trim,
mitered corners

Texture 1-11
plywood siding

12
6

12
24

Right Side Elevation

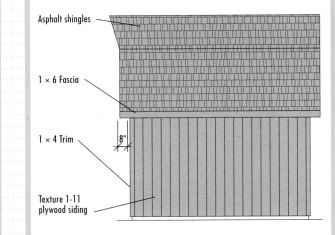

Asphalt shingles

1 × 6 Fascia

1 × 4 Trim

8"

Texture 1-11
plywood siding

Gable Overhang Detail

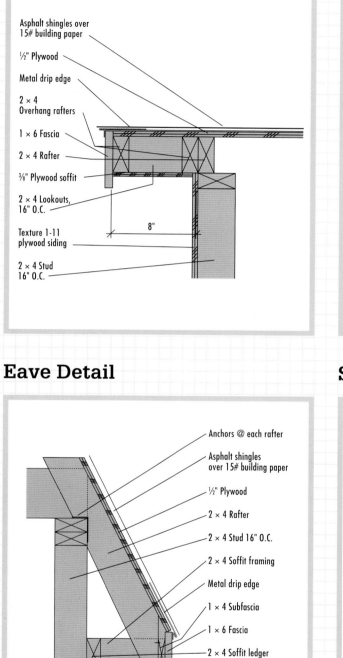

Asphalt shingles over 15# building paper

½" Plywood

Metal drip edge

2 × 4 Overhang rafters

1 × 6 Fascia

2 × 4 Rafter

⅜" Plywood soffit

2 × 4 Lookouts, 16" O.C.

Texture 1-11 plywood siding

2 × 4 Stud 16" O.C.

8"

Gable Overhang Rafter Details

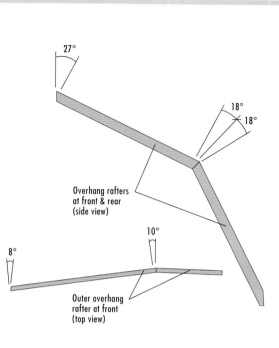

27°

18°

18°

Overhang rafters at front & rear (side view)

8°

10°

Outer overhang rafter at front (top view)

Eave Detail

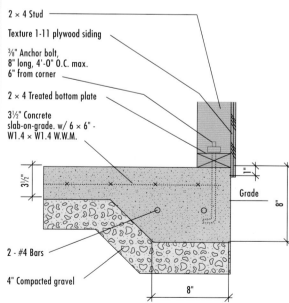

Anchors @ each rafter

Asphalt shingles over 15# building paper

½" Plywood

2 × 4 Rafter

2 × 4 Stud 16" O.C.

2 × 4 Soffit framing

Metal drip edge

1 × 4 Subfascia

1 × 6 Fascia

2 × 4 Soffit ledger

Soffit vent

⅜" Plywood soffit

Texture 1-11 plywood siding

Sill Detail

2 × 4 Stud

Texture 1-11 plywood siding

⅜" Anchor bolt, 8" long, 4'-0" O.C. max. 6" from corner

2 × 4 Treated bottom plate

3½" Concrete slab-on-grade. w/ 6 × 6" - W1.4 × W1.4 W.W.M.

3½"

Grade

1"

8"

2 - #4 Bars

4" Compacted gravel

8"

Attic Door Elevation

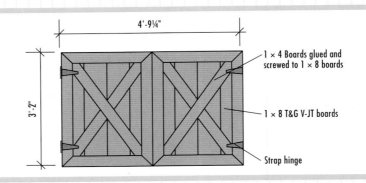

4'-9¼"

3'-2"

1 × 4 Boards glued and screwed to 1 × 8 boards

1 × 8 T&G V-JT boards

Strap hinge

Attic Door Jamb Detail

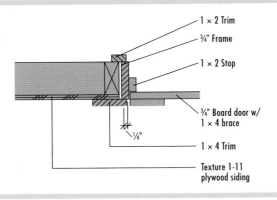

1 × 2 Trim

¾" Frame

1 × 2 Stop

¾" Board door w/ 1 × 4 brace

¼"

1 × 4 Trim

Texture 1-11 plywood siding

Garage Door Trim Detail

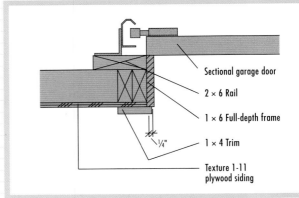

Sectional garage door

2 × 6 Rail

1 × 6 Full-depth frame

¼"

1 × 4 Trim

Texture 1-11 plywood siding

Attic Door Sill Detail

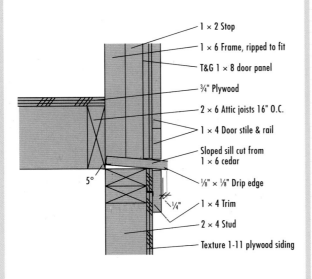

1 × 2 Stop

1 × 6 Frame, ripped to fit

T&G 1 × 8 door panel

¾" Plywood

2 × 6 Attic joists 16" O.C.

1 × 4 Door stile & rail

Sloped sill cut from 1 × 6 cedar

⅛" × ⅛" Drip edge

5°

¼"

1 × 4 Trim

2 × 4 Stud

Texture 1-11 plywood siding

Window Jamb Detail

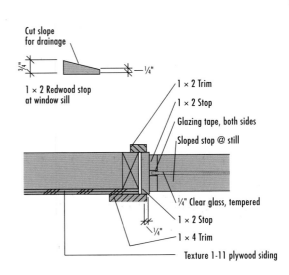

Cut slope for drainage

¾"

¼"

1 × 2 Redwood stop at window sill

1 × 2 Trim

1 × 2 Stop

Glazing tape, both sides

Sloped stop @ still

¼" Clear glass, tempered

1 × 2 Stop

¼"

1 × 4 Trim

Texture 1-11 plywood siding

Front Framing Elevation

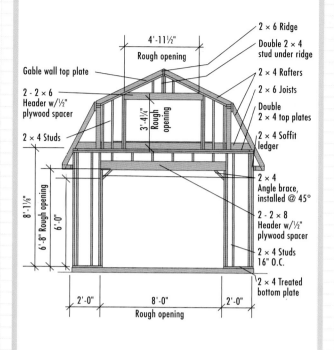

4'-11½"
Rough opening

Gable wall top plate

2 - 2 × 6 Header w/½" plywood spacer

2 × 4 Studs

3'-4¼" Rough opening

8'-1⅛" Rough opening

6'-0"

6'-8" Rough opening

2 × 6 Ridge

Double 2 × 4 stud under ridge

2 × 4 Rafters

2 × 6 Joists

Double 2 × 4 top plates

2 × 4 Soffit ledger

2 × 4 Angle brace, installed @ 45°

2 - 2 × 8 Header w/½" plywood spacer

2 × 4 Studs 16" O.C.

2 × 4 Treated bottom plate

2'-0"   8'-0"   2'-0"
Rough opening

Left Side Framing Elevation

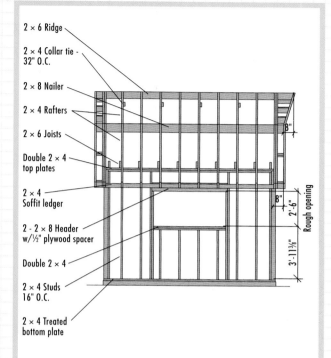

2 × 6 Ridge

2 × 4 Collar tie - 32" O.C.

2 × 8 Nailer

2 × 4 Rafters

2 × 6 Joists

Double 2 × 4 top plates

2 × 4 Soffit ledger

2 - 2 × 8 Header w/½" plywood spacer

Double 2 × 4

2 × 4 Studs 16" O.C.

2 × 4 Treated bottom plate

8"

8"

2'-6" Rough opening

3'-11¾"

Rear Framing Elevation

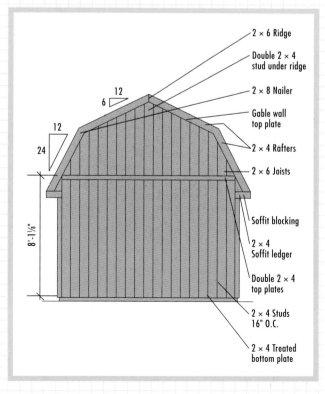

12
6

12
24

8'-1⅛"

2 × 6 Ridge

Double 2 × 4 stud under ridge

2 × 8 Nailer

Gable wall top plate

2 × 4 Rafters

2 × 6 Joists

Soffit blocking

2 × 4 Soffit ledger

Double 2 × 4 top plates

2 × 4 Studs 16" O.C.

2 × 4 Treated bottom plate

Right Side Framing Elevation

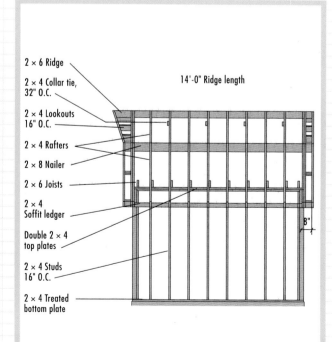

2 × 6 Ridge

2 × 4 Collar tie, 32" O.C.

2 × 4 Lookouts 16" O.C.

2 × 4 Rafters

2 × 8 Nailer

2 × 6 Joists

2 × 4 Soffit ledger

Double 2 × 4 top plates

2 × 4 Studs 16" O.C.

2 × 4 Treated bottom plate

14'-0" Ridge length

8"

How to Build the Gambrel Garage

Build the slab foundation at 144 × 144", following the steps on page 36. Set J-bolts into the concrete 1¾" from the outer edges and extending 2½" from the surface. Set a bolt 6" from each corner and every 48" in between (except in the door opening). Let the slab cure for at least three days before you begin construction.

Snap chalk lines on the slab for the wall plates. Cut two bottom plates and two top plates at 137" for the sidewalls. Cut two bottom and two top plates at 144" for the front and rear walls. Use pressure-treated lumber for all bottom plates. Cut 38 studs at 92⅝", plus two jack studs for the garage door at 78½" and two window studs at 75⅞". *Note: Add the optional slab now, as desired.*

Construct the built-up 2 × 8 headers at 99" (garage door) and 63" (window). Frame, install, and brace the walls with double top plates one at a time, following the FLOOR PLAN (page 160) and ELEVATION drawings (page 162). Use galvanized nails to attach the studs to the sole plates. Anchor the walls to the J-bolts in the slab with galvanized washers and nuts.

Build the attic floor. Cut ten 2 × 6 joists to 144" long, then clip each top corner with a 1½"-long, 45° cut. Install the joists as shown in the FRAMING ELEVATIONS, leaving a 3½" space at the front and rear walls for the gable wall studs. Fasten the joists with three 8d nails at each end.

Frame the attic kneewalls: Cut four top plates at 144" and two bottom plates at 137". Cut 20 studs at 26⅝" and four end studs at 33⅝". Lay out the plates so the studs fall over the attic joists. Frame the walls and install them 18⅛" from the ends of the joists, then add temporary bracing. *Option: You can begin building the roof frame by cutting two 2 × 8 nailers to 144" long. Fasten the nailers to the kneewalls so their top edges are 32⅝" above the attic joists.*

Cover the attic floor between the kneewalls with ¾" plywood. Run the sheets perpendicular to the joists, and stop them flush with the outer joists. Fasten the flooring with 8d ring-shank nails every 6" along the edges and every 12" in the field of the sheets.

Mark the rafter layouts onto the top and outside faces of the 2 × 8 nailers; see the FRAMING ELEVATIONS.

Cut the 2 × 6 ridge board at 168", mitering the front end at 16°. Mark the rafter layout onto the ridge. The outer common rafters should be 16" from the front end and 8" from the rear end of the ridge.

(continued)

Use the RAFTER TEMPLATES (page 161) to mark and cut two upper pattern rafters and one lower pattern rafter. Test-fit the rafters and make any needed adjustments. Use the patterns to mark and cut the remaining common rafters (20 total of each type). For the gable overhangs, cut an additional eight lower and six upper rafters following the GABLE OVERHANG RAFTER DETAILS (page 163).

Install the common rafters; then reinforce the joints at the knee walls with framing connectors. Also nail the attic joists to the sides of the floor rafters. Cut four 2 × 4 collar ties at 34", mitering the ends at 26.5°. Fasten them between pairs of upper rafters, as shown in the BUILDING SECTION (page 159) and FRAMING ELEVATIONS.

Snap a chalk line across the sidewall studs, level with the ends of the rafters. Cut two 2 × 4 soffit ledgers at 160" and fasten them to the studs on top of the chalk lines, with their ends overhanging the walls by 8". Cut 24 2 × 4 blocks to fit between the ledger and rafter ends, as shown in the EAVE DETAIL (page 163). Install the blocks.

Frame the gable overhangs. Cut 12 2 × 4 lookouts at 5" and nail them to the inner overhang rafters as shown in the LEFT and RIGHT SIDE FRAMING ELEVATIONS. Install the inner overhang rafters over the common rafters, using 10d nails. Cut the two front (angled) overhang rafters; see the GABLE OVERHANG RAFTER DETAILS. Install those rafters; then add two custom-cut lookouts for each rafter.

To complete the gable walls, cut top plates to fit between the ridge and the attic kneewalls. Install the plates flush with the outer common rafters. Mark the stud layout onto the walls and gable top plate; see the FRONT and REAR FRAMING ELEVATIONS. Cut the gable studs to fit and install them. Construct the built-up 2 × 6 attic door header at 62½"; then clip the top corners to match the roof slope. Install the header with jack studs cut at 40¼".

Install siding on the walls, holding it 1" below the top of the concrete slab. Add Z-flashing along the top edges, and then continue the siding up to the rafters. Below the attic door opening, stop the siding about ¼" below the top wall plate, as shown in the ATTIC DOOR SILL DETAIL (page 164). Don't nail the siding to the garage door header until the flashing is installed (Step 20).

Mill a ⅜"-wide × ¼"-deep groove into the 1 × 6 boards for the horizontal fascia along the eaves and gable ends (about 36 linear ft.); see the EAVE DETAIL. Use a router or table saw with a dado-head blade to mill the groove, and make the groove ⅞" above the bottom edge of the fascia.

Install the 1 × 4 subfascia along the eaves, keeping the bottom edge flush with the ends of the rafters and the ends flush with the outsides of the outer-most rafters; see the EAVE DETAIL. Add the milled fascia at the eaves, aligning the top of the groove with the bottom of the subfascia. Cut fascia to wrap around the overhangs at the gable ends but don't install them until Step 17.

(continued)

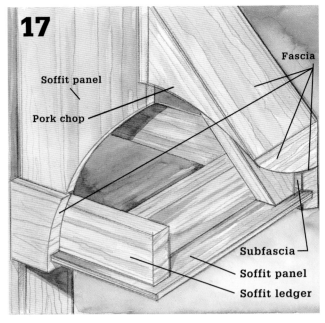

17

Fascia

Soffit panel

Pork chop

Subfascia

Soffit panel

Soffit ledger

Add fascia at the gable ends, holding it up ½" to be flush with the roof sheathing. Cut soffit panels to fit between the fascia and walls, and fasten them with 3d galvanized nails. Install the end and return fascia pieces at the gable overhangs. Enclose each overhang at the corners with a triangular piece of grooved fascia (called a pork chop) and a piece of soffit material. Install the soffit vents as shown in the EAVE DETAIL.

18

Sheath the roof, starting at one of the lower corners. Add metal drip edge along the eaves, followed by building paper; then add drip edge along the gable ends, over the paper. Install the asphalt shingles. Plan the courses so the roof transition occurs midshingle, not between courses; the overlapping shingles will relax over time. If desired, add roof vents (page 58).

19

Cover the Z-flashing at the rear wall with horizontal 1 × 4 trim. Finish the four wall corners with overlapping vertical 1 × 4 trim. Install the 2 × 6 rails that will support the garage door tracks, following the door manufacturer's instructions to determine the sizing and placement; see the GARAGE DOOR TRIM DETAIL (page 164).

20

For the garage doorframe, rip 1 × 8 trim boards to width so they cover the front wall siding and 2 × 6 rails, as shown in the GARAGE DOOR TRIM DETAIL. Install the trim, mitering the pieces at 22.5°. Install the 1 × 4 trim around the outside of the opening, adding flashing along the top; see the FRONT ELEVATION (page 162).

21

Install the garage door in the door opening, following the manufacturer's directions.

22

Build the window frame, which should be ½" narrower and shorter than the rough opening. Install the frame using shims and 10d galvanized casing nails, as shown in the WINDOW JAMB DETAIL (page 164). Cut eight 1 × 2 stop pieces to fit the frame. Bevel the outer sill stop for drainage. Order glass to fit, or cut your own plastic panel. Install the glazing and stops, using glazing tape for a watertight seal. Add the window trim.

23

For the attic doorframe, rip 1 × 6s to match the depth of the opening and cut the head jamb and side jambs. Cut the sill from full-width 1 × 6 stock; then cut a kerf for a drip edge (see the ATTIC DOOR SILL DETAIL). Fasten the head jamb to the side jambs and install the sill at a 5° slope between the side jambs. Install the doorframe using shims and 10d casing nails. Add shims or cedar shingles along the length of the sill to provide support underneath. The front edge of the frame should be flush with the face of the siding. Add 1 × 2 stops at the frame sides and top, ¾" from the front edges.

24

Build the attic doors as shown in the ATTIC DOOR ELEVATION (page 164), using glue and 1¼" screws. Each door measures 28⅝ × 38", including the panel braces. Cut the 1 × 8 panel boards about ⅛" short along the bottom to compensate for the sloping sill. Install the door with two hinges each. Add 1 × 4 horizontal trim on the front wall, up against the doorsill; then trim around both sides of the doorframe. Prime and paint as desired.

Convenience Shed

The Convenience Shed is so named for its exceptional versatility and ample storage space. This classic gabled outbuilding has a footprint that measures 12 × 16 ft. and it includes several features not found in most storage sheds. For starters, its 8-ft.-wide overhead garage door provides easy access for large equipment, supplies, projects or even a small automobile. The foundation and shed floor is a poured concrete slab, so it's ideal for heavy items like lawn tractors and stationary tools.

To the right of the garage door is a box bay window. This special architectural detail gives the building's facade a surprising house-like quality while filling the interior with natural light. And the bay's 33"-deep × 60"-wide sill platform is the perfect place for herb pots or an indoor flower box. The adjacent wall includes a second large window and a standard service door, making this end of the shed a pleasant, convenient space for all kinds of work or leisure.

Above the main space of the Convenience Shed is a fully framed attic built with 2 × 6 joists for supporting plenty of stored goods. The steep pitch of the roof allows for over 3 ft. of headroom under the peak. Access to the attic is provided by a drop-down staircase that folds up and out of the way, leaving the workspace clear below.

The garage door, service door, staircase, and both windows of the shed are pre-built factory units that you install following the manufacturers' instructions. Be sure to order all of the units before starting construction. This makes it easy to adjust the framed openings, if necessary, to match the precise sizing of each unit. Also consult your local building department to learn about design requirements for the concrete foundation. You may need to extend and/ or reinforce the perimeter portion of the slab or include a footing that extends below the frost line. An extended apron (as seen in the Gambrel Garage, page 156) is very useful if you intend to house vehicles in the shed.

Get creative in this large shed that can pass for a small garage. The building's ample space and generous headroom offer endless options, including a practice site for your Shed Band that's well out of earshot from the house.

Cutting List

DESCRIPTION	QTY./SIZE	MATERIAL
Foundation		
Drainage material	2.75 cu. yd.	Compactible gravel
Concrete slab	Field measure	3,000 psi concrete
Mesh	200 sq. ft.	6 × 6", W1.4 × W1.4 welded wire mesh
Reinforcing bar	As required by local code	As required by local code
Wall Framing		
Bottom plates	1 @ 16', 2 @ 12', 1 @ 10'	2 × 4 pressure-treated
Top plates	2 @ 14', 4 @ 12', 4 @ 10'	2 × 4
Standard wall studs	51 @ 8'* *may use 92⅝" precut studs	2 × 4
Diagonal bracing	5 @ 12'	1 × 4 (std. lumber)
Jack studs	5 @ 14'	2 × 4
Gable end studs	5 @ 8'	2 × 4
Header, overhead door	2 @ 10'	2 × 12
Header, windows	2 @ 10'	2 × 12
Header, service door	1 @ 8'	2 × 12
Header & stud spacers		See Sheathing, below
Box Bay Framing		
Half-wall bottom plate	1 @ 8'	2 × 4 pressure-treated
Half-wall top plate & studs	3 @ 8'	2 × 4
Joists	3 @ 8'	2 × 6
Window frame	4 @ 12'	2 × 4
Sill platform & top	1 sheet @ 4 × 8'	½" plywood
Rafter blocking	1 @ 8'	2 × 8
Roof Framing		
Rafters (& lookouts, blocking)	36 @ 10'	2 × 6
Ridge board	1 @ 18'	2 × 8
Attic		
Floor joists	16 @ 12'	2 × 6
Floor decking	6 sheets @ 4 × 8'	½" plywood
Staircase	1 unit for 22 × 48" rough opening	Disappearing attic stair unit

DESCRIPTION	QTY./SIZE	MATERIAL
Exterior Finishes		
Eave fascia	2 @ 18'	2 × 8 cedar
Gable fascia	4 @ 10'	1 × 8 cedar
Drip edge & gable trim	160 linear ft.	1 × 2 cedar
Siding	15 sheets @ 4 × 8'	⅝" Texture 1-11 plywood siding w/ vertical grooves 8" on center (or similar)
Siding flashing	30 linear ft.	Metal Z-flashing
Overhead door jambs	1 @ 10', 2 @ 8'	1 × 6 cedar
Overhead door stops	3 @ 8'	Cedar door stop
Overhead door surround	1 @ 10', 2 @ 8'	2 × 6
Corner trim	8 @ 8'	1 × 4 cedar
Door & window trim	4 @ 8', 5 @ 10'	1 × 4 cedar
Box bay bottom trim	1 @ 8'	1 × 10 cedar
Roofing		
Sheathing (& header, stud spacers)	14 sheets @ 4 × 8'	½" exterior-grade plywood roof sheathing
15# building paper	2 rolls	
Shingles	4⅔ squares	Asphalt shingles — 250# per sq. min.
Roof flashing	10'6"	
Doors & Windows		
Overhead garage door w/hardware	1 @ ⁹⁄₀ × ⁷⁄₀	
Service door	1 unit for 38 × 72⅞" rough opening	Prehung exterior door unit
Window	2 units for 57 × 41⅜"	Casement mullion window unit — complete
Fasteners & Hardware		
J-bolts w/nuts & washers	14	½"-dia. × 12"
16d galvanized common nails	3 lbs.	
16d common nails	15 lbs.	
10d common nails	2½ lbs.	
8d box nails	16 lbs.	
8d common nails	5 lbs.	
8d galvanized siding nails	10 lbs.	
1" galvanized roofing nails	10 lbs.	
8d galvanized casing nails	3 lbs.	
Entry door lockset	1	

Foundation Plan

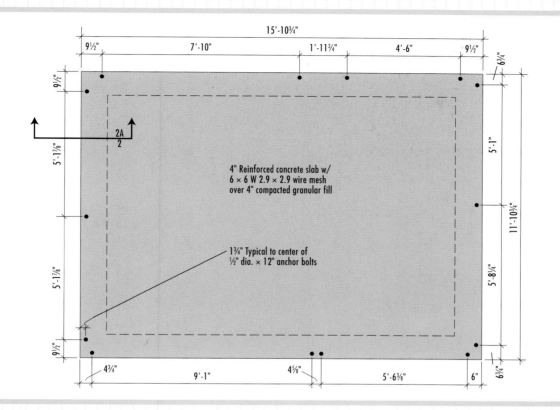

15'-10¾"

9½" 7'-10" 1'-11¾" 4'-6" 9½" 6¾"

9½"

5'-1⅞"

2A / 2

4" Reinforced concrete slab w/
6 × 6 W 2.9 × 2.9 wire mesh
over 4" compacted granular fill

5'-1"

11'-10¾"

1¾" Typical to center of
½" dia. × 12" anchor bolts

5'-8¼"

5'-1⅞"

9½"

6¾"

4¾" 9'-1" 4⅝" 5'-6⅜" 6"

Foundation Detail

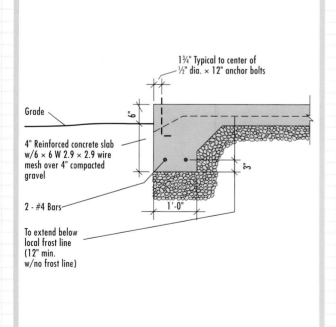

1¾" Typical to center of
½" dia. × 12" anchor bolts

Grade

6"

4" Reinforced concrete slab
w/6 × 6 W 2.9 × 2.9 wire
mesh over 4" compacted
gravel

2 - #4 Bars

3"

1'-0"

To extend below
local frost line
(12" min.
w/no frost line)

Building Section

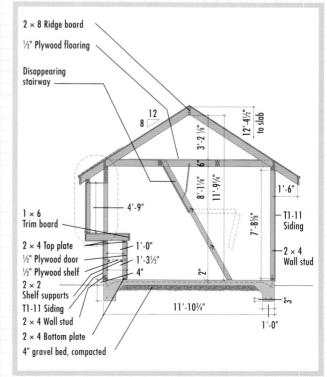

2 × 8 Ridge board

½" Plywood flooring

Disappearing
stairway

12
8

12'-4½"
to slab

3'-2⅛"

6"

8⅛"

11'-9¼"

1'-6"

4'-9"

1 × 6
Trim board

T1-11
Siding

2 × 4 Top plate 1'-0"

½" Plywood door 1'-3½"

½" Plywood shelf 4"

2 × 2
Shelf supports

T1-11 Siding

2 × 4 Wall stud

2 × 4 Bottom plate

4" gravel bed, compacted

2"

7'-8⅝"

2 × 4
Wall stud

11'-10¾" 3"

1'-0"

Front Elevation

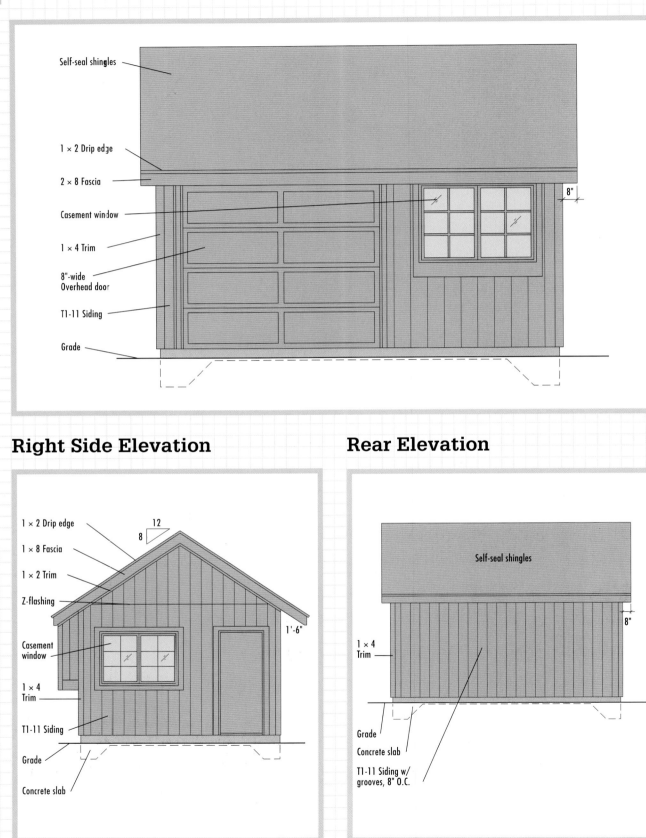

Self-seal shingles

1 × 2 Drip edge

2 × 8 Fascia

Casement window

1 × 4 Trim

8"-wide
Overhead door

T1-11 Siding

Grade

8"

Right Side Elevation

1 × 2 Drip edge

1 × 8 Fascia

1 × 2 Trim

Z-flashing

Casement
window

1 × 4
Trim

T1-11 Siding

Grade

Concrete slab

12
8

1'-6"

Rear Elevation

Self-seal shingles

8"

1 × 4
Trim

Grade

Concrete slab

T1-11 Siding w/
grooves, 8" O.C.

Wall Framing Plan

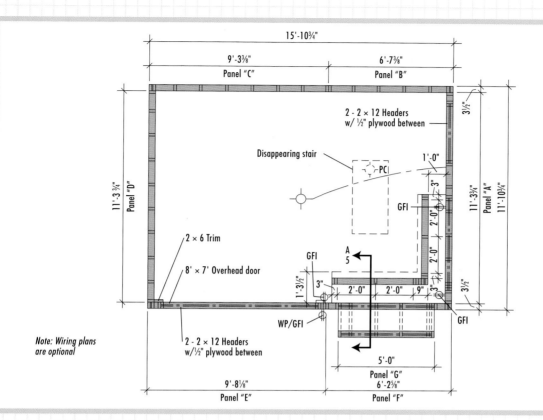

15'-10¾"

9'-3⅜"
Panel "C"

6'-7⅜"
Panel "B"

3½"

2 - 2 × 12 Headers
w/½" plywood between

Disappearing stair

PC

1'-0"

3"

GFI

11'-3¾"
Panel "A"
11'-10¾"

11'-3¾"
Panel "D"

2'-0"

2 × 6 Trim

A
5

GFI

2'-0"

8' × 7' Overhead door

GFI

1'-3½"

3"

2'-0"

2'-0"

9"

3"

3½"

Note: Wiring plans
are optional

2 - 2 × 12 Headers
w/½" plywood between

WP/GFI

GFI

5'-0"

Panel "G"
6'-2⅝"

9'-8⅛"
Panel "E"

Panel "F"

Back Side Framing

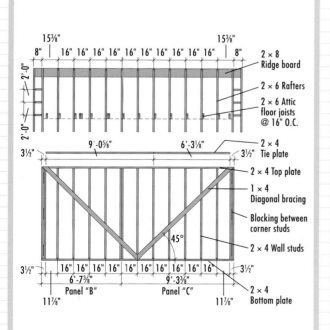

15⅜"

8" | 16" | 16" | 16" | 16" | 16" | 16" | 16" | 16"

15⅜"

8"

2 × 8
Ridge board

2 × 6 Rafters

2'-0"

2'-0"

2 × 6 Attic
floor joists
@ 16" O.C.

9'-0⅝"

6'-3⅛"

2 × 4
Tie plate

3½"

3½"

2 × 4 Top plate

1 × 4
Diagonal bracing

Blocking between
corner studs

45°

2 × 4 Wall studs

3½"

16" | 16" | 16" | 16" | 16" | 16" | 16" | 16" | 16"

3½"

6'-7⅜"
Panel "B"

9'-3⅜"
Panel "C"

2 × 4
Bottom plate

11⅞"

11⅞"

Left Side Framing

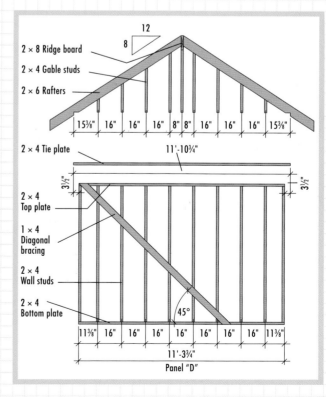

12
8

2 × 8 Ridge board

2 × 4 Gable studs

2 × 6 Rafters

15⅜" | 16" | 16" | 16" | 8" | 8" | 16" | 16" | 16" | 15⅜"

2 × 4 Tie plate

11'-10¾"

3½"

3½"

2 × 4
Top plate

1 × 4
Diagonal
bracing

2 × 4
Wall studs

45°

2 × 4
Bottom plate

11⅜" | 16" | 16" | 16" | 16" | 16" | 16" | 16" | 11⅜"

11'-3¾"
Panel "D"

Front Side Framing

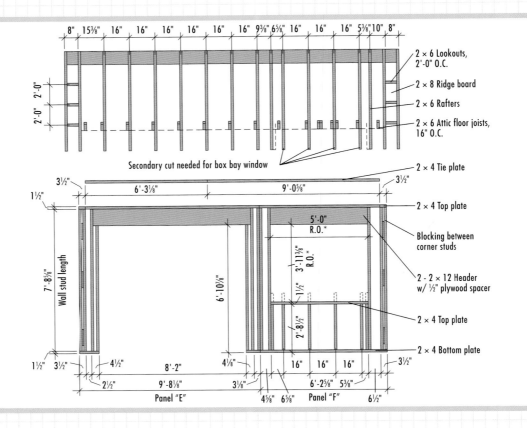

Secondary cut needed for box bay window

2 × 6 Lookouts, 2'-0" O.C.

2 × 8 Ridge board

2 × 6 Rafters

2 × 6 Attic floor joists, 16" O.C.

2 × 4 Tie plate

2 × 4 Top plate

Blocking between corner studs

2 - 2 × 12 Header w/ ½" plywood spacer

2 × 4 Top plate

2 × 4 Bottom plate

5'-0" R.O.*

3'-11⅛" R.O.*

Wall stud length

7'-8½"

6'-10⅛"

2'-8½"

Panel "E"

Panel "F"

Attic Floor Joist Framing

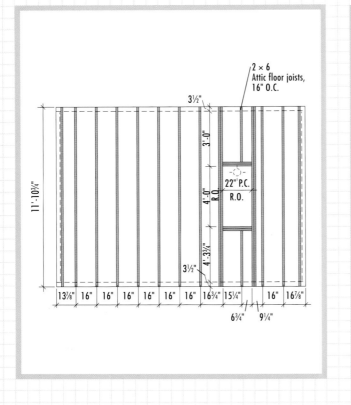

2 × 6 Attic floor joists, 16" O.C.

22" P.C. R.O.

4'-0" R.O.

11'-10¾"

Box Bay Window Framing

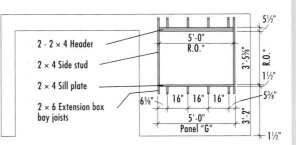

2 - 2 × 4 Header

2 × 4 Side stud

2 × 4 Sill plate

2 × 6 Extension box bay joists

5'-0" R.O.*

3'-5⅜" R.O.*

Panel "G"

5'-0"

3'-2"

Overhead Door Header Detail

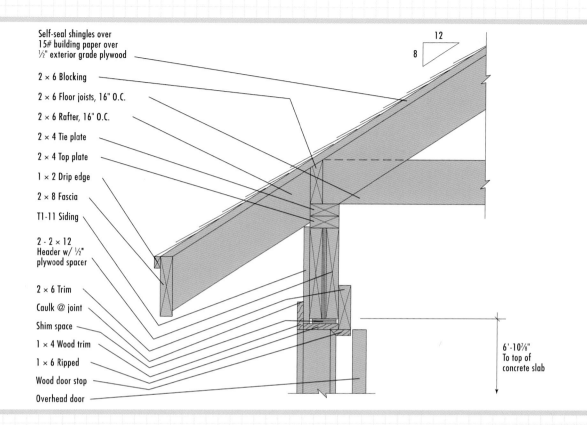

Self-seal shingles over 15# building paper over ½" exterior grade plywood

2 × 6 Blocking

2 × 6 Floor joists, 16" O.C.

2 × 6 Rafter, 16" O.C.

2 × 4 Tie plate

2 × 4 Top plate

1 × 2 Drip edge

2 × 8 Fascia

T1-11 Siding

2 - 2 × 12 Header w/ ½" plywood spacer

2 × 6 Trim

Caulk @ joint

Shim space

1 × 4 Wood trim

1 × 6 Ripped

Wood door stop

Overhead door

12 / 8

6'-10⅞"
To top of concrete slab

Overhead Door Jamb Detail

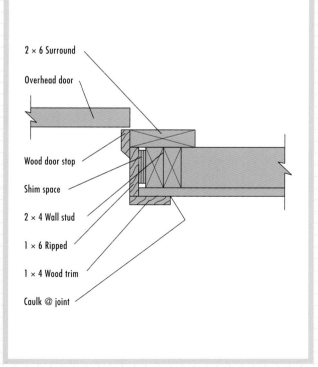

2 × 6 Surround

Overhead door

Wood door stop

Shim space

2 × 4 Wall stud

1 × 6 Ripped

1 × 4 Wood trim

Caulk @ joint

Service Door Header/Jamb Detail

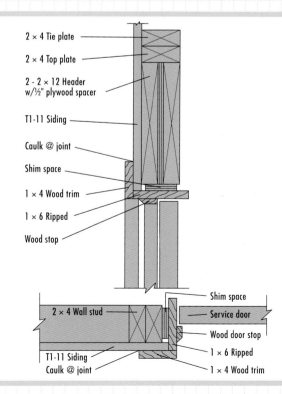

2 × 4 Tie plate

2 × 4 Top plate

2 - 2 × 12 Header w/½" plywood spacer

T1-11 Siding

Caulk @ joint

Shim space

1 × 4 Wood trim

1 × 6 Ripped

Wood stop

Shim space

Service door

Wood door stop

1 × 6 Ripped

2 × 4 Wall stud

T1-11 Siding

Caulk @ joint

1 × 4 Wood trim

Rafter Template

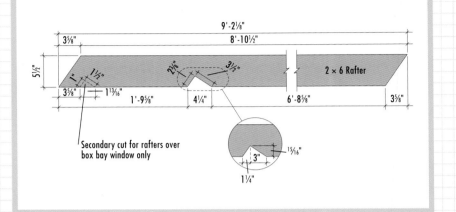

9'-2⅛"
8'-10½"

3⅝"
5½"
1"
1½"
3⅝"
1¹³⁄₁₆"
2⅝"
3½"
2 × 6 Rafter
1'-9⅝"
4¼"
6'-8⅝"
3⅝"

Secondary cut for rafters over box bay window only

3"
1¹⁵⁄₁₆"
1¼"

Counter Detail

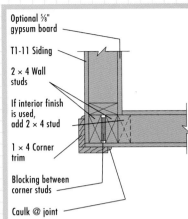

Optional ⅝" gypsum board

T1-11 Siding

2 × 4 Wall studs

If interior finish is used, add 2 × 4 stud

1 × 4 Corner trim

Blocking between corner studs

Caulk @ joint

Box Bay Window Detail

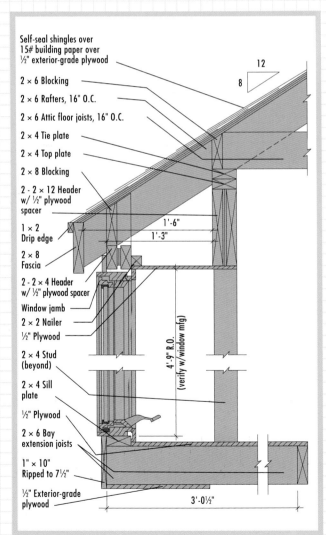

Self-seal shingles over 15# building paper over ½" exterior-grade plywood

2 × 6 Blocking

2 × 6 Rafters, 16" O.C.

2 × 6 Attic floor joists, 16" O.C.

2 × 4 Tie plate

2 × 4 Top plate

2 × 8 Blocking

2 - 2 × 12 Header w/ ½" plywood spacer

1 × 2 Drip edge

2 × 8 Fascia

2 - 2 × 4 Header w/ ½" plywood spacer

Window jamb

2 × 2 Nailer

½" Plywood

2 × 4 Stud (beyond)

2 × 4 Sill plate

½" Plywood

2 × 6 Bay extension joists

1" × 10" Ripped to 7½"

½" Exterior-grade plywood

12
8

1'-6"
1'-3"

4'-9" R.O. (verify w/ window mfg)

3'-0½"

Isometric

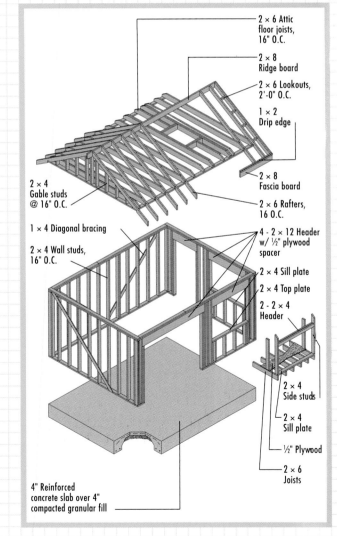

2 × 6 Attic floor joists, 16" O.C.

2 × 8 Ridge board

2 × 6 Lookouts, 2'-0" O.C.

1 × 2 Drip edge

2 × 8 Fascia board

2 × 6 Rafters, 16 O.C.

2 × 4 Gable studs @ 16" O.C.

1 × 4 Diagonal bracing

2 × 4 Wall studs, 16" O.C.

4 - 2 × 12 Header w/ ½" plywood spacer

2 × 4 Sill plate

2 × 4 Top plate

2 - 2 × 4 Header

2 × 4 Side studs

2 × 4 Sill plate

½" Plywood

2 × 6 Joists

4" Reinforced concrete slab over 4" compacted granular fill

How to Build the Convenience Shed

Build the concrete foundation using the specifications shown in the FOUNDATION DETAIL (page 175) and following the basic procedure on pages 36 to 39. The slab should measure 190¾" × 142¾". Set the 14 J-bolts into the concrete as shown in FOUNDATION PLAN (page 175). *Note: All slab specifications must comply with local building codes.*

Snap chalk lines for the bottom plates so they will be flush with the outside edges of the foundation. You can frame the walls in four continuous panels or break them up into panels "A" through "F", as shown in the WALL FRAMING PLAN (page 177). We completely assembled and squared all four walls before raising and anchoring them.

Frame the back wall(s) following the BACK SIDE FRAMING (page 177). Use pressure treated lumber for the bottom plate, and nail it to the studs with galvanized 16d common nails. All of the standard studs are 92⅝" long. Square the wall, then add 1 × 4 let-in bracing.

Raise the back wall and anchor it to the foundation J-bolts with washers and nuts. Brace the wall upright. Frame and raise the remaining walls one at a time, then tie all of the walls together with double top plates. Cover the outside of the walls with T1-11 siding.

(continued)

Cut fifteen 2 × 6 attic floor joists at 142¾". Cut the top corner at both ends of each joist: Mark 1⅞" along the top edge and ¹⁵⁄₁₆" down the end; connect the marks, then cut along the line. Clipping the corner prevents the joist from extending above the rafters.

Mark the joist layout onto the wall plates following the ATTIC FLOOR JOIST FRAMING (page 178). Leave 3½" between the outsides of the end walls and the outer joists. Toenail the joists to the plates with three 8d common nails at each end. Frame the rough opening for the staircase with doubled side joists and doubled headers; fasten doubled members together with pairs of 10d nails every 16". Install the drop-down staircase unit following the manufacturer's instructions.

Cover the attic floor with ½" plywood, fastening it to the joists with 8d nails.

Use the RAFTER TEMPLATE (page 180) to mark and cut two pattern rafters. Test-fit the rafters and adjust the cuts as needed. Cut all (24) standard rafters. Cut four special rafters with an extra bird's-mouth cut for the box bay. Cut four gable overhang rafters—these have no bird's-mouth cuts.

Cut the 2 × 8 ridge board at 206¾". Mark the rafter layout on the ridge and wall plates as shown in the FRONT SIDE FRAMING (page 178) and BACK SIDE FRAMING (page 177). Frame the roof following the steps on pages 48 to 51. Install 6½"-long lookouts 24" on center, then attach the overhang rafters. Fasten the attic joists to the rafters with three 10d nails at each end.

Mark the stud layout for the gable end walls onto the end wall plates following the SIDE FRAMING (page 177). Transfer the layout to the rafters, using a level. Cut each of the 2 × 4 studs to fit, mitering the top ends at 33.5°. Install the studs flush with the end walls.

Construct the 2 × 4 half-wall for the interior apron beneath the box bay: Cut two plates at 60" (pressure-treated lumber for bottom plate); cut five studs at 32½". Fasten one stud at each end, and space the remaining studs evenly in between. Mark a layout line 12" from the inside of the shed's front wall (see the BUILDING SECTION page 175). Anchor the half-wall to the slab using masonry screws or a powder-actuated nailer.

Cut six 2 × 6 joists at 36½". Toenail the joists to the inner and outer half-walls following the layout in the BOX BAY WINDOW FRAMING (page 178); the joists should extend 15" past the outer shed wall. Add a 60"-long 2 × 4 sill plate at the ends of the joists. Cut two 2 × 4 side studs to extend from the sill plate to the top edges of the rafters (angle top ends at 33.5°), and install them. Install a built-up 2 × 4 header between the side studs 41⅜" above the sill plate.

(continued)

13

Install a 2 × 2 nailer ½" up from the bottom of the 2 × 4 bay header. Cover the top and bottom of the bay with ½" plywood as shown in the BOX BAY WINDOW DETAIL. Cut a 2 × 4 stud to fit between the plywood panels at each end of the 2 × 4 shed wall header; fasten these to the studs supporting the studs and the header.

14

Bevel the side edge of the 2 × 6 blocking stock at 33.5°. Cut individual blocks to fit between the rafters and attic joists, and install them to seal off the rafter bays; see the OVERHEAD DOOR HEADER DETAIL (page 179). The blocks should be flush with the tops of the rafters. Custom-cut 2 × 8 blocking to enclose the rafter bays above the box bay header; see the BOX BAY WINDOW DETAIL.

15

Add 2 × 8 fascia to the ends of the rafters along each eave so the top outer edge will be flush with the top of the roof sheathing. Cover the gable overhang rafters with 1 × 8 fascia. Add 1 × 2 trim to serve as a drip edge along the eaves and gable ends so it will be flush with the top of the roof sheathing.

16

Add Z-flashing above the first row of siding, then cut and fit T1-11 siding for the gable ends. Cover the horizontal seam with 1 × 4 trim snugged up against the flashing.

17

To complete the trim details, add 1 × 2 along the gable ends and sides of the box bay. Use 1 × 4 on all vertical corners and around the windows, service door, and overhead door. Rip down 1 × 10s for horizontal trim along the bottom of the box bay. Also cover underneath the bay joists with ½" exterior-grade plywood.

18

Rip-cut 1 × 6 boards to 4⅛" wide for the overhead door jambs. Install the jambs using the door manufacturer's dimensions for the opening. Shim behind the jambs if necessary. Make sure the jambs are flush with the inside of the wall framing and extend ⅝" beyond the outside of the framing. Install the 2 × 6 trim as shown in the OVERHEAD DOOR HEADER DETAIL and OVERHEAD DOOR JAMB DETAIL.

19

Install the two windows and the service door following the manufacturers' instructions. Position the jambs of the units so they will be flush with the siding, if applicable. Install the overhead door, then add stop molding along the top and side jambs; see the SERVICE DOOR HEADER/JAMB DETAIL.

20

Install ½" plywood roof sheathing, starting at the bottom ends of the rafters. Add building paper and asphalt shingles.

Rustic Summerhouse

The quaint and cozy Rustic Summerhouse is a perfect spot for enjoying a meal, relaxing with the sunset, escaping into a good book, or taking a quick break from gardening or yard work. The entirely screened-in room is bug-free, large enough to comfortably seat six, strong enough to support a hammock for two, and stable enough to house a hot tub or whirlpool spa. This charming summerhouse, made with traditional rough-hewn materials, is the perfect finishing touch to any backyard or estate.

The building is constructed using post-and-beam construction techniques that have been passed down through the centuries, ensuring that the finished product will stand the test of time. The design's eleven screens ensure excellent airflow, keeping the interior comfortable even on hot days.

Attractively finished with board-and-batten siding and a corrugated metal roof, the Rustic Summerhouse's crowning achievement is the decorative cedar clapboard sunburst design above the door, handcrafted by each builder. Following the techniques discussed here to create this building design, your summerhouse will have its own completely unique finishing touch.

The materials are key to this building's quality. Hearty 2 × 6 flooring provides a solid base for even the most aggressive wear and tear, and rough-sawn 1 × 12 pine siding with two-inch battens gives the building its charm and character. Intermediate or expert builders may find this building to be quite quick to erect, whereas beginners may select this project as a fulfilling challenge with a fantastic payoff.

This cozy outdoor room is the perfect getaway or relaxation spot. Large enough to seat six for dinner, the Rustic Summerhouse is also the perfect retreat for one or two to sit and enjoy the view.

Whether close to your home, adjoining a garden or pond, or elsewhere on your property, this charming hideout will quickly become a focal point for your friends and family when enjoying the outdoors.

Cutting List

DESCRIPTION	QTY./SIZE	MATERIAL
Foundation/Floor		
Foundation base	2.5 cu. yds.	Compactible stone gravel
Concrete blocks	6	4 × 8 × 16" blocks
Skids	2 @ 14'	4 × 6 hemlock
Floor joists	8 @ 10'	2 × 6 hemlock
Rim joists	2 @ 14'	2 × 6 hemlock
Flooring	24 @ 14'	2 × 6 tongue-and-groove spruce or pine
Wall Framing		
Rear top plate beam	14'	4 × 4 hemlock
Front top plate beams	2 @ 62¾"	4 × 4 hemlock
Gable beams	2 @ 10'	4 × 4 hemlock
Rear wall horizontal nailers	4 @ 17¼"	2 × 4 hemlock
Front wall horizontal nailers	8 @ 7⅛"	2 × 4 hemlock
Window studs	8 @ 74"	2 × 4 hemlock
Front and rear wall window headers and sills	15 @ 36½"	2 × 4 hemlock
Side wall window headers and sills	18 @ 32½"	2 × 4 hemlock
Side wall spacer blocks	12 @ 12"	1 × 4 hemlock
Wall, corner & door posts	14 @ 74"	4 × 4 hemlock
Door studs	2 @ 82"	2 × 4
Door header 1	93"	2 × 4
Door header 2	112"	2 × 4
Roof Framing		
Ridge board	14'	1 × 8 pine
Dormer ridge board	59½"	1 × 8 pine
Common rafters	12 @ 66⅝"	2 × 6
Dormer common rafters	2 @ 65⅝"	2 × 6
Valley rafters	2 @ 87"	2 × 6
Jack 1 rafters	4 @ 12½"	2 × 4
Jack 2 rafters	4 @ 39½"	2 × 4
Collar ties	4 @ 4'	1 × 6

DESCRIPTION	QTY./SIZE	MATERIAL
Exterior Finishes		
1 × 4 door, window, and corner trim, ridge & temporary bracing	24 @ 12'	1 × 4 pine
Rear and front wall corner siding	6 @ 90"	1 × 12
Rear and front wall siding — under windows	16 @ 21"	1 × 12
Rear and front wall siding — above windows	12 @ 12"	1 × 12
Rear and side wall siding — between windows	8 @ 57"	1 × 6
Front wall siding — above windows	2 @ 18" and 24"	1 × 12
Front wall siding	2 @ 106"	1 × 12
Front wall siding	2 @ 109"	1 × 8
Front wall siding — above door	2 @ 23" and 27"	1 × 8
Front wall siding — above door	31"	1 × 8
Side wall corner siding	4 @ 94"	1 × 6
Side wall siding — under windows	18 @ 21"	1 × 12
Side wall siding — above windows	4 @ 22", 28", 34", and 40"	1 × 12
Side wall siding — above windows	2 @ 43"	1 × 12
Decorative sunburst boards	20 @ 4'	6"-wide red cedar clapboard
Sunburst spacer	2 @ 2'	1 × 6 pine
Sunburst spacer	2 @ 75"	1 × 5 pine
Kick plate	40½"	1 × 8 pine
Fascia	5 @ 16'	2 × 8 pine
Shadow board	5 @ 16'	2 × 4 pine
Window trim	6 @ 55½"	1 × 6 pine
Door casing	2 @ 81", 1 @ 38½"	1 × 5 pine
Doorstop	2 @ 80", 1 @ 36½"	1 × 2 pine
Rear wall battens	2 @ 82½"	¾ × 2" pine*
Under-window battens	40 @ 19"	¾ × 2" pine*
Gable battens	4 @ 11", 17", 23", 29", and 35"	¾ × 2" pine*

Cutting List

DESCRIPTION	QTY./SIZE	MATERIAL
Roofing		
Rear-side sheathing	5 @ 14'	1 × 12 pine
Rear-side sheathing — top ridge piece	14'	1 × 6 pine
Front-side sheathing	2 @ 33", 42¾", 55", 65½", and 76"	1 × 12 pine
Front-side sheathing — top ridge pieces	2 @ 75" and 81½"	1 × 6 pine
Dormer sheathing	2 @ 10½", 20½", 32", 42½", and 53"	1 × 12 pine
Dormer sheathing — top ridge pieces	2 @ 59"	1 × 6 pine
36"-wide roofing	11 @ 12'	Corrugated metal
Ridge cap	22 ft.	
24"-wide valley flashing	20 ft.	Aluminum
Windows		
2'8" screens	6	
3' screens	5	

DESCRIPTION	QTY./SIZE	MATERIAL
Door		
3' heavy-duty screen door	1	
Hardware		
16d common nails	15 lbs	
16d galvanized common nails	12 lbs	
8d galvanized common nails	17 lbs	
6d stainless steel nails	2 lbs	
1⅝" zinc screws	1 lb	
1½" metal roofing screws with rubber gasket, painted to match your roof color	450	
Metal roofing nails or staples	1 lb	
Black spring screen door hinges	2	
2½" decorative black screen door hinges	2	
Black screen door knob and latch	1	

Battens ripped on-site from 2 × 4 lumber

Floor Plan

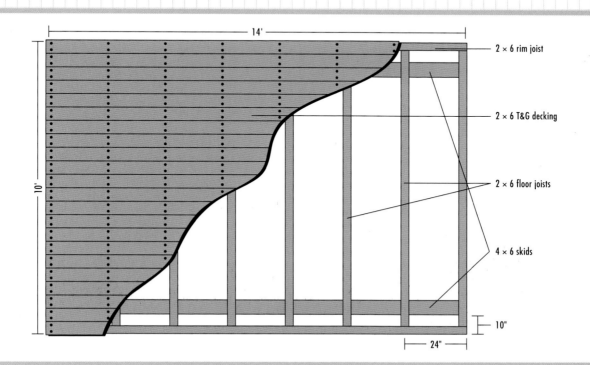

Front Elevation

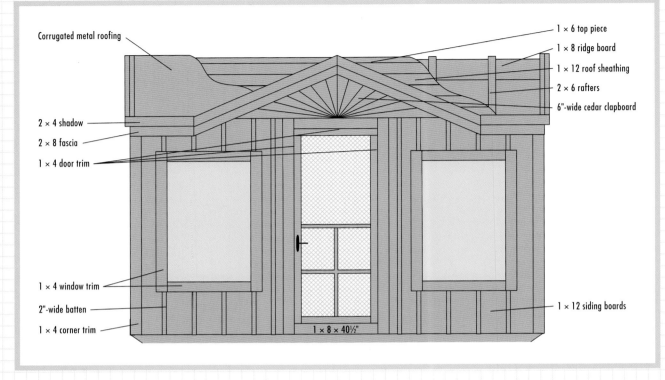

Corrugated metal roofing

1 × 6 top piece

1 × 8 ridge board

1 × 12 roof sheathing

2 × 6 rafters

6"-wide cedar clapboard

2 × 4 shadow

2 × 8 fascia

1 × 4 door trim

1 × 4 window trim

2"-wide batten

1 × 4 corner trim

1 × 8 × 40½"

1 × 12 siding boards

Rear Elevation

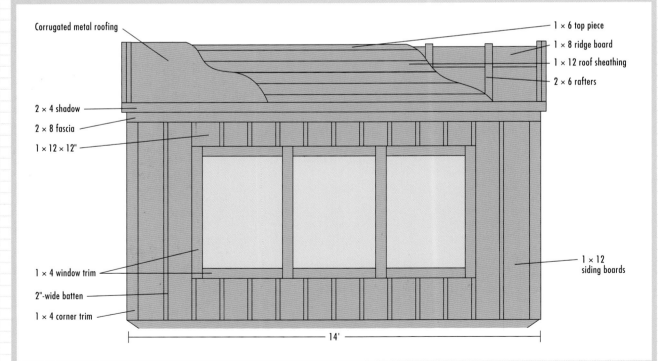

Corrugated metal roofing

1 × 6 top piece

1 × 8 ridge board

1 × 12 roof sheathing

2 × 6 rafters

2 × 4 shadow

2 × 8 fascia

1 × 12 × 12"

1 × 4 window trim

2"-wide batten

1 × 4 corner trim

1 × 12 siding boards

14'

Side Elevation

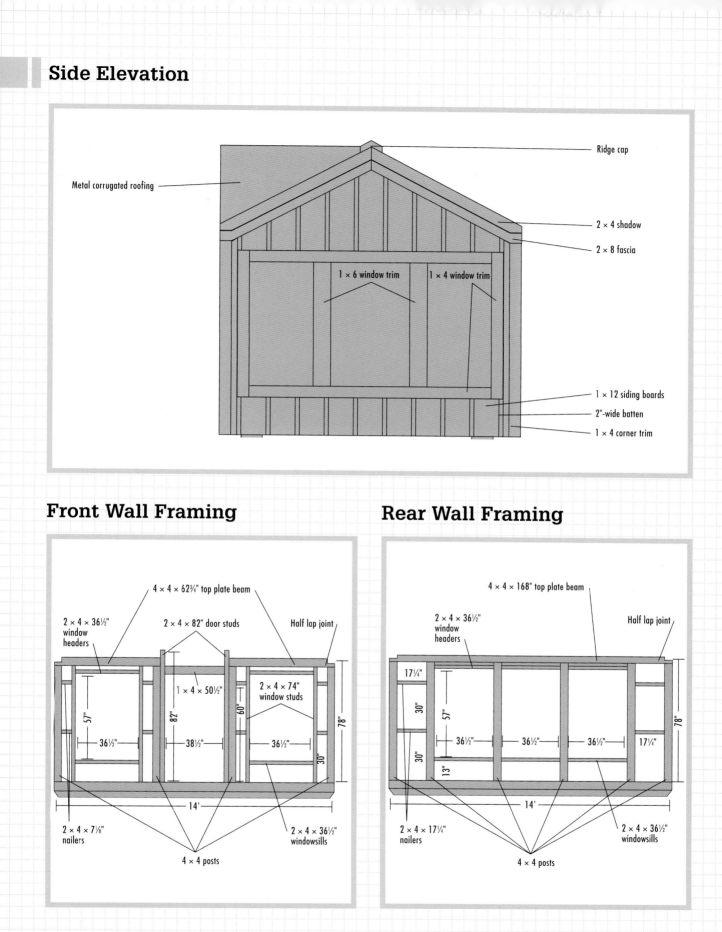

Ridge cap

Metal corrugated roofing

2 × 4 shadow

2 × 8 fascia

1 × 6 window trim

1 × 4 window trim

1 × 12 siding boards

2"-wide batten

1 × 4 corner trim

Front Wall Framing

4 × 4 × 62¾" top plate beam

2 × 4 × 36½" window headers

2 × 4 × 82" door studs

Half lap joint

1 × 4 × 50½"

2 × 4 × 74" window studs

57"

82"

60"

78"

36½"

38½"

36½"

30"

14'

2 × 4 × 7⅛" nailers

4 × 4 posts

2 × 4 × 36½" windowsills

Rear Wall Framing

4 × 4 × 168" top plate beam

2 × 4 × 36½" window headers

Half lap joint

17¼"

30"

57"

30"

13"

36½"

36½"

36½"

17¼"

78"

14'

2 × 4 × 17¼" nailers

4 × 4 posts

2 × 4 × 36½" windowsills

Side Wall Framing

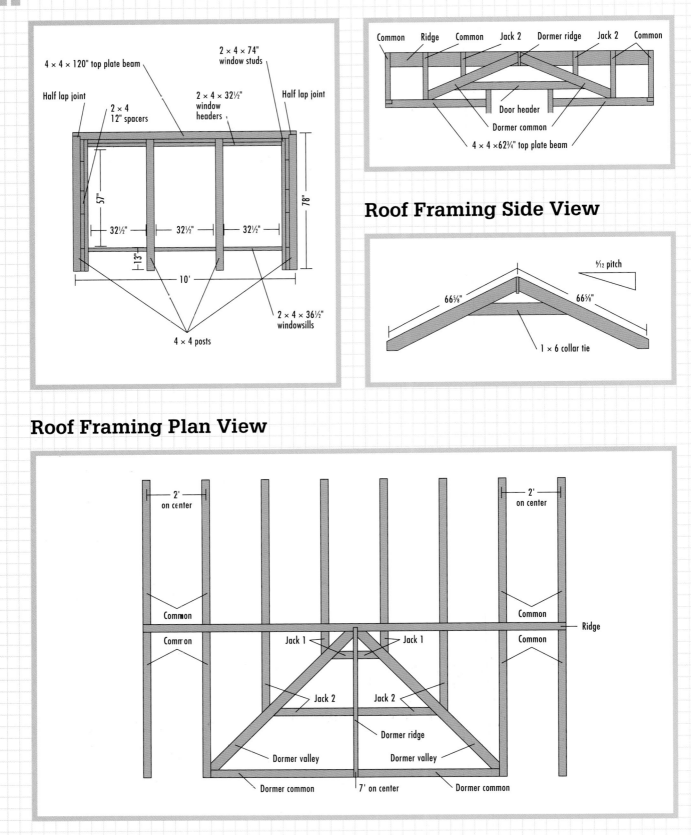

4 × 4 × 120" top plate beam

Half lap joint

2 × 4 12" spacers

2 × 4 × 74" window studs

2 × 4 × 32½" window headers

Half lap joint

57"

32½"   32½"   32½"

13"

78"

10'

2 × 4 × 36½" windowsills

4 × 4 posts

Roof Framing Front View

Common   Ridge   Common   Jack 2   Dormer ridge   Jack 2   Common

Door header

Dormer common

4 × 4 × 62¾" top plate beam

Roof Framing Side View

⁶⁄₁₂ pitch

66⅝"   66⅝"

1 × 6 collar tie

Roof Framing Plan View

2' on center

2' on center

Common   Ridge

Common   Jack 1   Jack 1   Common

Jack 2   Jack 2

Dormer ridge

Dormer valley   Dormer valley

Dormer common   7' on center   Dormer common

Roof Finishing Detail

Corrugated Metal Roofing Cutting Template

Common Rafter Template

Dormer Common Rafter Template

Door Jamb Detail

Door Elevation

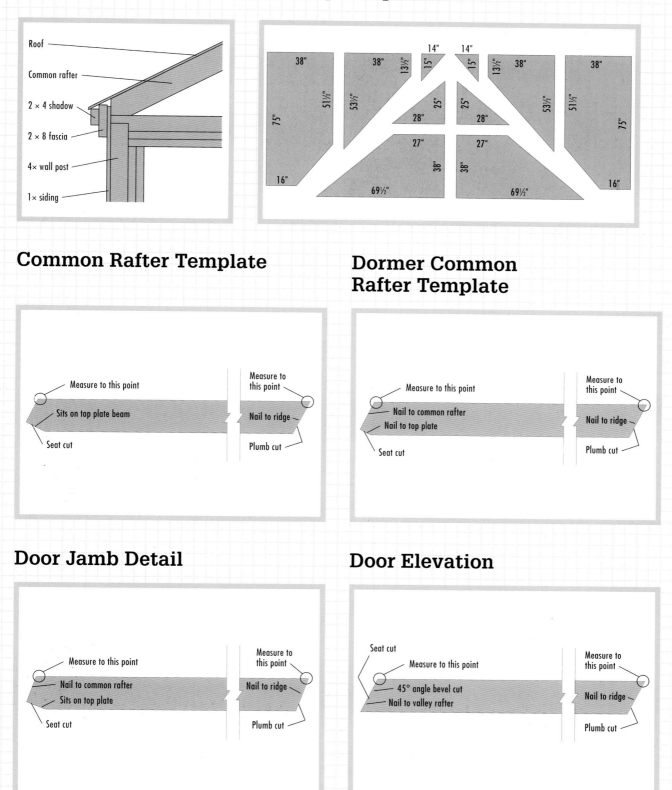

How to Build a Rustic Summerhouse

Prepare the 12 × 16-ft. foundation site with a level, 4"-deep layer of compacted gravel. Measure 12" in from the edges of the foundation site on all sides and outline the building's footprint. Position six concrete blocks approximately 6" within the outlines at the corners to form a rough 9 × 13-ft. footprint for the building to sit upon.

Prepare and position the skids. Cut the 4 × 6 skids (see page 28) to exactly 168" and cut rough 45° angles on the bottom edges of both ends of each skid with a reciprocating saw. Position the skids on the blocks with the angled cut facing down, roughly 10" inside of the outline, checking that they are level and parallel with one another. Cut eight 2 × 6 floor joists at 120" and cut two 2 × 6 rim joists at 168".

Floor joist

Rim joist

Lay out the floor joists perpendicular to the skids, starting at one end and positioning them every 24" on-center, overhanging the skids equally on each side. Nail the rim joists to the floor joists using three 16d common nails at each end. Check for level. Use wood shims under the skids to increase deck height, if necessary. Square the deck frame by measuring across the diagonals. When both corner-to-corner measurements are equal, the floor is square. Secure the squared deck by toenailing each joist to the skids.

Install 2 × 6 tongue-and-groove decking perpendicular to the floor joists. Hold the first piece of decking flush to the rim joists and cut it to fit. Nail decking to each joist with two 16d galvanized common nails. Rip the last piece to fit before installing.

Align the 4 × 4 corner posts (cut to length at 74") flush to the edges of each corner. Toenail each corner post to the deck on both outer sides with three 16d common nails. Use additional nails on the interior sides of the posts, if necessary.

Cut half-lap joints into the 4 × 4 beams with a circular saw and mark wall post and framing locations on beams as follows: for the 14-ft.-long rear top plate beam (see Diagrams, pages 190 to 193).

Place the rear wall top plate beam on the rear wall corner posts, with the half-lap joint and layout markings facing up. Endnail through the half-laps and into the top of the corner posts using three 16d common nails at each post.

(continued)

8

Set both center posts for the front wall. Measuring from the end of the deck, mark the post locations on the deck floor. Set 4 × 4 posts at these locations and toenail them to the deck on the outside using three 16d common nails each.

9

Position each front top plate beam, with the half-lap joint facing up over the corner post (the end over the center posts will not have a lap). Endnail the front top plate beams into the top of the corner posts and toenail into the center posts with three 16d common nails at each end (inset).

10

Attach 120"-long 4 × 4 side wall on the building sides, fitting the half-lap joints face down into the half-lap joints on the front and rear top plate beams. Endnail the side wall top plate into the front and rear top plate beams using three 16d common nails at each end.

11

Set the wall rear and side wall posts at the locations marked on the top plate beams; check for plumb and toenail to the deck and the top plate beam. If necessary, toenail additional nails on the interior sides of the posts to secure them in place. Check the deck for level in multiple places.

12

Temporary bracing

Level and attach 1 × 4 temporary front wall bracing inside the door opening on the inside of the building. Position this board high enough to walk under during the rest of construction and do not remove it until construction is complete.

13

Tack temporary 1 × 4 bracing diagonally on the inside of the side walls between a corner post and the top plate beam. Hold the corner posts perfectly plumb, then position bracing so as not to interfere with attaching the siding or the rafters later on. Do not remove the bracing until construction is complete.

14

Install horizontal nailers on the rear wall; cut four 2 × 4 nailers to 17¼". Measure up from the deck floor between a rear wall corner post and the first interior post and mark nailer locations at 30" and 60". Attach nailers to both posts with their bottom faces flush to these marks by toenailing one 16d common nail into each edge and two nails into one face.

15

Frame the rear wall windows. Install the first window headers tight against the top plate beam in the three gaps between interior posts along the rear wall. Nail the headers directly into the top plate beam. Install the second header tight to the first in the same manner.

(continued)

Install the rear wall windowsills. Measure up from the deck and make a mark at 13" on all interior posts. Toenail the windowsills to the posts with the top face flush to this mark using one 16d common nail on each edge and two on a face.

Begin framing the side walls. Cut 2 × 4 spacers at 12"—these will be nailed directly to the corner posts facing the side wall. Attach one spacer at the top of the post, one at the bottom, and one centered between them; attach with two 8d common nails on each end. Install 74" window studs tight to the spacers; endnail studs to the spacers and toenail to the deck and to the top plate beam.

Frame the side-wall windows by installing a double window header and a windowsill in each gap. Install double window headers as in step 15 and windowsills as in step 16. Install temporary diagonal bracing to all walls as in step 13 (inset).

Install overhead bracing. Plumb all walls and adjust if necessary. Install a long 1 × 4 brace (approximately 10-ft.) between each side wall and the front wall. Attach the brace to the interior front wall posts (flush with the inside edge) and the rear wall top plate beam, directly above the opposite wall post, side-wall framing.

Install the front wall window framing. From each side, measure from the corner and mark positions of window studs on the deck (inset). Cut four window studs to 74" and install at the marks; toenail to the top plate beam and decking. Measuring from the deck, make a mark at 30" and at 60" on each corner post and window stud. Cut 2 × 4 nailers to 7⅛" and install between the corner posts and window studs with their bottom edge flush to these marks. Install the double window header and window sill between the window studs as in steps 15 and 16.

Prepare the door frame by installing two 82"-long 2 × 4 studs tight to the inside of each door post using two 16d common nails at the bottom, top, and center of each stud.

Install the rear-wall siding. Use 1 × 12 pine boards and set siding to hang below rim joists ¼" and at least 4" above the top plate. Attach siding with two 8d galvanized nails at each floor joist, nailer, and top plate. When the wall is finished, snap a chalk line 4" above the top plate and use a circular saw to trim siding along the chalk line. *Note: For this load-bearing wall, do not use siding smaller than 1 × 6.*

Mark and cut a pattern rafter (inset). Test-fit the pattern rafters and make any necessary adjustments before cutting the rest. Crown the 1 × 8 ridge and mark rafter locations every 24" on-center. Attach two 2 × 6 front rafters, one to each end of the side wall. Endnail the ridge to the two front rafters. Attach the rafters on the opposing side wall to the top plate first and then to the ridge. Plumb the rafters.

(continued)

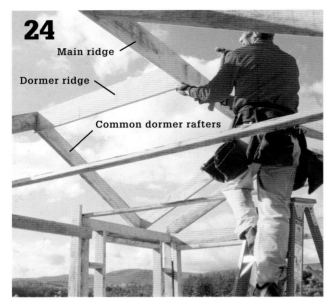

24

Main ridge

Dormer ridge

Common dormer rafters

Install rafters to the rear main wall top plate beam
and the main ridge at 6-ft. and 8-ft. Install 2 × 6 common
dormer rafters to the front wall; first toenail each seat cut
end to the front wall top plate beam at 2-ft. and 12-ft, then
endnail each through the end of the ′ × 8 dormer ridge. Last,
attach the dormer ridge to the main ridge at 7-ft. on-center.
Endnail the dormer ridge through the main ridge using three
8d common nails.

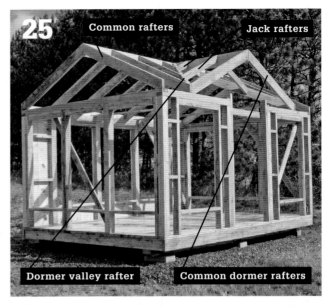

25 Common rafters — Jack rafters

Dormer valley rafter — Common dormer rafters

Install the remaining rafters. Attach front and rear rafters
to the main ridge and to the front and rear top plate beams
at 2-ft. and 12-ft. on-center. Then install dormer valley rafters
to the ridge at the junction of the two ridge poles and to the
front wall top plate beam. Install the remainder of the rear
common rafters and jack rafters as shown in ROOF FRAMING
PLAN VIEW, making sure to install each rafter and its opposite
together to maintain a straight ridge pole.

26

Brace the roof. Once all rafters are installed and you've
double-checked for level, nail temporary bracing from the top
of the main ridge at a 45° angle to a b ock attached to a floor
joist to hold the building square. Do not remove the temporary
bracing until construction is complete.

27

Finishing framing the door. Cut a 2 × 4 header at 93",
and miter-cut the ends at 63° to fit within the dormer rafters.
Position the door header on top of the door studs, tight within
the dormer rafters, and toenail in place. Cut a second door
header at 112" (with the same 63° miter-cut ends); position the
second door header behind the first so it extends to the outer
edge of the dormer rafters. Endnail to the dormer rafters on
both ends.

28

Ridge

Collar tie

Cut four 1 × 6 collar ties at 48" and miter-cut the ends at 26½°. Install collar ties tight to the ridge on the 2-ft., 4-ft., 10-ft., and 12-ft. rafters with five 8d common nails per rafter. Check each tie for level before fastening it.

29

Trim line

Install 1 × 12 siding on the side and front walls, setting it to hang below the rim joists ¼". Cut each siding piece to fit flush to the rafters and attach at the rim joist, horizontal nailer, top plate and rafters with four 8d galvanized common nails at each position. Allow front wall siding to extend above the top plate at least 4". Trim siding on the ends of the front wall as in step 22.

30

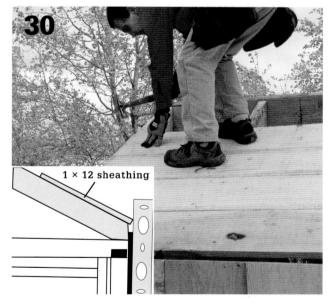

1 × 12 sheathing

Install 1 × 12 roof decking, beginning at the eave and working your way toward the ridge. Position the first piece flush with the rafter edge on the gable side; to position the decking on the eave side, hold a level or straightedge flush with the siding and place the first piece flush with the level. Attach decking with four 8d nails at each rafter. Install the rest of the boards flush with the first piece, cutting to fit.

31

Install the decorative sunburst above the door. Nail a level 1 × 6 piece of clapboard 3" above the door, flush to the subfascia on both sides. Blindnail to the siding using 6d stainless steel nails. Install the next piece with one end at the center of the first piece and the other end fanned up about 3" toward the roof, then install the opposing piece. Continue to install clapboard in this fashion as you move up toward the center; pieces will overlap at the bottom, reaching a thickness of about 6" when the sunburst is complete. Cap the sunburst by cutting and installing a piece to cover the central seam.

(continued)

32

Shadow

Fascia

Apply the 2 × 8 pine fascia and 2 × 4 shadow. Install fascia to the two side walls using the common rafter templates to match the angle of the rafters. Attach with three 16d galvanized common nails spaced every 24" on-center. Install fascia on the front and rear walls by nailing to a spacer at each rafter location with three 16d galvanized common nails. Install shadow board using the same technique, nailing it in place with two 16d galvanized common nails at each rafter (or every 24" on-center on the side walls).

33

Install the door, window, and corner trim. First, install the vertical 1 × 4 corner trim flush on the gable ends. Install the front and rear wall corner trim flush to the gable corner trim. Next, install the 1 × 5 door jamb trim to cover the siding and door framing on the interior of the door. Nail this in place. Finally, attach 1 × 4 exterior window and door trim to the siding. Set the window trim to overhang 1" inside the frame and door trim flush with the jamb trim.

34

Rip 2" pine stock into strips ¾- to ⅝"-thick to create the siding battens. Install the battens over the seams where two siding boards meet. Cut battens to fit up to the fascia and above and below the window trim. Attach them using 8d galvanized common nails following the nailing pattern of the siding. Avoid nailing into knots.

Install the corrugated metal roofing. First, install metal flashing in the valleys of the dormer, starting at the eaves using roofing nails spaced every 12". Leave the flashing at least 2" long at both the ridge and the eave overhang. Cut metal roofing according to the CORRUGATED METAL ROOFING CUTTING TEMPLATE on page 193; to cut roofing in the flats, score with a utility knife on the white side and flex until it snaps. To cut over ridges, use a circular saw with a metal abrasive blade. Install the first piece, allowing it to hang over the shadow board by 2" on both the gable end and the bearing wall. Screw the metal roofing into the sheathing with 1½" metal roofing screws with a rubber gasket, positioning the screws in the center of the flats and on all seams. Cut metal flashing with a utility knife as you install metal roofing over it. *Tip: Nail into the ridge of the roofing material only where two pieces of metal overlap.*

Install the ridge cap, fastening it into the ridges of the roofing material only. (Fastening the ridge cap in the flats will cause the roofing material to dent.) Attach the ridge with metal roofing screws every 8 to 12" on-center. Trim the ridge cap for length.

Install the screen door and window screens. Attach the door according to the manufacturer's instructions. Use adjustable spring hinges, if desired. Install a door knob and latch. Install window screens so they set tight against the exterior trim. You may need to have window screens custom-made. Allow the building to cure for one season and then paint or stain as desired.

Gothic Playhouse

Playhouses are all about stirring the imagination. Loaded with fancy American Gothic details, this charming little house makes a special play home for kids and an attractive backyard feature for adults. In addition to its architectural character (see Gothic Style, below), what makes this a great playhouse design is its size—the enclosed house measures 5 × 7½ ft. and includes a 5-ft.-tall door and plenty of headroom inside. This means your kids will likely "outgrow" the playhouse before they get too big for it. And you can always give the house a second life as a storage shed.

At the front of the house is a 30"-deep porch complete with real decking boards and a nicely decorated railing. Each side wall features a window and flower box, and the "foundation" has the look of stone created by wood blocks applied to the floor framing. All of these features are optional, but each one adds to the charm of this well-appointed playhouse.

As shown here, the floor of the playhouse is anchored to four 4 × 4 posts buried in the ground.

As an alternative, you can set the playhouse on 4 × 6 timber skids. Another custom variation you might consider is in the styling of the verge boards (the gingerbread gable trim). Instead of using the provided pattern, you can create a cardboard template of your own design. Architectural plan and pattern books from the Gothic period are full of inspiration for decorative ideas.

Gothic Style ▶

The architectural style known as American Gothic (also called Gothic Revival and Carpenter Gothic) dates back to the 1830s and essentially marks the beginning of the Victorian period in American home design. Adapted from a similar movement in England, Gothic style was inspired by the ornately decorated stone cathedrals found throughout Europe. The style quickly evolved in America as thrifty carpenters learned to re-create and reinterpret the original decorative motifs using wood instead of stone.

American Gothic's most characteristic feature is the steeply pitched roof with fancy scroll-cut bargeboards, or verge boards, which gave the style its popular nickname, "gingerbread." Other typical features found on Gothic homes (and the Gothic Playhouse) include board-and-batten siding, doors and windows shaped with Gothic arches, and spires or finials adorning roof peaks.

Hosting tea with the Mad Hatter or fending off dragons around the gables; the gothic playhouse is all about sparking the imagination.

Cutting List

DESCRIPTION	QTY./SIZE	MATERIAL
Foundation/Floor		
Drainage material	1 cu. yd.	Compactible gravel
Foundation posts	4 @ field measure	4 × 4 pressure-treated landscape timbers
Concrete	Field measure	3,000 psi concrete
Rim joists	3 @ 10', 1 @ 8'	2 × 12 pressure-treated, rated for ground contact
Floor joists	1 @ 10', 2 @ 8'	2 × 6 pressure-treated
Box sills (rim joists)	2 @ 12'	2 × 4 pressure-treated
Floor sheathing	2 sheets @ 4 × 8'	¾" ext.-grade plywood
Porch decking	5 @ 10'	1 × 6 pressure-treated decking
Foundation "stones"	7 @ 10'	⁵⁄₄ × 6" treated decking w/radius edge (R.E.D.), rated for ground contact
Framing		
Wall framing & railings	29 @ 12'	2 × 4
Rafters & spacers	7 @ 12'	2 × 4
Ridge board	1 @ 8'	1 × 6
Collar ties	1 @ 10'	1 × 4
Exterior Finishes		
Siding, window boxes & door trim	26 @ 10'	1 × 8 pressure-treated or cedar
Battens & trim	30 @ 8'	1 × 2 pressure-treated or cedar
Door panel, verge boards & fascia	10 @ 10'	1 × 6 pressure-treated or cedar
Door braces, trim & railing trim	2 @ 10'	1 × 4 pressure-treated or cedar
Railing balusters	4 @ 8'	2 × 2 pressure-treated or cedar
Window stops	2 @ 8'	⅜" pressure-treated or cedar quarter-round molding
Window glazing (optional)	4 @ 20 × 9½'	¼" plastic glazing
Spire		
Post	1 @ 8'	4 × 4 pressure-treated
Trim	1 @ 4'	1 × 2 pressure-treated

DESCRIPTION	QTY./SIZE	MATERIAL
Molding	1 @ 4'	Cap molding, pressure-treated
Balls	2 @ 3"-dia.	Wooden sphere, pressure-treated
Roofing		
Sheathing	4 sheets @ 4 × 8'	½" exterior-grade plywood roof sheathing
15# building paper	1 roll	
Drip edge	40 linear ft.	Metal drip edge
Shingles	1 square	Asphalt shingles — 250# per sq. min.
Fasteners & Hardware		
16d galvanized common nails	3½ lbs.	
16d common nails	5 lbs.	
10d common nails (for double top plates)	½ lb.	
10d galvanized finish/casing nails	4 lbs.	
8d galvanized common nails	1 lb.	
8d box nails	2 lbs.	
8d galvanized siding nails	8 lbs.	
1" galvanized roofing nails	3 lbs.	
2" deck screws (for porch decking)	1 lb.	
6d galvanized finish nails	2 lbs.	
3½" galvanized wood screws	24 screws	
1¼" galvanized wood screws	12 screws	
Dowel screws (for spire)	3 screws	Galvanized dowel screws
Lag screws w/washers	2 @ 6"	½" galvanized lag screws
Door hinges w/screws	3	Corrosion-resistant hinges
Door handle/latch	1	
Exterior wood glue		
Clear exterior caulk (for optional window panes)		
Construction adhesive		

Section

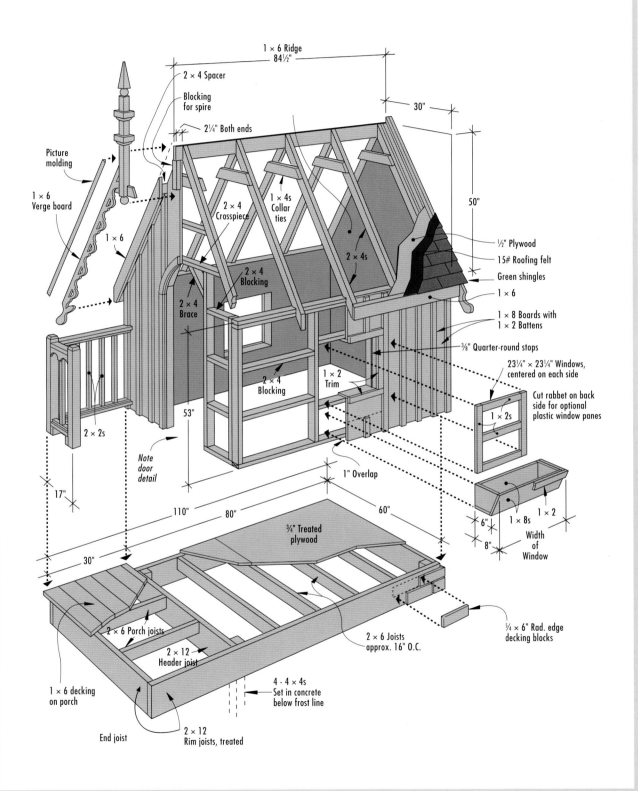

1 × 6 Ridge
84½"

2 × 4 Spacer

Blocking
for spire

2¼" Both ends

Picture
molding

30"

1 × 6
Verge board

50"

1 × 6

2 × 4
Crosspiece

1 × 4s
Collar
ties

½" Plywood

15# Roofing felt

2 × 4s

Green shingles

2 × 4
Blocking

1 × 6

1 × 8 Boards with
1 × 2 Battens

2 × 4
Brace

⅜" Quarter-round stops

23¼" × 23¼" Windows,
centered on each side

2 × 4
Blocking

1 × 2
Trim

Cut rabbet on back
side for optional
plastic window panes

1 × 2s

2 × 2s

53"

Note
door
detail

1" Overlap

1 × 2

6"

1 × 8s 1 × 2

8"

Width
of
Window

17"

110"

80"

60"

¾" Treated
plywood

30"

¼ × 6" Rad. edge
decking blocks

2 × 6 Porch joists

2 × 6 Joists
approx. 16" O.C.

2 × 12
Header joist

1 × 6 decking
on porch

4 - 4 × 4s
Set in concrete
below frost line

End joist

2 × 12
Rim joists, treated

Floor Plan

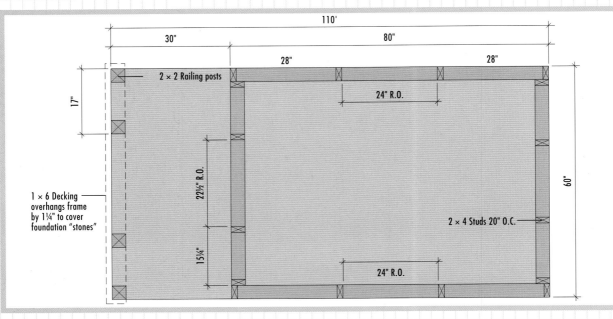

110'

30" | 80"

28" | 28"

2 × 2 Railing posts

17"

24" R.O.

22½" R.O.

1 × 6 Decking
overhangs frame
by 1¼" to cover
foundation "stones"

15¼"

60"

2 × 4 Studs 20" O.C.

24" R.O.

Verge Board Template

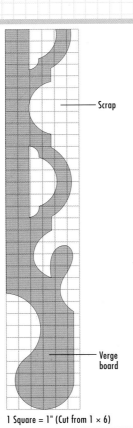

Scrap

Verge board

1 Square = 1" (Cut from 1 × 6)

Deck Railing Detail

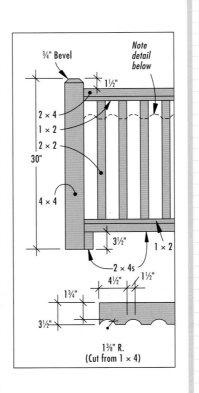

¾" Bevel

Note detail below

1½"

2 × 4
1 × 2
2 × 2
30"

4 × 4

3½"

1 × 2

2 × 4s

4½" | 1½"

1¾"

3½"

1⅜" R.
(Cut from 1 × 4)

Spire Detail

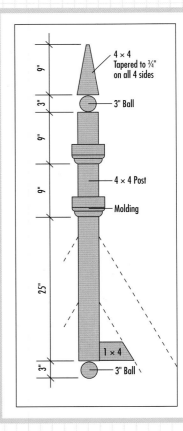

4 × 4
Tapered to ¾"
on all 4 sides

9"

3" | 3" Ball

9"

9" | 4 × 4 Post

Molding

25"

1 × 4

3" | 3" Ball

Door Detail

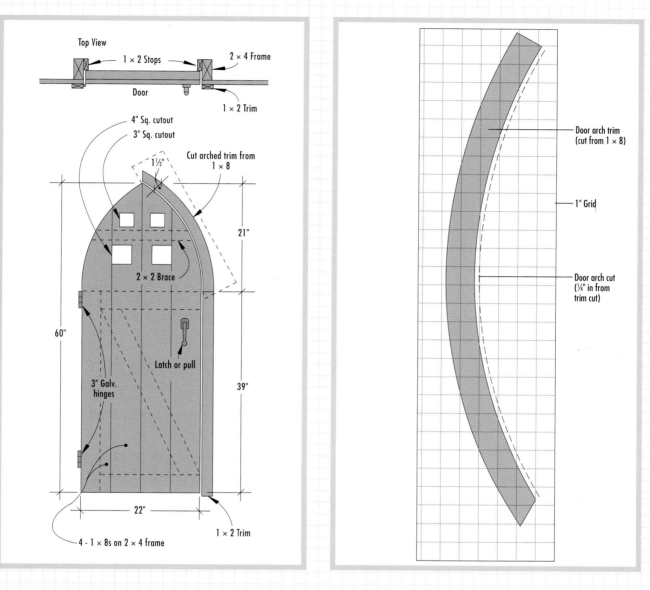

Top View

1 × 2 Stops
2 × 4 Frame
Door
1 × 2 Trim

4" Sq. cutout
3" Sq. cutout
Cut arched trim from 1 × 8
1½"
21"
2 × 2 Brace
Latch or pull
60"
39"
3" Galv. hinges
22"
4 - 1 × 8s on 2 × 4 frame
1 × 2 Trim

Door Arch Template

Door arch trim (cut from 1 × 8)

1" Grid

Door arch cut (¼" in from trim cut)

Board & Batten Detail

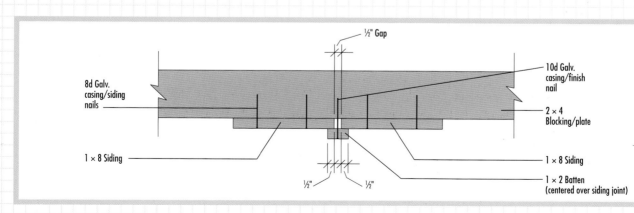

½" Gap

8d Galv. casing/siding nails

10d Galv. casing/finish nail

2 × 4 Blocking/plate

1 × 8 Siding

1 × 8 Siding

1 × 2 Batten (centered over siding joint)

½"   ½"

Front Framing

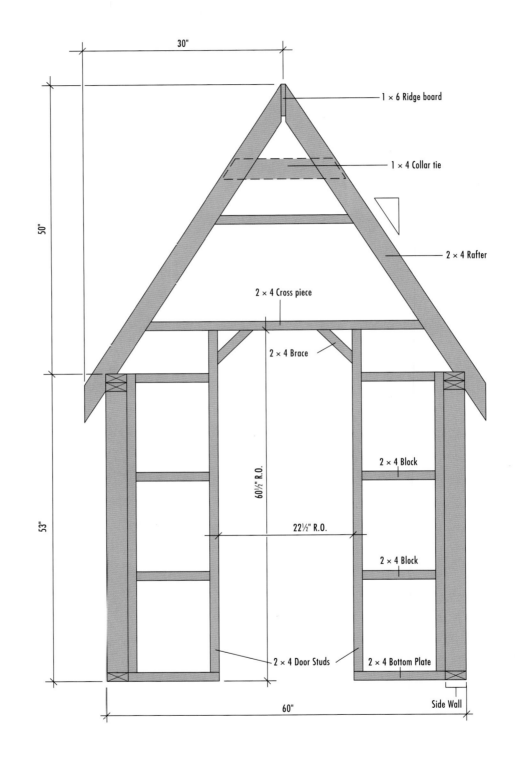

30"

1 × 6 Ridge board

1 × 4 Collar tie

2 × 4 Rafter

50"

2 × 4 Cross piece

2 × 4 Brace

2 × 4 Block

60½" R.O.

53"

22½" R.O.

2 × 4 Block

2 × 4 Door Studs

2 × 4 Bottom Plate

60"

Side Wall

Floor Framing Plan

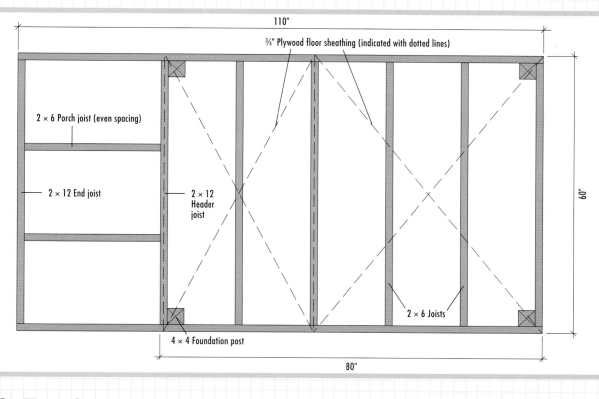

110"

¾" Plywood floor sheathing (indicated with dotted lines)

2 × 6 Porch joist (even spacing)

2 × 12 End joist

2 × 12 Header joist

60"

2 × 6 Joists

4 × 4 Foundation post

80"

Side Framing

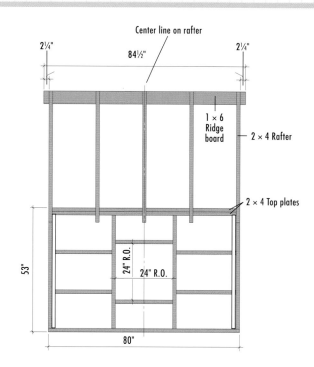

Center line on rafter

2¼"   84½"   2¼"

1 × 6 Ridge board

2 × 4 Rafter

2 × 4 Top plates

53"

24" R.O.

24" R.O.

80"

Rafter Template

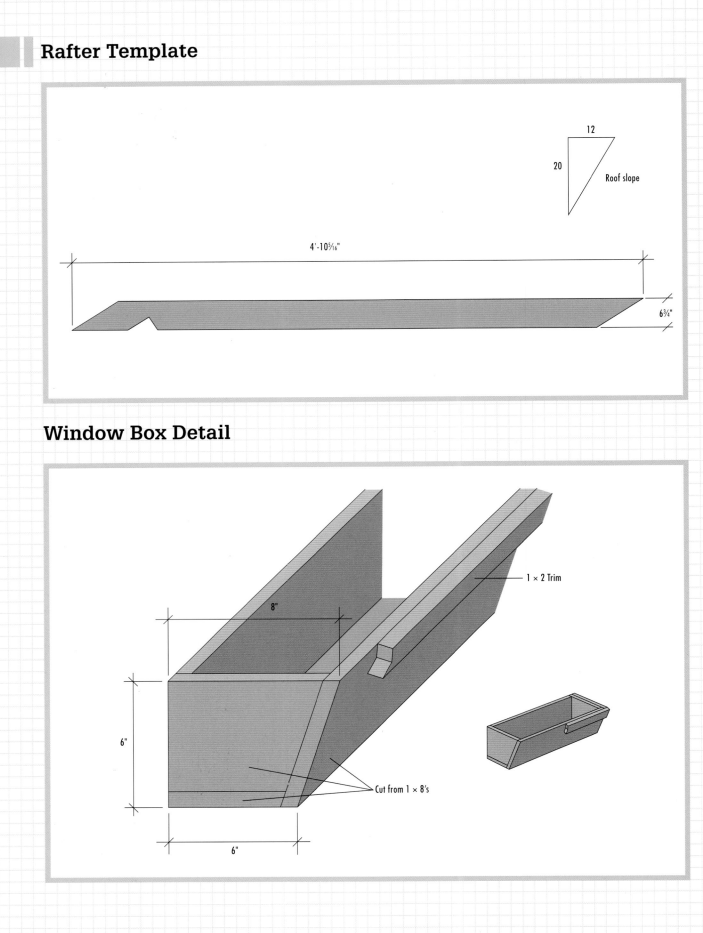

12

20

Roof slope

4'-10⁵⁄₁₆"

6¾"

Window Box Detail

8"

1 × 2 Trim

6"

6"

Cut from 1 × 8's

How to Build the Gothic Playhouse

Set up perpendicular mason's lines and batter boards to plot out the excavation area and the post hole locations, as shown in FLOOR FRAMING PLAN (page 211). Excavate and grade the construction area, preparing for a 4"-thick gravel base. Dig 12"-dia. holes to a depth below the frost line, plus 4". Add 4" of gravel to each hole. Set the posts in concrete so they extend about 10" above the ground.

After the concrete dries (overnight) add compactible gravel and tamp it down so it is 4" thick and flat. Cut two 2 × 12 rim joists for the floor frame, two 2 × 12 end joists and one header joist. Cut four 2 × 6 joists at 57" and two porch joists at 27¾". Assemble the floor frame with 16d galvanized common nails following FLOOR FRAMING PLAN.

Make sure the frame is square and level (prop it up temporarily), and then fasten it to the posts with 16d galvanized common nails.

Cover the interior floor with plywood, starting at the rear end. Trim the second piece so it covers ½ of the header joist. Install the 1 × 6 porch decking starting at the front edge and leaving a ⅛" gap between boards. Extend the porch decking 1¼" beyond the front and sides of the floor frame.

(continued)

Frame the side walls as shown in the SIDE FRAMING (page 211) and FLOOR PLAN (page 208). Each wall has four 2 × 4 studs at 48½", a top and bottom plate at 80", and a 2 × 4 window header and sill at 24". Install the horizontal 2 × 4 blocking, spaced evenly between the plates. Install only one top plate per wall at this time.

Build the rear wall. Raise the side and rear walls, and fasten them to each other and to the floor frame. Add double top plates. Both sidewall top plates should stop flush with the end stud at the front of the wall.

To frame the front wall, cut two treated bottom plates at 15¼", two end studs at 51½" and two door studs at 59". Cut a 2 × 4 crosspiece and two braces, mitering the brace ends at 45°. Cut six 2 × 4 blocks at 12¼". Assemble the wall as shown in the FRONT FRAMING (page 210). Raise the front wall and fasten it to the floor and sidewall frames.

Cut one set of 2 × 4 pattern rafters following the RAFTER TEMPLATE (page 212). Test-fit the rafters and make any necessary adjustments. Use one of the pattern rafters to mark and cut the remaining eight rafters. Also cut four 2 × 4 spacers—these should match the rafters but have no bird's-mouth cuts.

Cut the ridge board to size and mark the rafter layout following the SIDE FRAMING, and then screw the rafters to the ridge. Cut five 1 × 4 collar ties, mitering the ends at 31°. Fasten the collar ties across each set of rafters so the ends of the ties are flush with the rafter edges. Fasten the 2 × 4 crosspiece above the door to the two end rafters. Install remaining crosspieces as in the FRONT/REAR FRAMING.

Install the 1 × 8 siding boards so they overlap the floor frame by 1" at the bottom and extend to the tops of the side walls, and to the tops of the rafters on the front and rear walls. Gap the boards ½", and fasten them to the framing with pairs of 8d galvanized casing nails or siding nails. Install the four 2 × 4 spacers on top of the siding at the front and rear so they match the rafter placement.

Cut the arched sections of door trim from 1 × 8 lumber, following the arch template (page 209). Install the arched pieces and straight 1 × 2 side pieces flush with the inside of the door opening. Wrap the window openings with ripped 1 × 6 boards, and then frame the outsides of the openings with 1 × 2 trim. Install a 1 × 2 batten over each siding joint as shown in step 10.

Build the 1 × 2 window frames to fit snugly inside the trimmed openings. Assemble the parts with exterior wood glue and galvanized finish nails. If desired, cut a ¼" rabbet in the back side and install plastic windowpanes with silicone caulk. Secure the window frames in the openings with ⅜" quarter-round molding. Construct the window boxes as shown in the WINDOW BOX DETAIL (page 212). Install the boxes below the windows with 1¼" screws.

(continued)

To build the spire, start by drawing a line around a 4 × 4 post, 9" from one end. Draw cutting lines to taper each side down to ¾", as shown in the SPIRE DETAIL (page 208). Taper the end with a circular saw or handsaw, and then cut off the point at the 9" mark. Cut the post at 43". Add 1 × 2 trim and cap molding as shown in the detail, mitering the ends at the corners. Drill centered pilot holes into the post, balls, and point, and join the parts with dowel screws.

To cut the verge boards, enlarge the VERGE BOARD TEMPLATE (page 208) on a photocopier so the squares measure 1". Draw the pattern on a 1 × 6. Cut the board with a jigsaw. Test-fit the board and adjust as needed. Use the cut board as a pattern to mark and cut the remaining verge boards. Install the boards over the front and rear fascia, then add picture molding along the top edges.

Add a 1 × 2 block under the front end of the ridge board. Center the spire at the roof peak, drill pilot holes, and anchor the post with 6" lag screws. Cut and install the 1 × 6 front fascia to run from the spire to the rafter ends, keeping the fascia ½" above the tops of the rafters. Install the rear fascia so it covers the ridge board. Cut and install two 1 × 4 brackets to fit between the spire post and front fascia, as shown in the SPIRE DETAIL.

Cut the 1 × 6 eave fascia to fit between the verge boards, and install it so it will be flush with the top of the roof sheathing. Cut and install the roof sheathing. Add building paper, metal drip edge, and asphalt shingles.

Mark the deck post locations 1¼" in from the ends and front edge of the porch decking, as shown in the FLOOR PLAN. Cut four 4 × 4 railing posts at 30". Bevel the top edges of the posts at 45°, as shown in DECK RAILING DETAIL (page 208). Fasten the posts to the decking and floor frame with 3½" screws. Cut six 2 × 4 treated blocks at 3½". Fasten these to the bottoms of the posts, on the sides that will receive the railings.

Assemble the railing sections following the DECK RAILING DETAIL. Each section has a 2 × 4 top and bottom rail, two 1 × 2 nailers, and 2 × 2 balusters spaced so the edges of the balusters are no more than 4" apart. You can build the sections completely and then fasten them to the posts and front wall, or you can construct them in place starting with the rails. Cut the shaped trim boards from 1 × 4 lumber, using a jigsaw. Notch the rails to fit around the house battens as needed.

Construct the door with 1 × 6 boards fastened to 2 × 4 Z-bracing, as shown in the DOOR DETAIL. Fasten the boards to the bracing with glue and 6d finish nails. Cut the square notches and the top of the door with a jigsaw. Add the 2 × 2 brace as shown. Install the door with two hinges, leaving a ¼" gap all around. Add a knob or latch as desired.

Make the foundation "stones" by cutting 116 6"-lengths of ⁵⁄₄ × 6 deck boards (the pieces in the top row must be ripped down 1"). Round over the cut edges of all pieces with a router. Attach the top row of stones using construction adhesive and 6d galvanized finish nails. Install the bottom row, starting with a half-piece to create a staggered joint pattern. If desired, finish the playhouse interior with plywood or tongue-and-groove siding.

Metal & Wood Kit Sheds

The following pages walk you through the steps of building two new sheds from kits. The metal shed measures 8 × 9 ft. and comes with every piece in the main building pre-cut and pre-drilled. All you need is a ladder and a few hand tools for assembly. The wood shed is a cedar building with panelized construction—most of the major elements come in preassembled sections. The walls panels have exterior siding installed, and the roof sections are already shingled. For both sheds, the pieces are lightweight and maneuverable, but it helps to have at least two people for fitting everything together.

As with most kits, these sheds do not include foundations as part of the standard package. The metal shed can be built on top of a patio surface or out in the yard, with or without an optional floor. The wood shed comes with a complete wood floor, but the building needs a standard foundation, such as wooden skid, concrete block, or concrete slab foundation. To help keep either type of shed level and to reduce moisture from ground contact, it's a good idea to build it over a bed of compacted gravel. A 4"-deep bed that extends about 6" beyond the building footprint makes for a stable foundation and helps keep the interior dry throughout the seasons.

Before you purchase a shed kit, check with your local building department to learn about restrictions that affect your project. It's recommended—and often required—that lightweight metal sheds be anchored to the ground. Shed manufacturers offer different anchoring systems, including cables for tethering the shed into soil, and concrete anchors for tying into a concrete slab.

Kit sheds offer the storage you need, a quick build, and an attractive addition to your backyard. The metal shed kit shown here is constructed on pages 222 to 227.

This all-cedar kit shed is constructed on pages 228 to 235.

Building a Metal or Wood Kit Shed

If you need an outbuilding but don't have the time or inclination to build one from scratch, a kit shed is the answer. Today's kit sheds are available in a wide range of materials, sizes, and styles—from snap-together plastic lockers to Norwegian pine cabins with divided-light windows and loads of architectural details. Equally diverse is the range of quality and prices for shed kits. One thing to keep in mind when choosing a shed is that much of what you're paying for is the materials and the ease of installation. Better kits are made with quality, long-lasting materials, and many come largely preassembled. Most of the features discussed below will have an impact on a shed's cost.

The best place to start shopping for shed kits is on the Internet. Large manufacturers and small-shop custom designers alike have websites featuring their products and available options. A quick online search should help you narrow down your choices to sheds that fit your needs and budget. From there, you can visit local dealers or builders to view assembled sheds firsthand. When figuring cost, be sure to factor in all aspects of the project, including the foundation, extra hardware, tools you don't already own, and paint and other finishes not included with your kit.

High-tech plastics, like polyethylene and vinyl are often combined with steel and other rigid materials to create tough, weather-resistant—and washable—kit buildings.

If you're looking for something special, higher-end shed kits allow you to break with convention without breaking your budget on a custom-built structure.

Features to Consider ▸

Here are some of the key elements to check out before purchasing a kit shed:

MATERIALS

Shed kits are made of wood, metal, vinyl, various plastic compounds, or any combination thereof. Consider aesthetics, of course, but also durability and appropriateness for your climate. For example, check the snow load rating on the roof if you live in a snowy climate, or inquire about the material's UV resistance if your shed will receive heavy sun exposure. The finish on metal sheds is important for durability. Protective finishes include paint, powder-coating, and vinyl. For wood sheds, consider all of the materials, from the framing to the siding, roofing, and trimwork.

EXTRA FEATURES

Do you want a shed with windows or a skylight? Some kits come with these features, while others offer them as optional add-ons. For a shed workshop, office, or other workspace where you'll be spending a lot of time, consider the livability and practicality of the interior space, and shop accordingly for special features.

WHAT'S INCLUDED?

Many kits do not include foundations or floors, and floors are commonly available as extras. Other elements that may not be included:

- Paint, stain, etc.—Also, some sheds come pre-painted (or pre-primed), but you won't want to pay extra for a nice paint job if you plan to paint the shed to match your house.
- Roofing—Often the plywood roof sheathing is included but not the building paper, drip edge, or shingles.

Most shed kits include hardware (nails, screws) for assembling the building, but always check this to make sure.

ASSEMBLY

Many kit manufacturers have downloadable assembly instructions on their websites, so you can really see what's involved in putting their shed together. Assembly of wood sheds varies considerably among manufacturers—the kit may arrive as a bundle of pre-cut lumber or with screw-together prefabricated panels. Easy-assembly models may have wall siding and roof shingles already installed onto panels.

EXTENDERS

Some kits offer the option of extending the main building with extenders, or expansion kits, making it easy to turn an 8 × 10-ft. shed into a 10 × 12-ft. shed, for example.

FOUNDATION

Check with the manufacturer for recommended foundation types to use under their sheds. The foundations shown in the Building Basics section (page 22) should be appropriate for most kit sheds.

Shed hardware kits make it easy to build a shed from scratch. Using the structural gussets and framing connectors, you avoid tricky rafter cuts and roof assembly. Many hardware kits come with lumber cutting lists so you can build the shed to the desired size without using plans.

How to Assemble a Metal Kit Shed

Prepare the building site by leveling and grading as needed, and then excavating and adding a 4"-thick layer of compactible gravel. If desired, apply landscape fabric under the gravel to inhibit weed growth. Compact the gravel with a tamper and use a level and a long, straight 2 × 4 to make sure the area is flat and level.

Note: Always wear work gloves when handling shed parts—the metal edges can be very sharp. Begin by assembling the floor kit according to the manufacturer's directions—these will vary quite a bit among models, even within the same manufacturer. Be sure that the floor system parts are arranged so the door is located where you wish it to be. Do not fasten the pieces at this stage.

Once you've laid out the floor system parts, check to make sure they're square before you begin fastening them. Measuring the diagonals to see if they're the same is a quick and easy way to check for square.

Fasten the floor system parts together with kit connectors once you've established that the floor is square. Anchor the floor to the site if your kit suggests. Some kits are designed to be anchored after full assembly is completed.

Begin installing the wall panels according to the instructions. Most panels are predrilled for fasteners, so the main trick is to make sure the fastener holes align between panels and with the floor.

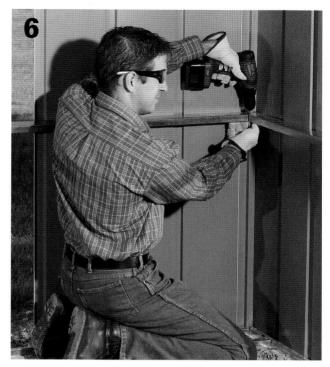

Tack together mating corner panels on at least two adjacent corners. If your frame stiffeners require assembly, have them ready to go before you form the corners. With a helper, attach the frame stiffener rails to the corner panels.

Install the remaining fasteners at the shed corners once you've established that the corners all are square.

Lay out the parts for assembling the roof beams and the upper side frames and confirm that they fit together properly. Then, join the assemblies with the fasteners provided.

(continued)

9

Attach the moving and nonmoving parts for the upper door track to the side frames if your shed has sliding doors.

10

Fasten the shed panels to the top frames, making sure that any fasteners holes are aligned and that crimped tabs are snapped together correctly.

11

Fill in the wall panels between the completed corners, attaching them to the frames with the provided fasteners. Take care not to overdrive the fasteners.

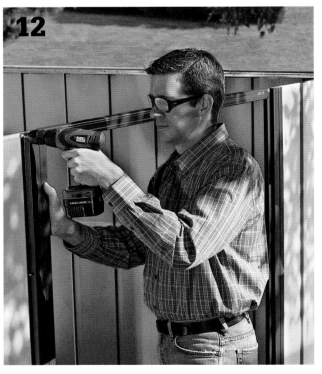

12

Fasten the doorframe trim pieces to the frames to finish the door opening. If the fasteners are colored to match the trim, make sure you choose the correct ones.

Insert the shed gable panels into the side frames and the door track and slide them together so the fastener holes are aligned. Attach the panels with the provided fasteners.

Fit the main roof beam into the clips or other fittings on the gable panels. Have a helper hold the free end of the beam. Position the beam and secure it to both gable ends before attaching it.

Drive fasteners to affix the roof beam to the gable ends and install any supplementary support hardware for the beam, such as gussets or angle braces.

(continued)

Begin installing the roof panels at one end, fastening them to the roof beam and to the top flanges of the side frames.

Apply weatherstripping tape to the top ends of the roof panels to seal the joints before you attach the overlapping roof panels. If your kit does not include weatherstripping tape, look for adhesive-backed foam tape in the weatherstripping products section of your local building center.

As the overlapping roof panels are installed and sealed, attach the roof cap sections at the roof ridge to cover the panel overlaps. Seal as directed. *Note: Completing one section at a time allows you to access subsequent sections from below so you don't risk damaging the roof.*

Attach the peak caps to cover the openings at the ends of the roof cap and then install the roof trim pieces at the bottoms of the roof panels, tucking the flanges or tabs into the roof as directed. Install plywood floor, according to manufacturer instructions.

20

Assemble the doors, paying close attention to right/left differences on double doors. Attach hinges for swinging doors and rollers for sliding doors.

21

Install door tracks and door roller hardware on the floor as directed and then install the doors according to the manufacturer's instructions. Test the action of the doors and make adjustments so the doors roll or swing smoothly and are aligned properly.

Tips for Maintaining a Metal Shed ▸

Touch up scratches or any exposed metal as soon as possible to prevent rust. Clean the area with a wire brush, and then apply a paint recommended by the shed's manufacturer.

Inspect your shed once or twice a year and tighten loose screws, bolts, and other hardware. Loose connections lead to premature wear.

Sweep off the roof to remove wet leaves and debris, which can be hard on the finish. Also clear the roof after heavy snowfall to reduce the risk of collapse.

Seal open seams and other potential entry points for water with silicone caulk. Keep the shed's doors closed and latched to prevent damage from wind gusts.

Anchor the Shed ▸

Metal sheds tend to be light in weight and require secure anchoring to the ground, generally with an anchor kit that may be sold separately by your kit manufacturer. There are many ways to accomplish this. The method you choose depends mostly on the type of base you've built on, be it concrete or wood or gravel. On concrete and wood bases, look for corner gusset anchors that are attached directly to the floor frame and then fastened with landscape screws (wood) or masonry anchors driven into concrete. Sheds that have been built on a gravel or dirt base can be anchored with auger-type anchors that are driven into the ground just outside the shed. You'll need to anchor the shed on at least two sides. Once the anchors are driven, cables are strung through the shed so they are connected to the roof beam. The ends of the cables should exit the shed at ground level and then be attached to the anchors with cable clamps.

How to Build a Wood Kit Shed

Prepare the base for the shed's wooden skid foundation with a 4" layer of compacted gravel. Make sure the gravel is flat, smooth, and perfectly level. *Note: For a sloping site, a concrete block foundation may be more appropriate (check with your shed's manufacturer).*

Cut three 4 × 4 (or 6 × 6) pressure-treated timbers to match the length of the shed's floor frame. Position two outer skids so they will be flush with the outside edges of the frame, and center one skid in between. Make sure that each skid is perfectly level and the skids are level with one another.

Prepare for the Delivery ▸

Panelized shed kits are shipped on pallets. The delivery truck may have a forklift, and the driver can take off the load by whole pallets. Otherwise, you'll have to unload the pieces one at a time. Make sure to have two helpers on hand to help you unload (often drivers aren't allowed to help due to insurance liability).

Once the load is on the ground, carry the pieces to the building site and stack them on pallets or scrap-wood skids to keep them clean and dry. Look through the manufacturer's instructions and arrange the stacks according to the assembly steps.

Assemble the floor frame pieces with screws. First, join alternating pairs of large and small pieces to create three full-width sections. Fasten the sections together to complete the floor frame.

Attach the floor runners to the bottom of the floor frame, using exterior screws. Locate the side runners flush to the outsides of the frame, and center the middle runner in between. Set the frame on the skids with the runners facing down. Check the frame to make sure it is level. Secure the floor to the skids following the manufacturer's recommendations.

Cover the floor frame with plywood, starting with a large sheet at the left rear corner of the frame. Fasten the plywood with screws. Install the two outer deck boards. Lay out all of the remaining boards in between, then set even gapping for each board. Fasten the remaining deck boards.

Lay out the shed's wall panels in their relative positions around the floor. Make sure you have them right-side-up: the windows are on the top half of the walls; on the windowless panels, the siding tells you which end is up.

(continued)

Position the two rear corner walls upright onto the floor so the wall framing is flush with the floor's edges. Fasten the wall panels together. Raise and join the remaining wall panels one at a time. Do not fasten the wall panels to the shed floor in this step.

Place the door header on top of the narrow front wall panel so it's flush with the wall framing. Fasten the header with screws. Fasten the door jamb to the right-side wall framing to create a ½" overhang at the end of the wall. Fasten the header to the jamb with screws.

Confirm that all wall panels are properly positioned on the floor: The wall framing should be flush with edges of the floor frame; the wall siding overhangs the outsides of the floor. Fasten the wall panels by screwing through the bottom wall plate, through the plywood flooring, and into the floor framing.

Install the wall's top plates starting with the rear wall. Install the side wall plates as directed—these overhang the front of the shed and will become part of the porch framing. Finally, install the front wall top plates.

11

Assemble the porch rail sections using the screws provided for each piece. Attach the top plate extension to the 4 × 4 porch post, and then attach the wall trim/support to the extension. Fasten the corner brackets, centered on the post and extension. Install the handrail section 4" up from the bottom of the post.

12

Install each of the porch rail sections: Fasten through the wall trim/support and into the side wall, locating the screws where they will be least visible. Fasten down through the wall top plate at the post and corner bracket locations to hide the ends of the screws. Anchor the post to the decking and floor frame with screws driven through angled pilot holes.

13

Hang the Dutch door using two hinge pairs. Install the hinges onto the door panels. Use three pairs of shims to position the bottom door panel: ½" shims at the bottom, ⅜" shims on the left side, and ⅛" shims on the right side. Fasten the hinges to the wall trim/support. Hang the top door panel in the same fashion, using ¼" shims between the door panels.

14

Join the two pieces to create the rear wall gable, screwing through the uprights on the back side. On the outer side of the gable, slide in a filler shingle until it's even with the neighboring shingles. Fasten the filler with two finish nails located above the shingle exposure line, two courses up. Attach the top filler shingle with two (exposed) galvanized finish nails.

(continued)

Position the rear gable on top of the rear wall top plates and center it from side to side. Use a square or straightedge to align the angled gable supports with the angled ends of the outer plates. Fasten the gable to the plates and wall framing with screws. Assemble and install the middle gable wall.

Arrange the roof panels on the ground according to their installation. Flip the panels over and attach framing connectors to the rafters at the marked locations, using screws.

With one or two helpers, set the first roof panel at the rear of the shed, then set the opposing roof panel in place. Align the ridge boards of the two panels, and then fasten them together with screws. Do not fasten the panels to the walls at this stage.

18

Position one of the middle roof panels, aligning its outer rafter with that of the adjacent rear roof panel. Fasten the rafters together with screws. Install the opposing middle panel in the same way. Set the porch roof panels into place one at a time—these rest on a ½" ledge at the front of the shed. From inside the shed, fasten the middle and porch panels together along their rafters.

19

Check the fit of all roof panels at the outside corners of the shed. Make any necessary adjustments. Fasten the panels to the shed with screws, starting with the porch roof. Inside the shed, fasten the panels to the gable framing, then anchor the framing connectors to the wall plates.

20

Install the two roof gussets between the middle rafters of the shed roof panels (not the porch panels): First measure between the side walls—this should equal 91" for this kit (see resources). If not, have two helpers push on the walls until the measurement matches your requirement. Hold the gussets level, and fasten them to the rafters with screws.

(continued)

Add filler shingles at the roof panel seams. Slide in the bottom shingle and fasten it above the exposure line two courses up, using two screws. Drive the screws into the rafters. Install the remaining filler shingles the same way. Attach the top shingle with two galvanized finish nails.

Cover the underside of the rafter tails (except on the porch) with soffit panels, fastening to the rafters with finish nails. Cover the floor framing with skirting boards, starting at the porch sides. Hold the skirting flush with the decking boards on the porch and with the siding on the walls, and fasten it with screws.

Add vertical trim boards to cover the wall seams and shed corners. The rear corners get a filler trim piece, followed by a wide trim board on top. Add horizontal trim boards at the front wall and along the top of the door. Fasten all trim with finish nails.

At the rear of the shed, fit the two fascia boards over the ends of the roof battens so they meet at the roof peak. Fasten the fascia with screws. Install the side fascia pieces over the rafter tails with finish nails. The rear fascia overlaps the ends of the side fascia. Cover the fascia joints and the horizontal trim joint at the front wall with decorative plates.

Place the two roof ridge caps along the roof peak, overlapping the caps' roofing felt in the center. Fasten the caps with screws. Install the decorative gusset gable underneath the porch roof panels using mounting clips. Finish the gable ends with two fascia pieces installed with screws.

Complete the porch assembly by fastening each front handrail section to a deck post, using screws. Fasten the handrail to the corner porch post. The handrail should start 4" above the bottoms of the posts, as with the side handrail sections. Anchor each deck post to the decking and floor frame with screws (see *Drilling Counterbored Pilot Holes,* this page).

Drilling Counterbored Pilot Holes ▶

Use a combination piloting/counterbore bit to pre-drill holes for installing posts. Angle the pilot holes at about 60°, and drive the screws into the framing below whenever possible. The counterbore created by the piloting bit helps hide the screw head.

Shed Maintenance & Repair

Once you have built your shed, it is important to maintain your investment.

The most common issues for sheds involve water damage of some sort—rotting or rusting siding, rotting foundations, or sinking of foundations due to uneven ground settling or improper installation.

Trees and shrubs that are in contact with shed siding and roofs can cause wear and moisture build-up that leads to rot. Sweep the roof in spring and fall and any time you notice an accumulation of leaves or pine needles.

Common siding materials such as plywood, hardboard, and clapboard are not meant to be in constant contact with the ground. Snow piled against the side of a shed may seem harmless, but the water from melting snow will penetrate wood fibers or metal seams and, through freezing and thawing, separate any protective coating from the surface. Woodpiles stacked against shed siding will also lead to rot. The wood will prevent rain and snow from draining away.

Make sure you paint the lower edge of any siding materials. A bare wood edge of plywood siding will act like a wick to pull up any moisture it comes in contact with. The siding appears stable on the outside, with its surface coating intact, but sooner or later the interior moisture will lead to bubbling or cracking of the surface coating and eventually to rot and delamination in the plywood.

In this chapter:

- Paint a Metal Shed
- Jacking Up a Shed
- Install Wooden Barn Doors on a Steel Shed
- Replacing Rotting Siding
- Installing an Anchor Cable

Paint a Metal Shed

Metal sheds sometimes age ungracefully. Aluminum panels can become chalky and dull. Steel panels, if scratched, can begin to rust. The aluminum can be treated with an aluminum siding brightener, which can yield a nice result without painting. If the shed is rusty steel, painting is the answer. If the shed has been waxed, you will need to clean it with automotive wax remover or aluminum siding cleaner.

Metal sheds rust and become damaged. Proper repairs and preparation followed by a coat of fresh paint improves the appearance and extends shed life.

How to Paint a Metal Shed

Clear all debris from the shed. If the shed has been waxed, clean thoroughly with automotive wax remover or aluminum siding cleaning solution.

Sand, clean and prime all rusted areas with a primer rated for exterior metal.

Paint the shed. The best possible surface will be obtained using a paint sprayer, which can be rented at a rental center. If you do not want to spray, use a short nap roller.

Metal Shed Maintenance ▸

- Trim shrubs and tree branches
- Inspect roof for rust
- Sweep leaves and twigs off roof
- Inspect siding for scratches or rust
- Inspect flooring for damage or rot
- Clean debris from door tracks
- Lubricate door slides or wheel axles with silicone lubricant
- Wash and wax with high quality auto wax
- Check tightness of cable anchors

Jacking Up a Shed

The sinking shed is a common problem. Unless a shed is built on cement piers that extend below the frost line, it is likely that sooner or later the shed will sink if the ground is subject to freeze/thaw cycles. Usually one side or one corner will sink faster. The easiest solution is to jack up that side or corner of the shed and add some shimming material to level it. Ground contact lumber or cement blocks can be used as shims. You may decide to add another set of support blocks or skids. Remove heavy items from the shed before beginning; no need to jack up the riding mower!

If the skids or joists have rotted, they should be replaced. This is an involved process and not covered here.

Tools & Materials ▸

Bottle jack
Scrap plywood
Pressure treated lumber
Concrete block or brick

String level
Work gloves
Eye protection

Before

After

Leveling a sunken shed is a surprisingly simple fix.

How to Jack Up a Shed

1

Using nails and hammer, install a masonry string level across the base of the shed. Nails should be equidistant from the top and bottom of the baseboards.

2

Excavate the area around the shed base to expose the foundation, and clear the area to determine the problem; sometimes a sinking shed is due to rotting skids, not settling soil. Remove debris or dirt so you have a clear view of the foundation materials. Depending on the landscape, you may have to dig out an additional area to install the jack.

3

Dig a trench if you will need room to maneuver a jack handle. The jack needs a firm surface beneath it to dissipate the pressure. Stack two 12 × 12" squares of plywood under the jack. Make sure the wood above the jack is solid. Place a chunk of 2 × 4 or 2 × 6 lumber on top of the jack. Slowly pump up the jack. It is best not to move structures more than ¼" at a time. Allow the structure to rest for a day after each raising.

4

When the string reads level, insert the appropriate shimming material between the skid or joists and the gravel or concrete base. Ground-contact treated lumber or solid cement bricks or blocks are good alternatives.

Safety Tip ▶

To avoid crushing and related injuries, never work on, under or around a load supported only by a jack. Always use jack stands, or solid cement bricks or blocks to support the shed.

Install Wooden Barn Doors on a Steel Shed

One of the frustrations of metal shed ownership is that the doors seem to expire long before the shed. Most inexpensive metal sheds have doors that slide on plastic slides—not even wheels! It seems like the doors quickly become catawampus, and no longer slide well in their tracks or cheap slides.

One answer is to create a set of new wood doors for the shed.

Tools & Materials ▸

Cordless drill
2 × 4 lumber
Plywood siding
Deck screws
Sheet metal screws

Angle brackets
Galvanized
    butt hinges
Work gloves
Eye protection

Steel shed doors often expire long before the shed itself. A new set of wood doors is an opportunity for a stylish upgrade.

How to Install Wooden Barn Doors on a Steel Shed

Sliding doors are typically removed by unfastening the screws attaching the door to the top slides then tilting back and lifting the door out of the bottom track.

Use 2 × 4s to frame a door opening. Measure and cut two boards to the height of the opening. Align them in the shed door opening, and use blocking to attach these at the top to the roof beams. Attach a 2 × 4 between the two sides as a header. Attach the base of the side 2 × 4s to the bottom door track, using angle brackets and sheet metal screws.

Measure the opening, and create two doors of equal size to fit into it. Use 2 × 4s for framing, with a diagonal brace, and cover with plywood siding. Attach the doors to the frame using galvanized butt hinges. The old metal doors may be used, but you will need to cut them down to size. They may also be mounted on galvanized butt hinges. Attach hardware.

Replacing Rotting Siding

Sometimes even the best maintenance doesn't stop shed siding from rotting or deteriorating. Powerful sun rays on southern exposures can wreak havoc on even the best maintained shed. Woodpiles, shrubs, or snow piles can lead to contact rot that might not be noticed until too late. In the example shown here, a poorly designed shed has led to rot—beware of any design that includes horizontal members that are not protected by flashing, as they will collect leaves and water. As shown in these steps, the best possible approach is to totally replace the siding. The amount of work for partial replacement is equivalent to full replacement, so the only savings might be in material costs.

Remember that siding is typically not rated for ground contact, so make sure siding is not in contact with the ground. If it is, dig out the dirt and perhaps create a drainage feature around the shed to direct water away from the shed. Splashing water from the roof can also age the shed more quickly.

Here, a 1 × 6 base trim board was attached over the oriented strand board siding, creating a ledge on the top of the trim board that ultimately led to rot in the panel. Battens made from 1 × 2 were run vertically to cover vertical seams and at each stud location to create a board-and-batten effect.

Tools & Materials ▸

Circular saw	Siding
Pry bar	Exterior caulk
Hammer	Work gloves
Galvanized siding nails	Eye protection

Partial Replacement ▸

Alternately, you could remove only the bottom, rotted portion of the siding. This is only a short term fix, as this partial job is susceptible to future problems. Remove trim boards and mark a level, horizontal line about 6" above the rotted area. Use a circular saw set to the thickness of the siding and saw along the line. Remove the rotted wood. Cut a new piece of siding to fit. Insert a piece of Z flashing under the old siding. Slide the new siding under the flashing and nail to studs. Replace the trim.

Accumulating rot defaces and devalues your shed; fortunately there's a quick fix.

Replacing rotting siding is a common fix for wooden sheds. After painting it will look as good as new.

How to Replace Rotting Siding

Remove the trim boards and/or batten with a pry bar and hammer to gain access to the rotting portion. The corner boards may also have to be removed.

Determine where the damaged or rotted material ends and snap a chalk line at least 6" past that point to serve as your cutting line. Where possible, snap chalk lines that fall midway across a framing member.

Use a circular saw to make a straight cut along the chalk line. The saw setting should be just slightly deeper than the width of the panel (usually about a ½"). It is easiest and safest to make the cuts before removing the fasteners which hold the panels in place. Finish the cut with a jigsaw or handsaw where the circular saw cannot reach. Remove any screws if present and pry off the damaged material.

Cut 2 × 4 blocking to support the wall studs along the cutout lines. To secure the blocking, use a handheld drill and drive deck screws toe-nail style into the studs. The backers will be used to secure the replacement patch.

Measure and cut replacement panels using the same size and type material. To allow for expansion and contraction, leave no more than ⅛" gap between the patch board and the original siding. Use screws or nails to fasten the patch. Screws provide better holding power but are more difficult to conceal. Reattach trim and then prime and paint all exposed wood surfaces.

Tip: Make corrective repairs to fix problems so they don't recur. Use a pneumatic nailer to secure appropriate molding to the ledge of the base trim. Here, pieces of ¾ × ¾" quarter-round molding are set into thick beds of caulk on the top edges of the base trim and then secured with finish nails. This creates a surface that sheds water instead of allowing it to accumulate.

How to Repair Wood Clapboard Siding

Locate and mark framing members inside the wall (use a stud finder) so you can draw cutting lines around the damage that fall over studs. Starting at the bottom, cut clapboards at the cutting lines with a keyhole saw or a wallboard saw. For access, slip wood shims under the clapboard above the one you're cutting. *Note: The repair will look better if you stagger cutting lines so they don't fall on the same stud.*

Cut replacement clapboards to fit, using a miter saw or power miter saw.

Nail the replacement clapboards in the patching area (you can use tape to hold them in place if you like). Follow the same nailing pattern used for the boards around it. Set nail heads with a nailset.

Caulk the gaps between clapboards and fill nailholes with exterior putty or caulk. Prime and paint the repaired section to match.

Wooden Shed Maintenance ▶

- Trim shrubs and tree branches
- Sweep leaves and twigs off roof
- Inspect roofing for breaks and cracks

- Inspect siding for damage or rot
- Inspect flooring for damage or rot
- Oil door hinges

How to Repair Board & Batten Siding

With a flat pry bar, remove the battens on each side of the damaged area. To protect the painted surfaces, cut along the joints between the boards and battens with a utility knife before removing the battens.

Remove the damaged panel (or make vertical cuts with a circular saw underneath the batten locations if any of the battens are only decorative). Cut a replacement panel from matching material, sized to leave a ⅛" gap between the original panels and the new patch. Nail the panel in place, caulk the repair seams and reinstall the battens. Prime and paint to match.

How to Repair Tongue & Groove Siding

Back of groove area on patch is removed

To repair tongue-and-groove siding, first mark both ends of the damage and rip-cut the board down the middle, from end to end, with a circular saw or trim saw. Then use the trim saw to cut along the vertical lies. Finish all cuts with a keyhole saw. Split the damaged board with a pry bar or a wide chisel. Then pull the pieces apart and out of the hole. If the building paper below the damaged section was cut or torn, repair it.

Cut the replacement board to fit, then cut off the backside of the groove so the board can clear the tongue on the course below. Prime the board, let it dry, then nail it into place. Paint to match.

Installing an Anchor Cable

If you live in an area subject to high winds and your shed is not anchored to a concrete foundation, it should be anchored with a cable anchoring system. Most shed manufacturers sell a variety of anchoring systems for their sheds. The cable system is the easiest to install after construction. If you live in hurricane or tornado prone areas, note that local ordinances may cover what sort of shed anchoring system is allowable. In order for the anchoring system to work properly, the shed needs to be level and firmly supported. If it isn't, fix those issues before installing the cable anchors.

Tools & Materials ▶

Anchor kit (see Resources)
Adjustable wrench
Work gloves
Eye protection

Sheds that are not connected to a permanent concrete foundation can benefit from an anchor cable to hold them in place safely.

How to Install an Anchor Cable

Align the anchors 5" to 9" from the side of the shed and parallel with the first roof panel. Twist the anchors into the ground using a short rod or crowbar through the eye of the anchor. Twist until 3" of the anchor extends above ground.

Insert the cable under the roof panel at the rib, then over all the roof beams and out the opposite side along the rib.

Insert about 6" of cable through the eye of the anchor and attach the cable using the cable clamp. Pull the cable somewhat taut, and repeat with the anchor on the opposite side. Repeat with the second set of anchors. Do not over tighten, as you can damage the shed. Check the cables annually for tautness and loosen or tighten the anchors as needed.

Resources

Arrow Storage Products
www.arrowsheds.com
800-851-1085
Auger Anchor Kit

Asphalt Roofing Manufacturers Association
202-207-0917
www.asphaltroofing.org

The Betty Mills Company
2121 S. El Camino Real, Suite D-100
San Mateo, CA 94403
800-BettyMills
www.bettymills.com

The Big eZee
Metal Kit Sheds
101 N. Fourth St.
Breese, IL 62230
800-851-1085

Cedar Shake & Shingle Bureau
604-820-7700
www.cedarbureau.org

Certified Wood Products Council
503-224-2205
www.certifiedwood.org

HDA, Inc.
*Designs: Service Shed (p. 84), Salt Box Storage Shed
   (p. 106), Clerestory Studio (p. 128), Sunlight Garden
   Shed (p. 142), Convenience Shed (p. 172)*
St. Louis, MO
800-373-2646/plan sales
314-770-2228/technical assistance
www.houseplansandmore.com

Paint Quality Institute
www.paintquality.com

Simpson Strong-Tie Co.
800-999-5099
www.strongtie.com
Metal lumber hangers and fasteners

Southern Pine Council
*Designs by Bruce Pierce: Simple Storage Shed
   (p. 154 to 165), Gothic Playhouse (p. 166 to 179)*
Kemer, LA
www.southernpine.com

Spirit Elements
800-511-1440
www.spiritelements.com
Cedar Shed Kit

DuraMAX
Available at the Betty Mills Company
800-BettyMills
www.bettymills.com

Finley Products, Inc.
1018 New Holland Ave.
Lancaster, PA 17601
888-626-5301
www.2x4basics.com

Summerwood Products
735 Progress Avenue
Toronto, Ontario M1H 2W7
Canada
866-519-4634
www.summerwood.com

Photo Credits

Metric Conversion Charts

Converting Measurements

To Convert:	To:	Multiply by:
Inches	Millimeters	25.4
Inches	Centimeters	2.54
Feet	Meters	0.305
Yards	Meters	0.914
Square inches	Square centimeters	6.45
Square feet	Square meters	0.093
Square yards	Square meters	0.836
Cubic inches	Cubic centimeters	16.4
Cubic feet	Cubic meters	0.0283
Cubic yards	Cubic meters	0.765
Pounds	Kilograms	0.454

To Convert:	To:	Multiply by:
Millimeters	Inches	0.039
Centimeters	Inches	0.394
Meters	Feet	3.28
Meters	Yards	1.09
Square centimeters	Square inches	0.155
Square meters	Square feet	10.8
Square meters	Square yards	1.2
Cubic centimeters	Cubic inches	0.061
Cubic meters	Cubic feet	35.3
Cubic meters	Cubic yards	1.31
Kilograms	Pounds	2.2

Lumber Dimensions

Nominal - U.S.	Actual - U.S. (in inches)	Metric
1 × 2	3/4 × 1 1/2	19 × 38 mm
1 × 3	3/4 × 2 1/2	19 × 64 mm
1 × 4	3/4 × 3 1/2	19 × 89 mm
1 × 6	3/4 × 5 1/2	19 × 140 mm
1 × 8	3/4 × 7 1/4	19 × 184 mm
1 × 10	3/4 × 9 1/4	19 × 235 mm
1 × 12	3/4 × 11 1/4	19 × 286 mm
2 × 2	1 1/2 × 1 1/2	38 × 38 mm
2 × 3	1 1/2 × 2 1/2	38 × 64 mm

Nominal - U.S.	Actual - U.S. (in inches)	Metric
2 × 4	1 1/2 × 3 1/2	38 × 89 mm
2 × 6	1 1/2 × 5 1/2	38 × 140 mm
2 × 8	1 1/2 × 7 1/4	38 × 184 mm
2 × 10	1 1/2 × 9 1/4	38 × 235 mm
2 × 12	1 1/2 × 11 1/4	38 × 286 mm
4 × 4	3 1/2 × 3 1/2	89 × 89 mm
4 × 6	3 1/2 × 5 1/2	89 × 140 mm
6 × 6	5 1/2 × 5 1/2	140 × 140 mm
8 × 8	7 1/4 × 7 1/4	184 × 184 mm

Metric Plywood

Standard Sheathing Grade	Sanded Grade
7.5 mm (5/16")	6 mm (4/17")
9.5 mm (3/8")	8 mm (5/16")
12.5 mm (1/2")	11 mm (7/16")
15.5 mm (5/8")	14 mm (9/16")
18.5 mm (3/4")	17 mm (2/3")
20.5 mm (13/16")	19 mm (3/4")
22.5 mm (7/8")	21 mm (13/16")
25.5 mm (1")	24 mm (15/16")

Counterbore, Shank & Pilot Hole Diameters

Screw Size	Counterbore Diameter for Screw Head	Clearance Hole for Screw Shank	Pilot Hole Diameter	
			Hard Wood	Soft Wood
#1	.146 (9/64)	5/64	3/64	1/32
#2	1/4	3/32	3/64	1/32
#3	1/4	7/64	1/16	3/64
#4	1/4	1/8	1/16	3/64
#5	1/4	1/8	5/64	1/16
#6	5/16	9/64	3/32	5/64
#7	5/16	5/32	3/32	5/64
#8	3/8	11/64	1/8	3/32
#9	3/8	11/64	1/8	3/32
#10	3/8	3/16	1/8	7/64
#11	1/2	3/16	5/32	9/64
#12	1/2	7/32	9/64	1/8

Index

Also From **CREATIVE PUBLISHING international**

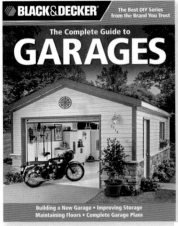

ISBN 978-1-58923-475-4

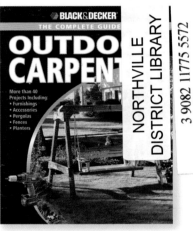

ISBN 978-1-58923-458-1

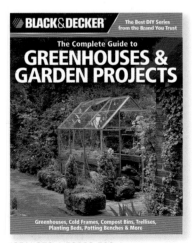

ISBN 978-1-58923-599-1

To view other titles
in the *Black &
Decker Complete
Guide* book series
scan this code

**Creative Publishing
international**

400 First Avenue North • Suite 300 • Minneapolis, MN 55401 • www.creativepub.com